HANDBOOK OF
UNITED STATES
ECONOMIC AND
FINANCIAL INDICATORS

HANDBOOK OF UNITED STATES ECONOMIC AND FINANCIAL INDICATORS

FREDERICK M. O'HARA, JR.

AND

ROBERT SICIGNANO

Greenwood Press

Westport, Connecticut • London, England

Library of Congress Cataloging in Publication Data

O'Hara, Frederick M.
  Handbook of United States economic and financial
indicators.

  Includes index.
    1. Economic indicators—United States—Handbooks,
manuals, etc. I. Sicignano, Robert. II. Title.
HC106.8.047   1985   330.973   84-22469
ISBN 0-313-23954-1 (lib. bdg.)

Library of Congress Catalog Card Number: 84-22469
  ISBN: 0-313-23954-1

First published in 1985

Greenwood Press
A Division of Congressional Information Service, Inc.
88 Post Road West, Westport, Connecticut 06881

Printed in the United States of America

10 9 8 7 6 5 4 3 2

CONTENTS

Preface   vii

How to Use the *Handbook*   ix

Main Entries   3

Appendix A.   Nonquantitative Indicators   191
Appendix B.   Abbreviations List and Guide to Sources   195
Appendix C.   List of Compilers of Indicators   209

Index   215

PREFACE

The <u>Handbook of Economic and Financial Indicators</u> brings together for the first time reference data on the major measures of economic activity in the United States. The basic economic indicators, most of which were developed during the early part of this century by the National Bureau of Economic Research, have over the years been added to, refined, and redefined by governmental agencies, quasi-governmental agencies, trade associations, small and large consulting firms, financial publishing companies, and many others. This volume presents the more important of these indicators as a tool for researchers, librarians, and economists who need quick answers about the various types of indicators and how to find their current and historic values. The more than 200 measures found here are compiled by some 55 sources. Bibliographic citations are provided at the ends of most entries for readers requiring more in-depth information.

We have defined an indicator as any standard measure of economic activity that reveals to the user where the economy has been, where it is now, or where it is heading in the future. The forms that these indicators take are many: volumes, ratios, indexes, composites, etc. The common thread that runs through all these measures is that they are all used for evaluative purposes to measure economic activity over the short or long terms.

We have placed together in one volume both economic and financial indicators. It is not only more convenient to have them together, but the differences between them are sometimes clouded; no purpose would be served by separating them. Hence, the Speculation Index is treated in the same manner and format as the Gross National Product.

Recognizing that the need often arises for information about certain tongue-in-cheek indicators (the Hemline Index, the Superbowl Predictor, etc.), we have included an appendix that treats these nonquantitative indicators in a manner parallel to the treatment of serious indicators. We felt compelled to include some reference to these unorthodox (and sometimes satirical) indicators because reference questions about them do indeed crop up from time to time (at least once a year in the case of the Superbowl Predictor) and because the economics literature occasionally refers to these marginal indicators.

In compiling the Handbook, we examined the indicators and the literature in which they are presented and discussed for two years, and we weighed each indicator for its usefulness as a true indicator of economic or financial activity. Standard sources were consulted, and periodical literature from 1950 to the present was searched. All of the tables and charts in current national and financial newspapers and magazines were extensively studied. In all, more than 300 periodicals were examined.

A master list of indicators was then compiled. Some information about the indicators was verified through the literature, while other information was verified by direct correspondence with the compilers of the indicators. If no validation could be made, the indicator was not included in the Handbook. As a result, several indicators published by some financial advisors and investment firms could not be included. Such cases, however, were in a minority.

To be included in the Handbook, an indicator had to fulfill the folowing criteria: (1) that it meet the precise definition stated above; (2) that enough literature surround the indicator to adequately define it and briefly state its composition; (3) that the actual value of the indicator be readily available to the researcher in a convenient form (tables or graphs) and in publications that are accessible to most libraries and research institutions; (4) that it appear in these publications on a recurring basis; and (5) that sufficient bibliographic references be available for each entry so that more research could be undertaken if desired. Even if one or more of these criteria were not met, an indicator was still included if we felt that the reader would benefit from the information available about it. As a result, a few entries appear without reference to their being regularly published statistical data. If the indicator is published only irregularly, the abbreviation "irr" is noted in the Cumulation information.

The authors would like to acknowledge the help of Alton Huntley whose review of the manuscript and suggestions for its improvement are greatly appreciated.

Economic indicators and all other facets of modern society are changing rapidly. Computerized data bases are complementing traditional printed sources of information about indicators, new indicators are being devised, and older ones are being modified to reflect changes in our society. As a result, any description of our financial and economic systems and their indicators is at least slightly out of date by the time it reaches print. And writers, being human, make errors of their own. Any suggestions a reader might have for improving or updating the present work would be graciously welcomed by the authors.

HOW TO USE THE *HANDBOOK*

The book is arranged alphabetically by indicator. Because some indicators are invariably known by several names, cross references are included in the text, and an exhaustive subject index appears at the end of the work covering the various terms and concepts implied by the indicators.

Each entry contains a maximum of nine elements: the name or names of the indicator; a brief description of the indicator; the derivation of the indicator or how it is produced; a short statement of how the indicator is used; the publisher (compiler) of the indicator; the name of the publication in which the indicator's values originally appear; the frequency with which the statistics are issued; a list of descriptive cumulations listing all of the national publications of record that regularly publish or project the indicator arranged according to how the information is provided; and finally, a bibliography, when available, to direct researchers to more information. Bibliographic entries were chosen for technical descriptions of the different facets and uses of particular indicators. Occasionally, however, general reading is recommended to provide an introduction to the subject at hand.

Different publications express values of indicators in a variety of ways. It is important, therefore, to know not only whether there are cumulations in a particular source, but also in what form they appear (percent change, units, dollars, etc.).

More than 125 periodicals and other materials were selected as readily available sources of these statistics. The cumulations are divided into tabular and graphic modes of presentation. Projections are included, when available, and constitute a third division. Within each of these divisions, the left-hand column contains the name of each periodical in an abbreviated form (see Appendix B for the complete title, publisher, and publisher's address). The right-hand column is divided into three parts: the periodicity of data to be found in each source (i.e., whether the data for a week, month, etc. appear in this publication); whether or not cumulations of many periods are to be found in each source (i.e., are data for two or more periods printed here); and in what units each statistic is presented.

For example, an entry for the Gross National Product is presented as follows:

TABLES
EI   Quarterly and yearly, cum, $

This entry indicates that in each issue of the periodical Economic Indicators, tables show quarterly and yearly statistics, historical data for this indicator are cumulated and presented, and the values are quoted in dollars. When no historical data are presented, "cum" is omitted. Sometimes an indicator is quoted in more than one form or expressed in more than one system of units by a given periodical. In such cases, all forms and methods of expression are reflected in the Cumulations by the inclusion of multiple entries.

Main Entries

A

Accession Rate, Manufacturing

<DESCRIPTION>

The number of additions (temporary and permanent) to the employment rolls per hundred extant employees during a given month.

<DERIVATION>

Cooperating manufacturers are surveyed by state employment security agencies; respondents provide the number of accessions during the month. Included in the data are employees that received pay for any part of the pay period including the twelfth of the month, new hires, rehires, or personnel that have transferred between establishments of the same company. The number of accessions is divided by the total number of employees and multiplied by 100. The data are seasonally adjusted by the ratio-to-moving-average method.

<USE>

One of the three components (the other two are layoff rate and quit rate) in the Bureau of Labor Statistics' calculation of labor turnover. A leading indicator.

<PUBLISHER>

U.S. Department of Labor, Bureau of Labor Statistics

<ANNOUNCED IN>

Employment and Earnings

<ANNOUNCEMENT FREQUENCY>

Monthly

<CUMULATIONS>

TABLES

BCD	Monthly, cum, rate
Bus Stats	Monthly and yearly, cum, rate
Emp & Earn	Monthly and yearly, cum, rate
SCB	Monthly and yearly, cum, rate
Emp & Earn	Yearly, cum, rate
Hist Stats	Yearly, cum, rate
Stat Abstr	Yearly, cum, rate

GRAPHS

BCD	Monthly, cum, rate

<MORE INFORMATION>

U.S. Dept. of Commerce, Bureau of Economic Analysis, Handbook of Cyclical U.S. Indicators, USGPO, Washington, D.C., 1977.

Rudolph C. Mendelssohn, "Three BLS Series as Business Cycle Turn Signals," Monthly Labor Rev. 82, 973-976 (Sept. 1959).

Bureau of Labor Statistics, A Guide to Seasonal Adjustment of Labor Force Data, Bull. 2114, U.S. Department of Labor, Washington, D.C., 1982.

Bureau of Labor Statistics and Bureau of the Census, Concepts and Methods Used in Labor Force Statistics Derived from the Current Population Survey, BLS Rept. 463 and Current Pop. Rept. (Ser. P-23) 62, U.S. Department of Labor and U.S. Department of Commerce, Washington, D.C., 1976.

Bureau of Labor Statistics, Workers, Jobs, and Statistics, Rept. 698, U.S. Department of Labor, Washington, D.C., 1983.

Advisory Service Index [Same as Sentiment Index of the Leading Services]
<DESCRIPTION>
The percentage of investment advisory services or stock-investment newsletters that are bearish.
<DERIVATION>
Each week, about 125 of the leading stock advisory services' publications are surveyed, and their recommendations are classified as bullish or bearish. The results of the survey are tabulated as the percentages of the services that are bullish and bearish. The percentage of services expressing bearish sentiments is then graphed alongside the Dow-Jones Industrial Average.
<USE>
When inverted, the bearish sentiment follows the major stock price averages very closely and is therefore used as a contrary indicator of market behavior.
<PUBLISHER>
Chartcraft, Inc.
<ANNOUNCED IN>
Investors Intelligence
<ANNOUNCEMENT FREQUENCY>
Weekly
<CUMULATIONS>
TABLES
Inv Intell   Weekly, cum, %
<MORE INFORMATION>
M. J. Pring, Technical Analysis Explained, An Illustrated Guide for the Investor, McGraw-Hill, New York, 1980, pp. 212-214.

After-Tax Corporate Profits [See Corporate Profits]

Agricultural Employment
<DESCRIPTION>
An estimate of the number of persons in the U.S. for whom the practice of agriculture is the principal employment.
<DERIVATION>
The statistics for this indicator are derived from the data of the Current Population Survey conducted monthly by the Bureau of the Census. The Survey covers about 60,000 occupied

households and has a response rate of about 97.5%. The Agricultural Employment data count the number of responders whose primary employment is in agriculture and who are age 16 or older. It comprises the self-employed, persons who work for wages or salaries, and those who put in 15 hours or more per week as unpaid workers on family farms. Inmates of institutions (such as penal farms) are not included. The data are adjusted to compensate for the number of nonrespondents, to reflect the known distribution of characteristics of the U.S. population, and to reflect the expected changes in each item between the preceding month's value and the current month's value (an estimate that is based on the part of the sample that is common to both months). The data are seasonally adjusted.

<USE>
Used to assess the productivity of the agricultural labor force. (About 4% of the population produces most of the country's food needs as well as the food exports that, as a class, are the nation's largest foreign exchange earner.) Also used to detect and evaluate the effects on the agricultural industry of structural and technological changes. This productivity and these effects have additional import in expectations about future food supply, consumer prices, real estate prices, and several other aspects of the national economy.

<PUBLISHER>
U.S. Department of Labor, Bureau of Labor Statistics
<ANNOUNCED IN>
Employment and Earnings
<ANNOUNCEMENT FREQUENCY>
Monthly
<CUMULATIONS>
TABLES

Emp & Earn	Monthly, nos.
Bus Stats	Monthly, cum, nos.
SCB	Monthly, cum, nos.
Hist Stats	Yearly, cum, nos.
Stat Abstr	Yearly, cum, nos.

<MORE INFORMATION>
P. A. Daly, Agricultural Employment: Has the Decline Ended?, Monthly Labor Review, 11-17 (Nov. 1981).

"Labor Force, Employment, and Unemployment from the Current Population Survey," Chap. 1 in BLS Handbook of Methods, Vol. I, U.S. Dept. of Labor, Washington, D.C., 1982.

Geoffrey Moore, "Employment: The Neglected Indicator," Wall Street Journal, 10 (Feb. 3, 1972).

G. H. Moore and J. Shiskin, "Why the Leading Indicators Really Do Lead," Across the Board, 71-75 (May 1978).

Julius Shiskin, "Employment and Unemployment: The Doughnut or the Hole," Monthly Labor Review, 3-10 (Feb. 1976).

Bureau of Labor Statistics, Workers, Jobs, and Statistics, Rept. 698, U.S. Department of Labor, Washington, D.C., 1983.

Bureau of Labor Statistics, A Guide to Seasonal Adjustment of Labor Force Data, Bull. 2114, U.S. Department of Labor, Washington, D.C., 1982.

Bureau of Labor Statistics and Bureau of the Census, Concepts and Methods Used in Labor Force Statistics Derived

from the Current Population Survey, BLS Rept. 463 and Current
Pop. Rept. (Ser. P-23) 62, U.S. Department of Labor and U.S.
Department of Commerce, Washington, D.C., 1976.

Aircraft, New Orders
<DESCRIPTION>
The value in dollars of the new orders placed in a given
month with U.S. developers or producers of airplanes,
missiles, spacecraft, and the engines for such vehicles.
<DERIVATION>
Companies in the target industry are surveyed monthly and
report their new orders (including backlog) received for
prime contracts and subcontracts less terminations during the
period. All orders and backlog reported must be supported by
binding legal documents. Data are also provided for
conversions, modifications, site activation, other aerospace
products and services (including drones), and research and
development.
<USE>
Used to gage the employment activity of heavy industry and to
form projections of the gross national product.
<PUBLISHER>
Aerospace Industries Association of America and the U.S.
Department of Commerce, Bureau of the Census
<ANNOUNCED IN>
Survey of Current Business
<ANNOUNCEMENT FREQUENCY>
Monthly
<CUMULATIONS>
TABLES
Bus Stats   Monthly and yearly, $
SCB   Monthly and yearly, $
Stat Abstr   Yearly, cum, $
GRAPHS
Aero F&F   Yearly, cum, $
<MORE INFORMATION>
  U.S. Dept. of Commerce, Bureau of Economic Analysis,
Handbook of Cyclical U.S. Indicators, USGPO, Washington,
D.C., 1977.

Aircraft Shipments
<DESCRIPTION>
The number and dollar value of the complete civilian aircraft
and foreign-customer military planes shipped by reporting
U.S. aircraft manufacturers in a given month.
<DERIVATION>
Manufacturers are surveyed monthly, and report the number of
aircraft shipped, the dollar value of the shipments, and the
airframe weight shipped. The number of shipments and dollar
values are totalled and published. Dollar values do not
include the values of the spare parts shipped with the
aircraft but include engines. Airframe weight does not
include aircraft's load, engine, propellers, wheels, or other
accessories.

<USE>
An indicator of activity in the heavy industry sector of the
economy.
<PUBLISHER>
U.S. Department of Commerce, Bureau of the Census, and the
U.S. Department of Transportation, Federal Aviation Agency
<ANNOUNCED IN>
Complete Aircraft and Aircraft Engines, Cir. M37G
<ANNOUNCEMENT FREQUENCY>
Monthly
<CUMULATIONS>
TABLES

Ind W	Latest month and year ago, nos.
Bus Stats	Monthly and yearly, cum, $
SCB	Monthly and yearly, cum, $
Aero F&F	Yearly, cum, $
Aero F&F	Yearly, cum, nos.
FAA Stats	Yearly, cum, $
FAA Stats	Yearly, cum, nos.
Stat Abstr	Yearly, cum, $

Airline Passenger Miles [See Revenue Passenger Miles]

American Stock Exchange Advance-Decline Line
<DESCRIPTION>
An indication of how many stock prices have increased during
a given period on the American Stock Exchange versus the
number of prices that have decreased.
<DERIVATION>
Daily or weekly data for all of the issues on the Exchange
are analyzed to determine the numbers of advances and of
declines; the number of declines is subtracted from the
number of advances; the resulting value is added to an
arbitrary base reference number appropriate for the Exchange.
<USE>
Considered to be an accurate leading indicator for market
turns and directions. Used to forecast peaks and troughs in
the stock market and to measure price trends.
<PUBLISHER>
American Stock Exchange
<ANNOUNCED IN>
American Stock Exchange news release
<ANNOUNCEMENT FREQUENCY>
Daily
<CUMULATIONS>
TABLES

MG Fin Wkly	Daily, cum, nos.
S&P Stats	Daily, cum, nos.
NYT	Latest daily, nos.
WSJ	Latest daily, nos.
Barron's	Latest week, nos.

GRAPHS

MG Fin Wkly	Daily, cum, nos.
S&P Outlook	Monthly, cum, nos.

<MORE INFORMATION>
William Gordon, The Stock Market Indicators as a Guide to Market Timing, Investors Press, Palisades Park, N. J., 1968, pp. 45-65.

Michael Hayes, The Dow Jones - Irwin Guide to Stock Market Cycles, Dow Jones - Irwin, Homewood, Ill., 1977, pp. 101-106.

Martin J. Pring, Technical Analysis Explained, An Illustrated Guide for the Investor, McGraw-Hill, New York, 1980, pp. 164-169.

American Stock Exchange Big Block Activity
<DESCRIPTION>
The number of transactions on the American Stock Exchange that exceed 10,000 shares during a day.
<DERIVATION>
American Stock Exchange members report all large-block buy and sell orders electronically. The orders are transmitted to the Exchange floor, where they are tallied daily.
<USE>
Because such large transactions are almost always the actions of institutions, these statistics are taken to indicate the gross market activity of traders with large and sophisticated analytical resources. This statistic is a coincident indicator that generally confirms movements in other stock-market indicators.
<PUBLISHER>
American Stock Exchange
<ANNOUNCED IN>
American Stock Exchange news release
<ANNOUNCEMENT FREQUENCY>
Daily
<CUMULATIONS>
TABLES

Barron's	Daily, cum, no. of transactions
AMEX	Yearly, cum, no. of shares
AMEX	Yearly, cum, no. of transactions
AMEX	Yearly, cum, % of total volume

GRAPHS

MG Fin Wkly	Monthly and yearly, cum, no. of transactions
AMEX	Yearly, cum, % of round lot volume

<MORE INFORMATION>
Martin J. Pring, Technical Analysis Explained, An Illustrated Guide for the Investor, McGraw-Hill, New York, 1980, pp. 158-159.

Martin E. Zweig, "Trusty Market Indicator, Bring the Record of the Big-Block Index up to Date," Barron's, 11-12 (Jan. 24, 1983).

Dudley R. Bohlen, "Large Block Transactions: A Premier Contrary Indicator," pp. 42-1 to 42-5 in The Encyclopedia of Stock Market Techniques, Investors Intelligence, Larchmont, N.Y., 1983.

American Stock Exchange Market Value Index [Replaced the American Stock Exchange Price Change Index]
<DESCRIPTION>
A measure of the change in the aggregate market value of outstanding common shares, American Depository Receipts, and warrants on the American Stock Exchange.
<DERIVATION>
The share price for common shares, American Depositary Receipts, and warrants is multiplied by the number of shares outstanding for 860 corporations listed on the American Stock Exchange. Rights, preferred stocks, and when-issued stocks are not included. This calculation is then indexed to the value for Sept. 4, 1973, which was assigned an index value of 100.00. Because of the method of calculating the market value, the index is not affected by new listings, delistings, splits, suspensions or halts of trading, or distributions of dividends. Sixteen subsidiary indexes (for eight industrial groupings and eight geographic areas) are also calculated.
<USE>
A measure of the overall market strength and of speculative activity.
<PUBLISHER>
American Stock Exchange
<ANNOUNCED IN>
American Stock Exchange news release
<ANNOUNCEMENT FREQUENCY>
Daily
<CUMULATIONS>
TABLES
Barron's   Daily, index nos.
MG Fin Wkly   Daily, index nos.
NYT   Daily and weekly, index nos.
NYT   Daily and weekly, high-low, % change
WSJ   Daily and year ago, index nos.
WSJ   Daily and year ago, % change
Forbes   Latest month and year ago, % change
AMEX   Monthly, cum, index nos.
Inc   Monthly, cum, % change
FR Bull   Monthly and yearly, cum, index nos.
Stat Abstr   Yearly, cum, index nos.
GRAPHS
AMEX   Yearly, cum, index nos.
MG Fin Wkly   Daily, cum, index nos.
Inc   Monthly, cum, % change
Moody's Ind   Monthly and yearly, ranges
<MORE INFORMATION>
   B. A. Schoomer, Jr., "The American Stock Exchange Index System," Fin. Anal. J. 20, 57-61 (May-June 1967).
   "Market Guides," Barron's, 9+ (Sept. 26, 1966).
   Barry Bosworth, "The Stock Market and the Economy," Brookings Papers on Economic Activity 2, 257-290 (1975).
   John Kirk, "American Exchange's Market Indicators Explained," Banking, 4 (Sept. 1966).

American Stock Exchange Odd-Lot Index
<DESCRIPTION>
A measure of the portion of the daily or weekly sales on the American Stock Exchange that are made up of 100 shares or less.
<DERIVATION>
The daily or weekly total of odd-lot transactions on the Exchange is divided by the total number of transactions occurring on the Exchange during that period.
<USE>
To predict future movements in stock market activity; a contrary indicator of market activity.
<PUBLISHER>
American Stock Exchange
<ANNOUNCED IN>
American Stock Exchange news release
<ANNOUNCEMENT FREQUENCY>
Daily
<CUMULATIONS>
TABLES
Barron's   Latest week's end, nos.
MG Fin Wkly Weekly and daily, cum, nos.
<MORE INFORMATION>
   Michael Hayes, The Dow Jones - Irwin Guide to Stock Market Cycles, Dow Jones - Irwin, Homewood, Ill., 1977, pp. 168-172.
   William Gordon, The Stock Market Indicators as a Guide to Market Timing, Investors Press, Palisades Park, N. J., 1968, pp. 61-71.

American Stock Exchange Price Change Index [See American Stock Exchange Market Value Index]

American Stock Exchange Price-Earnings Ratio
<DESCRIPTION>
A measure of the value of the stocks purchased on the American Stock Exchange; more accurately, a measure of the speculative nature of the purchases on that exchange.
<DERIVATION>
The average price for all of the stocks included in the Dow Jones Industrial Average is divided by the average earnings reported for those stocks.
<USE>
As a gage of speculative activity in the market and to assess turning points of the market in the near term. The higher the ratio, the more speculative the market is considered to be because increased investment is not being reflected in increased returns (earnings) from the corporations' performances. Conversely, a lower ratio indicates better value of purchases in the market.
<PUBLISHER>
American Stock Exchange
<ANNOUNCED IN>
American Stock Exchange news release
<ANNOUNCEMENT FREQUENCY>
Daily

<CUMULATIONS>
TABLES
MG Fin Wkly Latest week and year ago, nos.
<MORE INFORMATION>
  Michael Hayes, The Dow Jones - Irwin Guide to Stock Market
Cycles, Dow Jones - Irwin, Homewood, Ill., 1977, p. 54.

American Stock Exchange Seat Sales
<DESCRIPTION>
The price paid in dollars for one seat on or membership in
the American Stock Exchange; such membership is required to
actively trade on the Exchange, and the number of seats is
limited. Prices paid are determined by supply and demand, and
the sales are private ones between individuals.
<DERIVATION>
Seats on the American Stock Exchange can be transferred by an
auction system. The price paid for a seat is determined by
prevailing stock-market conditions and by supply and demand.
Brokers involved in these sales report them and the prices to
the Exchange.
<USE>
An indicator of expected future profitability of the
exchange; used mostly for historical comparisons of
stock-market activity and current strength of the market.
<PUBLISHER>
American Stock Exchange
<ANNOUNCED IN>
American Stock Exchange news release
<ANNOUNCEMENT FREQUENCY>
Monthly
<CUMULATIONS>
TABLES
ASE Stat Rev Yearly, cum, $
GRAPHS
MG Fin Wkly Yearly, cum, $

American Stock Exchange Short Interest Ratio
<DESCRIPTION>
The portion of the American Stock Exchange's volume made up
of short selling.
<DERIVATION>
The monthly uncovered short positions on the American Stock
Exchange expressed in shares are divided by the average daily
volume for each day of the preceding month.
<USE>
A buy or sell signal; a measure of the demand for future
trading. Short sellers eventually have to cover their
positions. In a rising market, this necessity increases the
demand for the shorted stocks, increasing their prices. In a
declining market, no such immediate demand for the stocks
exists, and their values are likely to decline.
<PUBLISHER>
American Stock Exchange
<ANNOUNCED IN>
American Stock Exchange news release

<ANNOUNCEMENT FREQUENCY>
Monthly (midmonth)
<CUMULATIONS>
GRAPHS
MG Fin Wkly Monthly, cum, nos.
<MORE INFORMATION>
   Michael Hayes, The Dow Jones - Irwin Guide to Stock Market
Cycles, Dow Jones - Irwin, Homewood, Ill., 1977, pp. 147-150.
   J. B. Cohen, E. D. Zinbarg, and Arthur Zeikel, Investment
Analysis and Portfolio Management, Irwin, Homewood, Ill.,
1977.
   William Gordon, The Stock Market Indicators as a Guide to
Market Timing, Investors Press, Palisades Park, N. J., 1968,
pp. 93-110.
   Thomas J. Kerrigan, "The Short Interest Ratio and Its
Component Parts," Financial Analysts Journal, 45-49
(Nov./Dec. 1974).
   Randall O. Smith, "Short Interest and Stock Market Prices,"
Financial Analysts Journal, 151-154 (Nov./Dec, 1968).

American Stock Exchange Volume
<DESCRIPTION>
The total number of common and preferred stock shares bought
and sold daily on the American Stock Exchange.
<DERIVATION>
Records of sales are used to tally and sum the number of
individual shares traded during each day.
<USE>
Used in conjunction with price trends to determine market
advances and declines.
<PUBLISHER>
American Stock Exchange
<ANNOUNCED IN>
American Stock Exchange news release
<ANNOUNCEMENT FREQUENCY>
Daily
<CUMULATIONS>
TABLES
NYT   Daily and weekend, nos.
WSJ   Daily and weekend, nos.
Barron's   Latest weekend, nos.
FR Bull   Monthly and yearly, cum, averages
MG Fin Wkly Weekly, cum, nos.
AMEX   Yearly, cum, nos.
Stat Abstr   Yearly, cum, nos.
<MORE INFORMATION>
   John Kirk, "American Exchange's Market Indicators
Explained," Banking, 4 (Sept. 1966).

American Stock Exchange Volume Momentum
<DESCRIPTION>
A measure of the current performance of the American Stock
Exchange in comparison with its performance during the recent
past.

<DERIVATION>
The average volume per day of shares bought and sold on the
American Stock Exchange for the past month is divided by the
monthly volume of shares on that exchange averaged over the
past six months.
<USE>
To determine trends in market activity; used in conjunction
with the Price Momentum. Total volume usually falls prior to
declines and rises before advances.
<PUBLISHER>
American Stock Exchange
<ANNOUNCED IN>
Media General Financial Weekly
<ANNOUNCEMENT FREQUENCY>
Monthly
<CUMULATIONS>
GRAPHS
MG Fin Wkly Monthly, cum, ratio nos.
<MORE INFORMATION>
   John   Kirk,   "American   Exchange's   Market   Indicators
Explained," Banking, 4 (Sept. 1966).

AMEX Index [See American Stock Exchange Market Value Index]

Appliance Factory Sales
<DESCRIPTION>
Total dollar sales for a given month of the major appliance
manufacturing industry including exports.
<DERIVATION>
Manufacturers are surveyed monthly. Reports are classified by
type of product, and totals are calculated for the different
classifications. Totals by class are then summed. Grand total
may differ from the numerical sum of the class data because
of overlapping of the categories. Different appliances have
been included in the survey at different times.
<USE>
A leading indicator of consumer sentiment.
<PUBLISHER>
Association of Home Appliance Manufacturers
<ANNOUNCED IN>
Monthly Factory Shipments of Major Appliances
<ANNOUNCEMENT FREQUENCY>
Monthly
<CUMULATIONS>
TABLES
Ind W   Latest month and year ago, units
Bus Stats   Monthly and yearly, cum, units
SCB   Monthly and yearly, cum, units
Merch   Yearly, cum, $
Merch   Yearly, cum, units
<MORE INFORMATION>
   U.S. Dept. of Commerce, Bureau of Economic Analysis,
Handbook of Cyclical U.S. Indicators, USGPO, Washington,
D.C., 1977.

Arms Index [See Short-Term Trading Index]

Automobile Output
<DESCRIPTION>
The total number of automobiles produced domestically by all
automobile manufacturers during a given week.
<DERIVATION>
Each week, Ford, GM, Chrysler, American Motors, Volkswagen,
and Honda report to their industry trade association the
number of automobiles they produced that week in the U.S.
These figures are then summed. Automobiles that are
distributed in the U.S. but produced overseas are not
included in the tally.
<USE>
A component of the Consumer Durable Goods Output Index and a
leading indicator of future consumer spending.
<PUBLISHER>
Motor Vehicle Manufacturers Association
<ANNOUNCED IN>
Auto News
<ANNOUNCEMENT FREQUENCY>
Weekly
<CUMULATIONS>
TABLES
Barron's	Latest week and year ago, units
Ind W	Latest week and year ago, units
NYT	Latest week and year ago, units
Auto News	Latest week, month, and year, units
Facts File	Monthly, units
S&P Stats	Monthly and yearly, cum, units
MVMA	Yearly, cum, units

GRAPHS
Ind W	Latest monthly and yearly, units
MVMA	Yearly, cum, units

Automobile Sales [Also called Ten-Day Auto Sales]
<DESCRIPTION>
Total domestic auto sales by the manufacturers to dealers
expressed in the number of automobiles for the latest ten
days.
<DERIVATION>
The auto industry is polled three times each month. Each time
the domestic automobile manufacturers report the number of
units sold in the U.S. during the previous ten days. All
makes of automobiles are included in the survey. These
reported figures are then summed and announced within a few
days of reporting.
<USE>
A measure of total consumer spending and of overall business
activity
<PUBLISHER>
Ward's Communications, Inc.
<ANNOUNCED IN>
Ward's Automotive Reports

<ANNOUNCEMENT FREQUENCY>
Thrice monthly
<CUMULATIONS>
TABLES

Auto News	Latest ten days and year ago, units
Barrons	Latest and year ago, units
Bus Stats	Monthly and yearly, cum, units
SCB	Monthly and yearly, cum, units
Stat Bull	10 Day, cum, units
Auto News	10 Day and monthly, units
Pred Base	Yearly, cum, units
Pred Fore	Yearly, cum, units

GRAPHS

| Mo Econ Ind | Yearly, cum, units |

PROJECTIONS

Pred Fore	Yearly, units
Value Line	Quarterly and yearly, % change
Bus Rev WF	Yearly, units

<MORE INFORMATION>
   "The Rage for Faster Forecasts," Business Week, 135 (Oct. 18, 1982).

Automotive Factory Sales
<DESCRIPTION>
The number of vehicles shipped and sold or billed to customers, dealers, or allied divisions during a given month.
<DERIVATION>
Manufacturers report the number of vehicles (cars, trucks, buses, taxicabs, hearses, ambulances, fire trucks, etc.) shipped or billed during the month. These are tabulated by class (passenger cars, trucks and buses, etc.) and then totaled. Export sales are included. Sales to the federal government are included except for tactical military vehicles. Virtually the entire industry is covered.
<USE>
An especially good indicator of future consumer demand and a measure of overall economic health
<PUBLISHER>
Motor Vehicle Manufacturers Association of the U.S.
<ANNOUNCED IN>
Automotive News
<ANNOUNCEMENT FREQUENCY>
Monthly
<CUMULATIONS>
TABLES

Ward's Repts	Monthly, units
Bus Stats	Monthly and yearly, cum, units
SCB	Monthly and yearly, cum, units
Ward's Repts	Quarterly and yearly, cum, units
MVMA	Yearly, cum, units
Stat Abstr	Yearly, cum, units

<MORE INFORMATION>
   U.S. Dept. of Commerce, Bureau of Economic Analysis, Handbook of Cyclical U.S. Indicators, USGPO, Washington, D.C., 1977.

Average Daily Volume [See American Stock Exchange Volume and New York Stock Exchange Average Daily Volume]

Average Hourly and Weekly Earnings [Includes the Adjusted Hourly Earnings Index]
<DESCRIPTION>
The average gross hourly earnings of workers (1) in manufacturing and (2) all private nonagricultural industries; those earnings indexed to (expressed as a percentage of) those earnings in 1967; and the average gross weekly earnings of workers in the. (1) wholesale and retail trade, (2) construction, (3) manufacturing, and (4) all private nonagricultural industries. "Workers" include all production and nonsupervisory personnel in the mining; construction; manufacturing; transportation and public utilities; trade, finance, insurance, and real estate; and service industries.
<DERIVATION>
Monthly payroll figures are collected from a sampling of employers by the Bureau of Labor Statistics. These figures include all pay before any deductions are taken out. Total payrolls are divided by total hours reported for each industry. Real earnings are calculated by dividing these values by the Consumer Price Index and multiplying by 100. A stratified estimating procedure is used to avoid bias toward large industries or certain regions.
<USE>
Widely used in collective bargaining, in escalating the costs of labor covered by long-term contracts, and in general economic analyses.
<PUBLISHER>
U.S. Department of Labor, Bureau of Labor Statistics
<ANNOUNCED IN>
Bureau of Labor Statistics press release entitled "The Employment Situation"
<ANNOUNCEMENT FREQUENCY>
Monthly
<CUMULATIONS>
TABLES

EI	Monthly, avg. hourly, cum, $
EI	Monthly, avg. weekly, cum, $
EI	Monthly and year ago, latest,$
BW	Monthly and yearly, avg. hourly, cum, $
Emp & Earn	Monthly and yearly, avg. earnings, cum, $
Emp & Earn	Monthly and yearly, avg. hourly, cum, $
MLR	Monthly and yearly, avg. hourly, cum, $
Bus Stats	Monthly and yearly, avg. hourly, cum, $
SCB	Monthly and yearly, avg. hourly, cum, $
MLR	Monthly and yearly, avg. weekly, cum, $
Bus Stats	Monthly and yearly, avg. weekly, cum, $
SCB	Monthly and yearly, avg. weekly, cum, $
S&P Stats	Monthly and yearly, avg. weekly, cum, $
Stat Abstr	Yearly, avg. hourly, cum, % change
EI	Yearly, avg. hourly, cum, $
EI	Yearly, avg. weekly, cum, $

PROJECTIONS
Value Line   Quarterly, avg. hourly, % change
<MORE INFORMATION>
   Joint Economic Committee, 1980 Supplement to Economic Indicators, Historical and Descriptive Background, USGPO, Washington, D.C., 1980.
   Bureau of Labor Statistics, Handbook of Methods, Bulletin 1910, Department of Labor, Washington, D.C., 1976.
   Bureau of Labor Statistics, Workers, Jobs, and Statistics, Rept. 698, U.S. Department of Labor, Washington, D.C., 1983.

Average Manufacturing Workweek [See Workweek, Average Manufacturing]

Average Prime Rate Charged by Banks
<DESCRIPTION>
The interest rate that banks charge their most-credit-worthy business customers on short-term loans and the base on which those banks determine the rates they will charge to other business customers averaged nationwide.
<DERIVATION>
The prime rate charged by the majority of 30 large money-market banks on each day of the month is multiplied by the number of days that rate was in effect. Those values are summed, and the total is divided by the number of days. The average is expressed in percentage points and is not seasonally adjusted.
<USE>
Used to determine an estimated national base for the cost of money and to note trends in that cost.
<PUBLISHER>
Board of Governors of the Federal Reserve System
<ANNOUNCED IN>
Selected Interest Rates, Statistical Release H.15 (519)
<ANNOUNCEMENT FREQUENCY>
Monthly
<CUMULATIONS>
TABLES
MG Fin Wkly   Latest period, %
WSJ   Latest period, %
World Fin M   Monthly and yearly, cum, %
Moody's B&F   Quarterly and yearly, cum, %
S&P Cred Wk   Weekly, latest, %
Man Han   Weekly, latest, %
EI   Weekly and monthly, high-low, cum, %
FR Bull   Weekly and monthly, cum, %
Barron's   Weekly and year ago, latest, %
BW   Weekly and year ago, latest, %
Ind W   Weekly and year ago, latest, %
NYT   Weekly and year ago, latest, %
EI   Yearly, cum, %
GRAPHS
MG Fin Wkly   Monthly, %
Builder   Monthly and yearly, %

PROJECTIONS
Fin Ind   Quarterly and yearly, %
Value Line   Quarterly and yearly, %
Bus Rev WF   Yearly, %
<MORE INFORMATION>
  Joint Economic Committee, 1980 Supplement to Economic Indicators, Historical and Descriptive Background, USGPO, Washington, D.C.,1980.

Average Weekly Hours

<DESCRIPTION>
The average number of hours spent working each week by American workers. "Workers" include all production and nonsupervisory personnel in the mining; construction; manufacturing; transportation and public utilities; trade, finance, insurance, and real estate; and service industries. Includes all time for which the employees are paid. One of the 12 leading economic indicators.
<DERIVATION>
The Bureau of Labor Statistics collects employment figures each month from a sample of employers for a specific pay period. The total hours of work paid for by each industry is divided by the number of production and related workers for that industry. The resulting values are then seasonally adjusted by multiplying them by an adjustment factor.
<USE>
Used as a leading indicator of the effects of changes in economic activity in the manufacturing sector of the U.S. economy because the cutting back of overtime and the workweek is a frequent initial response by manufacturers to decreased demand for products. These data are also used in compiling other indicators, such as average earnings and current production estimates.
<PUBLISHER>
U.S. Department of Labor, Bureau of Labor Statistics
<ANNOUNCED IN>
Employment and Earnings
<ANNOUNCEMENT FREQUENCY>
Monthly
<CUMULATIONS>
TABLES
Ind W   Latest and year ago, hours
Stat Bull   Latest month, % change
MLR   Monthly and yearly, cum, hours
Bus Stats   Monthly and yearly, cum, hours
EI   Monthly and yearly, cum, hours
SCB   Monthly and yearly, cum, hours
Stat Abstr   Monthly and yearly, cum, hours
Pred Base   Yearly, cum, hours
Pred Fore   Yearly, cum, hours
PROJECTIONS
Pred Fore   Yearly, hours
<MORE INFORMATION>
  Joint Economic Committee, 1980 Supplement to Economic Indicators, Historical and Descriptive Background, USGPO, Washington, D.C., 1980.

"Official Indicators: What Are They? Can They Predict the Future?" U.S. News and World Report, 66-67 (Aug.16, 1976).

Bureau of Labor Statistics, A Guide to Seasonal Adjustment of Labor Force Data, Bull. 2114, U.S. Department of Labor, Washington, D.C., 1982.

Bureau of Labor Statistics and Bureau of the Census, Concepts and Methods Used in Labor Force Statistics Derived from the Current Population Survey, BLS Rept. 463 and Current Pop. Rept. (Ser. P-23) 62, U.S. Department of Labor and U.S. Department of Commerce, Washington, D.C., 1976.

Bureau of Labor Statistics, Workers, Jobs, and Statistics, Rept. 698, U.S. Department of Labor, Washington, D.C., 1983.

B

Bad Guess Theorem [See Appendix A. Nonquantitative Indicators]

Balance of Trade
<DESCRIPTION>
The difference in the dollar values of the goods that are exported from the United States and the goods that are imported into the United States.
<DERIVATION>
United States Merchandise Imports is subtracted from United States Merchandise Exports to give a net balance. Data exclude military grants and are derived from census data that are adjusted for differences in valuation, coverage, and timing.
<USE>
Used to assess the performance of the nation's international transactions, including gold movements, foreign trade, and foreign exchange.
<PUBLISHER>
U. S. Department of Commerce, Bureau of Economic Analysis
<ANNOUNCED IN>
Survey of Current Business
<ANNOUNCEMENT FREQUENCY>
Monthly
<CUMULATIONS>
TABLES
Highlights	Monthly, $
Bus Stats	Monthly and yearly, cum, $
SCB	Monthly and yearly, cum, $
BCD	Quarterly, cum, $
EI	Quarterly and yearly, cum, $
Hist Stats	Yearly, cum, $
Stat Abstr	Yearly, cum, $

GRAPHS
BCD	Yearly, cum, $

<MORE INFORMATION>
   Walter S. Salant and Associates, The United States Balance of Payments in 1968, The Brookings Institution, Washington, D.C., 1963.

Bank Debits
<DESCRIPTION>
The dollar value of all the checks that depositors write on their bank accounts during a specified period.
<DERIVATION>
The Federal Reserve System regularly surveys about 1600 banks in more than 200 centers of financial activity across the country. New York City is not included because of the effects there on banking transactions by the heavy trading of securities. Respondents provide dollar amounts of bank debits and demand deposits less debits to U.S. Government accounts and interbank transactions. Withdrawal slips are not included among the debits.
<USE>
An indicator of current business activity.
<PUBLISHER>
Board of Governors of the Federal Reserve System
<ANNOUNCED IN>
Federal Reserve Bulletin
<ANNOUNCEMENT FREQUENCY>
Monthly
<CUMULATIONS>
TABLES
FR Bull   Monthly and yearly, cum, $
S&P Stats   Monthly and yearly, cum, $
<MORE INFORMATION>
   G. Garvy, Debits and Clearing Statistics and Their Use, Board of Governors of the Federal Reserve System, Washington, D.C., 1959.

Bank Loans [See Commercial and Industrial Loans Outstanding, Weekly Reporting Large Commercial Banks]

Barron's Confidence Index
<DESCRIPTION>
A comparison of the yields of higher- and lower-grade bonds.
<DERIVATION>
The average yield on Barron's ten best-grade corporate bonds is divided by the average yield on ten intermediate-grade bonds.
<USE>
Used to forecast movements in the corporate-bond markets. The higher the Index, the more confident one might be in the markets and the more likely one might be to purchase lower-grade bonds. Conversely, the lower the Index, the less confidence might be placed in the corporate-bond markets, and the riskier it might be to purchase lower-grade bonds.
<PUBLISHER>
Dow Jones and Co.
<ANNOUNCED IN>
Barron's National Business and Financial Weekly
<ANNOUNCEMENT FREQUENCY>
Weekly

<CUMULATIONS>
TABLES
Barron's   Latest week, % change
Barron's   Latest week and a year ago, index nos.
GRAPHS
MG Fin Wkly Monthly, cum, index nos.
<MORE INFORMATION>
   F. Amling, Investments, An Introduction to Analysis and
Management, Prentice Hall, Englewood Cliffs, N.J., 1974.
   Jack E. Gaumnitz and Carlos A. Salabar, "The Barron's
Confidence Index, An Examination of Its Value as a Market
Indicator," Financial Analysts J. 22, 16 (Sept.-Oct. 1969).
   William Gordon, The Stock Market Indicators as a Guide to
Market Timing, Investors Press, Palisades Park, N. J., 1968,
pp. 79-90.
   Joseph E. Granville, "Market Forecaster? Barron's
Confidence Index Has Compiled an Uncanny Record," Barron's,
9+ (Sept. 7, 1959).

Barron's Fifty-Stock Average
<DESCRIPTION>
A weighted average of the price of 50 selected stocks.
<DERIVATION>
Fifty stocks are selected, and a $100 investment in each is
assumed. The average price per share for the collective
investment is then calculated. As a reslt, equal percentage
movements of different stocks have the same effect on the
calculated average even though those stocks may have
radically different prices per share. The issues included are
changed periodically to compensate for the effects of market
movements on the weighting of the selected portfolio.
<USE>
An overall indicator of stock-price activity.
<PUBLISHER>
Dow Jones and Co.
<ANNOUNCED IN>
Barron's National Business and Financial Weekly
<ANNOUNCEMENT FREQUENCY>
Weekly
<CUMULATIONS>
Barron's   Daily, averages

Barron's Group Stock Averages
<DESCRIPTION>
The average price of a selected group of stocks.
<DERIVATION>
Several hundred stocks have been selected to represent
various sectors of the stock market (aircraft manufacturers,
pharmaceutical firms, banks, etc.). The closing prices for
each of these stocks is noted on each Thursday, and a simple
arithmetic average is calculated. Adjustments to the data are
made to compensate for splits, large dividend payments, and
other anomalies.

<USE>
A price indicator of key-industry market sectors.
<PUBLISHER>
Dow Jones and Co.
<ANNOUNCED IN>
Barron's National Business and Financial Weekly
<ANNOUNCEMENT FREQUENCY>
Weekly
<CUMULATIONS>
TABLES
Barron's   Latest two weeks, avg
Barron's   Latest week, % change

Barron's Twenty Low-Priced Stocks Index
<DESCRIPTION>
The average price of twenty selected low-priced stocks listed
on major exchanges.
<DERIVATION>
In July of 1960, twenty stocks were selected that met four
criteria: a price of $15 or less, a ratio of current assets
to current liabilities of 2 to 1 or better, a satisfactory
earnings record, and a price substantially below the 1959
high. These stocks have been changed as issues disappeared
from the market or their prices became too large. The values
of these stocks as of Thursday are totalled up to calculate
the index. The index is adjusted for stock splits by
multiplying the previous week's value of a stock that has
been split by a compensating factor.
<USE>
A measure of speculative activity on the stock market; a
lagging indicator of market price trends.
<PUBLISHER>
Dow Jones and Co.
<ANNOUNCED IN>
Barron's National Business and Financial Weekly
<ANNOUNCEMENT FREQUENCY>
Weekly
<CUMULATIONS>
TABLES
Barron's   Latest two weeks and year ago, index nos.
<MORE INFORMATION>
  A. Merjos, Swinging Index, Barron's, 9+, Nov. 23, 1970.

Big Block Activity [See American Stock Exchange Big Block
Activity and New York Stock Exchange Big Block Activity]

Bond Buyer Twenty-Bond Index
<DESCRIPTION>
The yield of a representative bond having a maturity of about
20 years and selling at a price close to par.
<DERIVATION>
Originally, the bonds of the 20 largest cities were selected,
but substitutions have been made as cities paid off their

debts or had no debt outstanding with a sufficiently long maturity. The index now includes cities, states, counties, and a territory. The yields of the bonds on each Thursday are noted and averaged.
<USE>
Used as a yardstick to compare the yields of various municipal bonds.
<PUBLISHER>
The Bond Buyer
<ANNOUNCED IN>
The Bond Buyer
<ANNOUNCEMENT FREQUENCY>
Weekly
<CUMULATIONS>
TABLES
Barron's	Latest week and year ago, %
Man Han	Latest week, %
Man Han	Latest week, % change
Bus Stats	Monthly and yearly, cum, %
SCB	Monthly and yearly, cum, %
Bond Buyer	Weekly, cum, %
Wk Bond Buyr	Weekly, cum, %
Stat Abstr	Yearly, cum, %

<MORE INFORMATION>
   David M. Darst, The Complete Bond Book, A Guide to All Types of Fixed-Income Securities, McGraw-Hill, New York, 1975.

Brokerage House Rule [See Appendix A. Nonquantitative Indicators]

Building Cost Index
<DESCRIPTION>
A measure of the combined effect of wage and price changes on the value of the construction dollar.
<DERIVATION>
Four costs are calculated, those of: 68.38 hours of skilled labor at the average rate for such labor in 20 selected cities; 25 cwt of standard structural steel shapes at the average price for such steel at three selected mills; 22.56 cwt of Portland cement at the average price for such cement in 20 selected cities; and 1088 board feet of two-by-four lumber at the average price for such lumber in 20 selected cities. These costs are weighted 56:26:3:15, respectively. These weights are adjusted periodically to reflect economic conditions. The calculated total is then indexed to the totals in 1913 and 1967, producing two series, a 1913 = 100 series and a 1967 = 100 series. Monthly indexes are the indexes calculated for the first week of the month. Annual indexes are straight mathematical averages of the component months. The skilled-labor and materials components are also broken out and published as separate indexes. A related index, the Construction Cost Index, uses much of the same data in its derivation; it uses a different labor base.

<USE>
Used to judge underlying trends of construction costs in the
U.S. and to estimate costs of future construction projects.
<PUBLISHER>
McGraw-Hill Information Systems Co.
<ANNOUNCED IN>
Engineering News-Record
<ANNOUNCEMENT FREQUENCY>
Weekly (U.S.; 1913 = 100)
Monthly (City-by-city; 1967 = 100)
<CUMULATIONS>
TABLES
Eng News-Rec Latest week, index nos.
Eng News-Rec Latest and year ago, % change
Bus Stats   Monthly and yearly, cum, index nos.
Const Rev   Monthly and yearly, cum, index nos.
SCB   Monthly and yearly, cum, index nos.
Stat Abstr   Yearly, cum, index nos.
PROJECTIONS
Eng News-Rec Yearly, index nos.
<MORE INFORMATION>
  "Construction Costs Tracked for U.S.," Engineering
News-Record, 210 (12), 114-121 (Mar. 24, 1983).

Building Permits [See Housing Permits]

Business Executives' Expectations [See Measure of Business
Confidence]

Business Failures
<DESCRIPTION>
The number of court proceedings or voluntary actions entered
into during a month that are likely to result in a loss to
creditors.
<DERIVATION>
Dun & Bradstreet surveys the records of the federal
bankruptcy courts and tallies the number of industrial and
commercial enterprises that are petitioned into those courts
along with the number of concerns that are forced out of
business through the actions of state courts involving
foreclosure, execution, attachments with insufficient assets
to cover all claims, receivership, reorganization,
rearrangement. To these numbers are added the number of
voluntary discontinuances with known loss to creditors and
voluntary compromises with creditors out of court, where this
information can be obtained. The information is reported both
as the total number of failed businesses and as an index
number. The index number is the number of failed businesses
per 10,000 businesses listed in the Dun & Bradstreest
Reference Book; it shows the annual rate at which business
concerns would fail if the rate of that month prevailed for
the year. The index is seasonally adjusted.

<USE>
An indicator of overall business activity; inversely tied to
the expansion and contraction of business activity.
<PUBLISHER>
Dun & Bradstreet, Inc.
<ANNOUNCED IN>
Monthly Business Failures
<ANNOUNCEMENT FREQUENCY>
Monthly
<CUMULATIONS>
TABLES

Barron's	Latest and year ago, nos.
Ind W	Latest and year ago, nos.
MG Fin Wkly	Latest and year ago, nos.
D&B Mon	Monthly, cum, nos.
Bus Stats	Monthly and yearly, cum, nos.
Bus Stats	Monthly and yearly, cum, %
S&P Stats	Monthly and yearly, cum, nos.
SCB	Monthly and yearly, cum, nos.
SCB	Monthly and yearly, cum, %
D&B Failure	Yearly, cum, nos.
Hist Stats	Yearly, cum, nos.
Stat Abstr	Yearly, cum, nos.

GRAPHS

D&B Failure	Yearly, cum, index nos.

<MORE INFORMATION>
   Victor Zannowitz and Lionel J. Lerner, "Cyclical Changes in
Business Failures and Corporate Profits," Chap. 12 in
Geoffrey H. Moore, Business Cycle Indicators, Princeton
University Press, Princeton, N.J., 1961.

Business Inventory-Sales Ratio [See Inventory-Sales Ratio]

Business Loans [See Commercial and Industrial Loans
Outstanding, Weekly Reporting Large Commercial Banks]

Business Week Index
<DESCRIPTION>
A weighted average of the production activity in eleven major
U.S. industries.
<DERIVATION>
The values of 13 statistical components are determined. These
components are rail freight traffic, intercity trucking,
machinery production, electric power output, defense and
space equipment contracts, crude oil refinery runs, raw steel
production, automobile assemblies, lumber production, paper
production, paperboard production, coal production, and truck
assemblies. These values are weighted with empirically
derived statistical weights to normalize the data. The
normalized values are seasonally adjusted with weekly
seasonal factors, summed, and divided by a constant to give
the index. Together, the production series make up about 46%
of the weight of the index, transport about 40%, and
electricity use about 14%.

<USE>
An immediate indicator of the well-being of the industrial economy; foreshadows the short-term swings and major turning points in the industrial sector that determine the direction and force of the economy as a whole.
<PUBLISHER>
Business Week
<ANNOUNCED IN>
Business Week
<ANNOUNCEMENT FREQUENCY>
Weekly
<CUMULATIONS>
TABLES

BW	Latest two weeks, month ago, and year ago, index nos.
S&P Outlook	Latest week and year ago, index nos.
S&P Stats	Monthly and yearly, cum, index nos.

GRAPHS

BW	Weekly, monthly, yearly, cum, index nos.

<MORE INFORMATION>
  "The Index Shows a Strong Recovery," Business Week, 50-57 (Oct. 21, 1972).

Business Week Leading Index

<DESCRIPTION>
A weighted average of seven leading indicators charted as a four-week moving average with the most recent week being given the greatest weight.
<DERIVATION>
Seven leading indicators were selected: Unemployment Insurance Programs, Initial Claims; Moody's Aaa Corporate Bond Yields; seven components of Money Supply M2 that are available from the Federal Reserve System on a weekly basis; Standard & Poor's 500; Federal Reserve System data on homebuilding and commercial construction loans; Business Failures; and the Journal of Commerce's index of industrial materials' prices. These indicators are weighted, normalized, and combined. Several are seasonally adjusted, and four are used as either the absolute difference from the previous week or the rate of change. All of the components are adjusted to account for their different degrees of volatility, and the index as a whole is adjusted for trend.
<USE>
To quickly anticipate meaningful changes in the trend of the national economy; it is claimed that the index predicts the peaks of the business cycle by at least seven months and the end of recessions by an average of three months.
<PUBLISHER>
Business Week
<ANNOUNCED IN>
Business Week
<ANNOUNCEMENT FREQUENCY>
Weekly
<CUMULATIONS>
TABLES

BW	Latest week, month, year, index nos.

GRAPHS
BW   Weekly, monthly, yearly, index nos.
<MORE INFORMATION>
  "A New Economic Index That Provides Early Forecasts,"
Business Week, 154-158 (Nov. 14, 1983).

Buying Plans Index
<DESCRIPTION>
A periodic survey to determine families' appraisals of
present business conditions, future business conditions,
plans to make major purchases in the near future, and plans
to take a vacation in the near future.
<DERIVATION>
Each month, 10,000 households are surveyed and asked how they
feel business conditions and employment opportunities are at
the present time and how they feel those conditions and
opportunities will be six months hence. They are also asked
if they plan to purchase a home or automobile, buy an
appliance, or take a vacation during the followin six months.
The panel constitutes a representative sample of the U.S.
population. The responses are tallied and expressed as
percentages. Data from a survey are directly comparable with
the data from previous surveys. The index was originally
compiled bimonthly.
<USE>
An indicator of future consumer-related production activity.
<PUBLISHER>
The Conference Board
<ANNOUNCED IN>
Consumer Attitudes and Buying Plans
<ANNOUNCEMENT FREQUENCY>
Bimonthly
<CUMULATIONS>
TABLES
Consumer Att Monthly, cum, index nos.
Stat Bull   Monthly, cum, index nos.
GRAPHS
CABP   Monthly, cum, index nos.
Stat Bull   Monthly, cum, index nos.
<MORE INFORMATION>
  "Consumer Attitudes and Buying Plans," Conference Board
Record, 34-35 (Feb. 1968).

C

Capacity Utilization [See Manufacturers' Capacity Utilization: Bureau of Economic Analysis and Manufacturers' Capacity Utilization: Federal Reserve Board]

Capacity Utilization Rate [See Manufacturers' Capacity Utilization: Bureau of Economic Analysis and Manufacturers' Capacity Utilization: Federal Reserve Board]

Capital Appropriations
<DESCRIPTION>
An estimate of the amount of money manufacturers in the U.S. are planning to spend on new plant and equipment.
<DERIVATION>
The 1000 largest U.S. manufacturing corporations are surveyed quarterly by The Conference Board to determine the levels of funds appropriated for new plant and equipment in the budgets and plans of those corporations. The actual expenditures for new plant and equipment are also obtained. All areas of manufacturing except petroleum are included. The amounts reported are summed, and an adjustment is made for cancellations. The results are reported as millions of constant 1958 dollars.
<USE>
A leading indicator of general economic activity and of future investment. The empirical values are used to predict future appropriations, which are helpful in judging the future course of overall economic activity and in forecasting activity of the capital-goods producing industries.
<PUBLISHER>
The Conference Board
<ANNOUNCED IN>
Capital Appropriations
<ANNOUNCEMENT FREQUENCY>
Quarterly
<CUMULATIONS>
TABLES
Cap Approp   Quarterly, cum, $
Cap Approp   Quarterly, cum, % change

GRAPHS
Cap Approp   Quarterly, cum, $
Cap Approp   Quarterly, cum, % change
<MORE INFORMATION>
    Elliot   S.   Grossman,   Capital   Appropriations   and
Expenditures: A Quarterly Forecasting Model, The Conference
Board, New York, 1975.
    Elliot S. Grossman, "Getting a Better Bead on a Leading
Indicator," Conference Board Record, 2-6 (Mar. 1975).

Capital Expenditures
<DESCRIPTION>
An estimate of the amount of money manufacturers in the U.S.
have spent on new plant and equipment during a given quarter.
<DERIVATION>
The 1000 largest U.S. manufacturing corporations are surveyed
quarterly by The Conference Board to determine the levels of
funds expended for new plant and equipment. The planned
expenditures for new plant and equipment are also obtained.
All areas of manufacturing except petroleum are included. The
amounts reported are summed. The results are reported as
millions of constant 1958 dollars.
<USE>
Helpful in judging the future course of overall economic
activity and in forecasting activity of the capital-goods
producing industries.
<PUBLISHER>
The Conference Board
<ANNOUNCED IN>
Capital Appropriations
<ANNOUNCEMENT FREQUENCY>
Quarterly
<CUMULATIONS>
TABLES
Cap Approp   Quarterly, cum, $
Cap Approp   Quarterly, cum, % change
GRAPHS
Cap Approp   Quarterly, cum, $
Cap Approp   Quarterly, cum, % change
<MORE INFORMATION>
    E. S. Grossman, Capital Appropriations and Expenditures: A
Quarterly Forecasting Model, The Conference Board, New York,
1975.

Carloadings [Also called Freight-Car Loadings]
<DESCRIPTION>
The total number of railroad car loadings by Class 1
railroads for all commodities.
<DERIVATION>
All Class 1 railway carriers (railroads that have annual
gross revenues of $50 million or more) report the number of
car loadings to the Association of American Railroads weekly.
The Association then totals these figures. Class 1 haulers
handle 97% of the railroad traffic in the U.S.

<USE>
A leading indicator of general business activity.
<PUBLISHER>
Association of American Railroads
<ANNOUNCED IN>
Rail News Update
<ANNOUNCEMENT FREQUENCY>
Weekly
<CUMULATIONS>
TABLES
Moody Trans   Monthly and yearly, cum, nos.
Wkly Car   Weekly, cum, nos.
Rail Age   Year to date, nos.
Rail Age   Year to date, % change
Ybk Rail   Yearly, cum, nos.
Stat Abstr   Yearly, cum, nos.
GRAPHS
Moody Trans   Monthly and yearly, cum, nos.

Change in Business Loans
<DESCRIPTION>
The actual differences during the month in the total amount
of commercial and industrial loans outstanding.
<DERIVATION>
About 320 banks report their outstanding loans to commercial
and industrial customers to the Federal Reserve on a weekly
basis (see Commercial and Industrial Loans Outstanding,
Weekly Reporting Large Commercial Banks). These figures are
totalled for the previous month and seasonally adjusted. The
month's total is subtracted from the total for the preceeding
month, and the change is converted to a simple annual rate
measured in billions of dollars.
<USE>
Considered to be an indicator of future businesss activity
because businesses usually finance additional inventory and
borrow in anticipation of increased volume of production.
<PUBLISHER>
Board of Governors of the Federal Reserve System
<ANNOUNCED IN>
Federal Reserve Bulletin
<ANNOUNCEMENT FREQUENCY>
Weekly
<CUMULATIONS>
TABLES
Stat Bull   Latest quarter and year ago, % change
Man Han   Latest week and year ago, $
BCD   Monthly, cum, $
FR Bull   Weekly, cum, $
GRAPHS
BCD   Monthly, cum, $
<MORE INFORMATION>
  Richard M. Snyder, Measuring Business Changes, Wiley, New
York, 1955, p. 272 ff.

Change in Inventories on Hand and on Order [See Inventory Change]

Change in Sensitive Prices
<DESCRIPTION>
The change in an index of prices charged in primary markets for 13 specified classes of crude materials.
<DERIVATION>
A sample of specified commodities from 13 classes of crude materials (hides and skins, potash, crude natural rubber, wastepaper, iron ore, iron and steel scrap, nonferrous metal scrap, sand, gravel and crushed stone, bituminous coal, anthracite coal, natural gas, and crude petroleum) are priced by reporters in a sample of primary markets in the U.S. These prices are gathered for the Tuesday of the week containing the 13th of the month or are an average of prices throughout the month. The actual wholesale selling prices quoted by representative manufacturers or on organized exchanges or markets are the prices gathered. The price data are weighted based on the value of shipments and combined. The total is indexed to a value of 100 for 1967 and seasonally adjusted. The indicator is expressed as a percent change from the previous month and as a four-term weighted moving average placed at the terminal month.
<USE>
Used as one of the components of the Leading Indicators Composite Index. A leading indicator at peaks, troughs, and overall.
<PUBLISHER>
U.S. Department of Labor, Bureau of Labor Statistics
<ANNOUNCED IN>
Business Conditions Digest
<ANNOUNCEMENT FREQUENCY>
Monthly
<CUMULATIONS>
TABLES
Stat Bull   Latest quarter and year ago, % change
S&P Stats   Monthly and yearly, cum, % change
<MORE INFORMATION>
  Handbook of Cyclical Indicators, U.S. Department of Commerce, Bureau of Economic Analysis, Washington, D.C., 1977, pp. 60-61.
  "Official Indicators: What Are They? Can They Predict the Future?" U.S. News and World Report, 66-67 (Aug. 16, 1976).

Change in Total Liquid Assets
<DESCRIPTION>
The month-to-month change in the holdings of currency, demand deposits, time deposits, savings bonds, negotiable certificates of deposit, short-term marketable U.S. securities, open-market paper, federal funds and repurchasing agreements, and money-market-fund shares by the private domestic nonfinancial sector.
<DERIVATION>
Month-to-month percent changes are computed for the total liquid assets version of the money supply (in dollars). These changes are then smoothed by taking a four-term weighted moving average (1-2-2-1) placed at the terminal month of the span.

<USE>
Used as one of the components of the Leading Indicators
Composite Index. A measure of the availability of funds for
consumer spending and capital investment.
<PUBLISHER>
Board of Governors of the Federal Reserve System
<ANNOUNCED IN>
News Release H6, Monetary Aggregates
<ANNOUNCEMENT FREQUENCY>
Monthly
<CUMULATIONS>
TABLES
BCD   Monthly, cum, % change
GRAPHS
BCD   Yearly, cum, % change
<MORE INFORMATION>
  Handbook of Cyclical Indicators, U.S. Department of
Commerce, Bureau of Economic Analysis, Washington, D.C.,
1977.

Chemical Week Weekly Index of Chemical Prices
<DESCRIPTION>
A measure of the aggregate change in the prices of chemicals.
<DERIVATION>
A sample of the chemical industry is surveyed weekly to
determine the current prices of a specific selection
(unweighted) of chemicals. The value of this chemical
marketbasket is then indexed to the cost of a similar
marketbasket in 1967; the 1967 index value is fixed at 100.
<USE>
Used as an indicator of the cost of doing business. Many
industries are dependent on feedstock chemicals for their
manufacturing processes; when the prices of those feedstocks
go up, the cost of manufacturing goes up, also.
<PUBLISHER>
McGraw-Hill Economics
<ANNOUNCED IN>
Chemical Week
<ANNOUNCEMENT FREQUENCY>
Monthly
<CUMULATIONS>
TABLES
Chem W   Latest week, week ago, month ago, year ago,
               index nos.
GRAPHS
Chem W   Weekly, cum, index nos.

Coal Production (Bituminous)
<DESCRIPTION>
An estimate (based on carloadings and average tonnage carried
by car) of the U.S. production in tons of bituminous coal and
lignite during a given month.
<DERIVATION>
The coal industry is surveyed weekly by the Association of

American Railroads to determine the number of carloadings performed at mine mouths. This number of carloadings is then multiplied by the average coal tonnage carried per car as calculated by the Interstate Commerce Commission. The Energy Information Administration (EIA) independently surveys the industry to determine the methods of coal distribution. From its data, the EIA calculates the ratio of coal that is shipped by rail. The amount estimated to be shipped by rail is then divided by this ratio to produce an estimate of all production.
<USE>
Used to determine the energy mix used to meet the country's energy requirements and as an indirect measure of industrial activity.
<PUBLISHER>
U.S. Department of Energy, Energy Information Administration
<ANNOUNCED IN>
Monthly Energy Review
<ANNOUNCEMENT FREQUENCY>
Monthly
<CUMULATIONS>
TABLES

BW	Latest week, month and year ago, tonnage
Ind W	Latest week and year ago, tonnage
NYT	Latest week and year ago, tonnage
MG Fin Wkly	Latest week and year ago, tonnage
Mo En Rev	Monthly, cum, tonnage
Bus Stats	Monthly and yearly, cum, tonnage
Energy Info	Monthly and yearly, cum, tonnage
S&P Stats	Monthly and yearly, cum, tonnage
SCB	Monthly and yearly, cum, tonnage
Coal Age	Year to date, tonnage
Int Energy	Yearly, tonnage
Key Coal	Yearly, cum, tonnage
Pred Base	Yearly, cum, tonnage
Pred Fore	Yearly, cum, tonnage
Stat Abstr	Yearly, cum, tonnage

GRAPHS

Mo En Rev	Monthly, cum, tonnage
Coal Age	Weekly and monthly, cum, tonnage

PROJECTIONS

Pred Fore	Yearly, tonnage

<MORE INFORMATION>
  Richard M. Snyder, Measuring Business Changes, Wiley, New York, 1955, p. 193.

Coincident Indicators [see Coincident Indicators Composite Index]

Coincident Indicators Composite Index
<DESCRIPTION>
The average behavior of a group of economic indicators whose values have been noted to coincide with business-cycle turns.

<DERIVATION>
Four economic indicators were selected because their values
generally changed in a manner similar to changes in the
business cycles and at about the same time as those
business-cycle changes. Those indicators are the employees on
nonagricultural payrolls, the index of total industrial
production, the personal income (less transfer payments), and
the manufacturing and trade sales. Month-to-month percent
changes or differences are calculated for each component of
the composite index. The percent changes (or differences) for
each component are standardized to an absolute value of one
by dividing each monthly change by the average of these
changes. These standardized changes are then weighted
according to the economic significance, statistical adequacy,
cyclical timing, conformity to business cycles, smoothness,
and currency of each component. A weighted average of the
standardized changes is then computed for all the components.
<USE>
Indicates changes in the direction of aggregate economic
activity; viewed by many as an indicator of current and
future levels of economic activity.
<PUBLISHER>
U.S. Department of Commerce, Bureau of Economic Analysis
<ANNOUNCED IN>
Business Conditions Digest
<ANNOUNCEMENT FREQUENCY>
Monthly
<CUMULATIONS>
TABLES
BCD   Monthly, cum, index nos.
GRAPHS
BCD   Yearly, cum, index nos.
BCD   Yearly, cum, % change
<MORE INFORMATION>
  Geoffrey   H.   Moore,   Ed.,   Business   Cycle   Indicators,
Princeton University Press, Princeton, N.J., 1961.

**Commercial   and   Industrial   Loans   Outstanding,   Weekly
Reporting Large Commercial Banks** [Also called Bank Loans]
<DESCRIPTION>
A measure of the average dollar amount of business loans
outstanding each month.
<DERIVATION>
The Federal Reserve System receives from about 320 banks
reports that include data on the amount of commercial and
industrial loans outstanding as of each Wednesday and the
amount of loans sold outright during each week to the banks'
own foreign branches, nonconsolidated nonbank affiliates,
holding companies, and consolidated nonbank subsidiaries of
the holding companies. All of these are summed and seasonally
adjusted weekly. The arithmetic mean of the weekly values for
a month is calculated for the monthly value.
<USE>
A lagging indicator for peaks, for troughs, and overall.
<PUBLISHER>
Board of Governors of the Federal Reserve System

```
<ANNOUNCED IN>
Federal Reserve Bulletin
<ANNOUNCEMENT FREQUENCY>
Weekly
<CUMULATIONS>
TABLES
BCD          Monthly, cum, $
FR Bull      Monthly, cum, $
Bus Stats    Monthly and yearly, cum, $
SCB          Monthly and yearly, cum, $
Stat Abstr   Yearly, cum, $
GRAPHS
BCD          Yearly, cum, $
<MORE INFORMATION>
```

N. Jacoby, H. Neil, and R. J. Saulnier, Business Finance and Banking, rev.ed., National Bureau of Economic Research, New York, 1980.

Handbook of Cyclical Indicators, U.S. Department of Commerce, Bureau of Economic Analysis, Washington, D.C., 1977.

Nathaniel Chadwick, "An Infallible Indicator of Stock Market Trends," Banking, 39+ (Mar. 1971).

Composite Index of Coincident Indicators [see Coincident Indicators Composite Index]

Composite Index of Lagging Indicators [see Lagging Indicators Composite Index]

Composite Index of Leading Indicators [see Leading Indicators Composite Index]

Composite Coincident Indicators [see Coincident Indicators Composite Index]

Composite Lagging Indicators [see Lagging Indicators Composite Index]

Composite Leading Indicators [see Leading Indicators Composite Index]

Conference Board Diffusion Index [See Diffusion Index]

Conference Board Help Wanted Advertising Index [See Help Wanted Advertising Index]

Constant Maturities Treasury Securities
<DESCRIPTION>
An estimated yield to maturity for any Treasury security given the aggregate performance of such securities in current bond markets.
<DERIVATION>
Closing yields of selected outstanding Treasury securities are plotted on a graph with the date of maturity on the x-axis and the yield on the y-axis. A single, continuous yield curve is then drawn through the midst of the plotted points allowing a yield to be interpolated for any fixed maturity.
<USE>
Used to estimate the yield of a Treasury security for a given time to maturity.
<PUBLISHER>
Board of Governors of the Federal Reserve System
<ANNOUNCED IN>
Selected Interest Rates, Statistical Release H.15 (519)
<ANNOUNCEMENT FREQUENCY>
Weekly
<CUMULATIONS>
TABLES
EI   Weekly, monthly, yearly, cum, %
FR Bull   Weekly, monthly, yearly, cum, %
<MORE INFORMATION>
   Joint Economic Committee, 1980 Supplement to Economic Indicators, Historical and Descriptive Background, USGPO, Washington, D.C., 1980.

Construction Contract Awards
<DESCRIPTION>
The estimated total dollar value of awards for housing, industrial and commercial buildings, utilities, and public works throughout the U.S. for a given month.
<DERIVATION>
The data used to calculate this indicator are derived from the Dodge reports, sampling, permit filings, and publications, with the majority coming from the Dodge reports. The values reflect as closely as possible the actual construction costs exclusive of land, architect's fees, and equipment that is not an integral part of the structure. The data are indexed to a value of 100 for 1977 and are seasonally adjusted. The annual indexes are based on annual data and are not averages of the monthly figures.
<USE>
Used as an indicator of trends in future construction activity.
<PUBLISHER>
McGraw-Hill Information Systems Co., F. W. Dodge Div.; U.S. Department of Commerce
<ANNOUNCED IN>
Survey of Current Business
<ANNOUNCEMENT FREQUENCY>
Monthly

<CUMULATIONS>
TABLES
Bus Stats   Monthly and yearly, cum, $
Const Rev   Monthly and yearly, cum, $
SCB   Monthly and yearly, cum, $
Stat Abstr   Yearly, cum, $
<MORE INFORMATION>
   Richard M. Snyder, Measuring Business Changes, Wiley, New
York, 1955, p. 210.
   "The Methodology Underlying the Dodge Index of Construction
Contracts, Seasonally Adjusted," Construction Review, 5-7
(Nov. 1959).

Construction Cost Index
<DESCRIPTION>
A measure of the combined effect of wage and price changes on
the value of the construction dollar.
<DERIVATION>
Four costs are calculated, those of: 200 hours of common
labor at the average rate for such labor in 20 selected
cities; 25 cwt of standard structural steel shapes at the
average price for such steel at three selected mills; 22.56
cwt of Portland cement at the average price for such cement
in 20 selected cities; and 1088 board feet of two-by-four
lumber at the average price for such lumber in 20 selected
cities. These costs are weighted 74:15:2:9, respectively.
These weights are adjusted periodically to reflect economic
conditions. The calculated total is then indexed to the
totals in 1913 and 1967, producing two series, a 1913 = 100
series and a 1967 = 100 series. Monthly indexes are the
indexes calculated for the first week of the month. Annual
indexes are straight mathematical averages of the component
months. The common-labor and materials components are also
broken out and published as separate indexes. A related
index, the Building Cost Index, uses much of the same data in
its derivation; it uses a different labor base.
<USE>
Used to judge underlying trends of construction costs in the
U.S. and to estimate costs of future construction projects.
<PUBLISHER>
McGraw-Hill Information Systems Co.
<ANNOUNCED IN>
Engineering News-Record
<ANNOUNCEMENT FREQUENCY>
Weekly (U.S.; 1913 = 100)
Monthly (City-by-city; 1967 = 100)
<CUMULATIONS>
TABLES
Eng News-Rec Latest week, index nos.
Eng News-Rec Latest and year ago, % change
Bus Stats   Monthly and yearly, cum, index nos.
Const Rev   Monthly and yearly, cum, index nos.
SCB   Monthly and yearly, cum, index nos.
Stat Abstr   Yearly, cum, index nos.

PROJECTIONS
Eng News-Rec Yearly, index nos.
<MORE INFORMATION>
  "Construction Costs Tracked for U.S.," Engineering
News-Record 210 (12), 114-121 (Mar. 24, 1983).

Consumer Confidence Index
<DESCRIPTION>
The fraction of positive opinions expressed by respondents is
calculated from answers to questions about (1) the current
state of business conditions and employment opportunities,
(2) how these conditions and opportunities will change during
the following six months, and (3) how they feel their own
economic conditions will change during the same period.
<DERIVATION>
A questionnaire is mailed to 5000 representative sample homes
each month; answers to standardized questions are indexed to
answers received in 1969-1970 to show month-to-month
variations in opinions about economic outlook. The survey
is conducted by National Family Opinion, Inc.
<USE>
Used to foretell short-term shifts in the national growth
rate and guide production and marketing decision making.
<PUBLISHER>
The Conference Board
<ANNOUNCED IN>
Consumer Attitudes and Buying Plans
<ANNOUNCEMENT FREQUENCY>
Monthly
<CUMULATIONS>
TABLES
Ind W   Latest and year ago, index nos.
CABP   Monthly, cum, index nos.
Stat Bull   Monthly, cum, index nos.
GRAPHS
CABP   Yearly, cum, index nos.
Mo Econ Ind Yearly, cum, index nos.
Stat Bull   Yearly, cum, index nos.
<MORE INFORMATION>
  Fabian Linden, "The Measure of Consumer Confidence," Across
the
Board, April 1979, pp. 74-79.

Consumer Installment Credit
<DESCRIPTION>
Estimates of credit extended and credit repaid and the net
change in credit debt outstanding for credit given to
individuals through normal business channels usually for the
purchase of consumer goods. Excluded are long-term financings
(e.g., mortgages), purchases made with travel and
entertainment credit-cards, borrowings on life-insurance
policies, loans to farmers, and noninstallment credit.
<DERIVATION>
Benchmark surveys of credit outstanding for various classes
of creditors are conducted (e.g., every five years). These

benchmark values are then brought up to date by surveying a sample of the population of creditors on a monthly or annual basis. These intermediate estimates are then adjusted for season and trading day.
<USE>
Consumer installment credit is used as an indicator of near-term consumer purchasing power and the market for consumer goods often bought on the installment plan. Consumer debt also reflects the general financial position of consumers and is an important element in the demand for funds in the financial community.
<PUBLISHER>
Board of Governors of the Federal Reserve System
<ANNOUNCED IN>
Consumer Installment Credit, Statistical Release G.19
<ANNOUNCEMENT FREQUENCY>
Monthly
<CUMULATIONS>
TABLES

BCD	Monthly, cum, $
BCD	Monthly, cum, % change
Man Han	Monthly, cum, $
Bus Stats	Monthly and yearly, cum, $
FR Bull	Monthly and yearly, cum, $
SCB	Monthly and yearly, cum, $
S&P Stats	Monthly and yearly, cum, $
EI	Monthly and yearly, cum, $
Moody's B&F	Yearly, cum, $
Stat Abstr	Yearly, cum, $
Hist Stats	Yearly, cum, $

GRAPHS

Stat Abstr	Yearly, cum, $
BCD	Yearly, cum, $

<MORE INFORMATION>
   Board of Governors of the Federal Reserve System, Banking and Monetary Statistics, 1941-1970, Federal Reserve Board, Washington, D.C., 1971.
   Joint Economic Committee, 1980 Supplement to Economic Indicators, Historical and Descriptive Background, USGPO, Washington, D.C., 1980.
   John Kirk, "Economic Indicators: The How and the Why," Banking, 27-28 (Aug. 1964).

Consumer Price Index [Formerly called the Cost of Living Index.]
<DESCRIPTION>
A composite index number relates the cost for a specific mix in type and quantity of consumer goods and services to the cost for an equivalent mix in 1967. Covers the prices of everything people buy in the normal courses of their lives: food, clothing, transportation, fuel, household supplies, health services and materials, recreational goods and events, shelter, etc.
<DERIVATION>
The prices of about 400 precisely specified goods and services are determined by observation at points of purchase

and by other means nationwide. The costs incurred by (1) urban wage earners and clerical workers and (2) all urban households are then estimated by weighting, averaging, and summing the prices. The resulting index is then broken down into components for not only the above two classes of consumers nationwide but also for classes of goods and services, regions of the country, and 28 major metropolitan areas. The indexes are considered to be representative of the changes in costs faced by 90% of the U.S. urban households and 50% of the urban wage and clerical workers.
<USE>
As an escalator (cost of living allowance) for wages, pensions, Social Security benefits, rents, royalties, and child-support payments; as a guide to making business decisions and in setting governmental policies.
<PUBLISHER>
U.S. Department of Labor, Bureau of Labor Statistics
<ANNOUNCED IN>
Bureau of Labor Statistics press release
<ANNOUNCEMENT FREQUENCY>
Monthly
<CUMULATIONS>
TABLES

BW	Latest and year ago, index nos.
NYT	Latest and year ago, % change
NYT	Latest and year ago, index nos.
Barron's	Latest and year ago, index nos.
FR Bull	Latest and year ago, % change
Man Han	Latest and year ago, % change
CCH Labor	Monthly and yearly, cum, index nos.
BNA	Monthly and yearly, cum, index nos.
S&P Stats	Monthly and yearly, cum, index nos.
FR Bull	Monthly and yearly, cum, index nos.
Bus Stats	Monthly and yearly, cum, index nos.
SCB	Monthly and yearly, cum, index nos.
EI	Monthly and yearly, cum, index nos.
EI	Monthly and yearly, cum, % change
Int Econ Ind	Quarterly and yearly, cum, index nos.
Int Econ Ind	Quarterly and yearly, cum, % change
Ind W	Latest quarter and yearly, index nos.
Ind W	Latest quarter and yearly, % change
Stat Abstr	Yearly, cum, % change
Stat Abstr	Yearly, cum, index nos.
Bus Stats	Yearly, cum, index nos.

GRAPHS

Mo Econ Ind	Yearly, cum, index nos.
MG Fin Wkly	Yearly, cum, index nos.
EI	Yearly, cum, index nos.
Stat Abstr	Yearly, cum, % change

PROJECTIONS

Value Line	Quarterly and yearly, % change
Bus Rev WF	Yearly, index nos.
Ind W	Yearly, index nos.
Pred Fore	Yearly, index nos.

<MORE INFORMATION>
  CPI Detailed Report, Bureau of Labor Statistics, Washington, D.C., monthly.

Revising the Consumer Price Index, Bureau of Labor Statistics, Washington, D.C., 1978.

The Consumer Price Index: Concepts and Content over the Years, Bureau of Labor Statistics, Washington, D.C., May 1978.

Handbook of Methods, Bureau of Labor Statistics, Washington, D.C., 1976.

Consumer Prices, Major Industrial Countries
<DESCRIPTION>
Estimated change in the average cost of living in Canada, Japan, France, Germany, Italy, or England since a given reference date.
<DERIVATION>
Methods of calculating the price index vary from country to country. Generally, a particular "market basket," including rent and ordinary services is specified, and the cost for that given mix and quantity of goods and services is surveyed each month at a regular time. The weighted sum of the similar costs is then indexed to the cost found for the items some time in the past (ranging from 1970 to 1976). The sample population may or may not include rural families. The indexes are not seasonally adjusted.
<USE>
Used to determine changes and trends in the costs of goods and services purchased by the average wage earner in the respective foreign country.
<PUBLISHER>
U.S. Department of Commerce, International Trade Administration, Office of Planning and Research
<ANNOUNCED IN>
International Economic Indicators
<ANNOUNCEMENT FREQUENCY>
Monthly
<CUMULATIONS>
TABLES
Int Econ Ind Quarterly and yearly, cum, index nos.
Int Econ Ind Quarterly and yearly, cum, % change
Int Fin Stat Yearly, cum, index nos.
UN Stat Year Yearly, cum, index nos.
Int Fin Stat Yearly, cum, index nos.
Stat Abstr Yearly, cum, index nos.
<MORE INFORMATION>
Joint Economic Committee, 1980 Supplement to Economic Indicators, Historical and Descriptive Background, USGPO, Washington, D.C., 1980.

Contract Awards [See Construction Contract Awards]

Contracts and Orders for Plant and Equipment
<DESCRIPTION>
The value of new contract awards to building contractors, public-works contractors, and public-utilities contractors

and of new orders received by manufacturers in nondefense capital-goods industries. This value is expressed in current dollars and in 1972 dollars.
<DERIVATION>
The data for this indicator are made up of three components: data on commercial and industrial contracts (e.g., banks, office buildings, stores, warehouses, and factories); data on contracts for privately-owned nonbuilding construction (such as streets, bridges, dams, parks, sewerages, power plants, airports, and pipelines); and data on manufacturers' new orders (e.g., steam turbines and communications equipment). The construction contracts data cover new construction, additions, and major alterations; maintenance work is excluded. The data are derived from Dodge reports (which represent actual construction costs exclusive of land, architects' fees, and costs for equipment) supplemented by permit-place reports. Manufacturers' new orders are compiled by the Census Bureau [see Manufacturers' New Orders for Consumer Goods and Materials]. The three components of the data are seasonally adjusted, totalled, expressed in billions of dollars, and converted to 1972 dollars.
<USE>
Used as one of the components of the Leading Indicators Composite Index. A leading indicator of overall economic activity.
<PUBLISHER>
U.S. Department of Commerce, Bureau of Economic Analysis
<ANNOUNCED IN>
Business Conditions Digest
<ANNOUNCEMENT FREQUENCY>
Monthly
<CUMULATIONS>
TABLES
Stat Bull   Latest three months, % change
BCD   Monthly, cum, $
S&P Stats   Monthly and yearly, cum, $
GRAPHS
BCD   Yearly, cum, $
<MORE INFORMATION>
   G. H. Moore and J. Shiskin, "Why the Leading Indicators Really Do Lead," Across the Board, 71-75 (May 1978).
   "Official Indicators: What Are They? Can They Predict the Future?" U.S. News and World Report, 66-67 (Aug. 16, 1976).

Corporate Bond Yield Averages [See Moody's Corporate Aaa Bond Yield Averages]

Corporate Financing Plans
<DESCRIPTION>
An assessment of the actions that corporations' are likely to take to ensure the availability of operating funds.
<DERIVATION>
Fewer than 50 executives of U.S. companies are surveyed about their companies' sources of funds during the past 12 months

and their plans for financing their operations during the following 12 months. Specifically, they are asked what percentage of funds for the previous 12 months came from internal sources (retained earnings, charges, and sales of assets and securities) and what percentage came from external funds. Those that used external sources are asked what percentage of these external funds were comprised of bond issues, private placements, new equity, bank loans (long term and short term), commercial paper, and other sources. The responses are averaged and expressed as an overall percentage. The executives are then asked whether they see each of these figures staying the same, increasing 5 to 10%, increasing more than 10%, decreasing 5 to 10%, or decreasing more than 10%. The number of executives responding in each category is tabulated.
<USE>
Used as an indicator of U.S. capital- and bond-market activities.
<PUBLISHER>
The Conference Board
<ANNOUNCED IN>
Financial Indicators and Corporate Financing Plans
<ANNOUNCEMENT FREQUENCY>
Semiannual
<CUMULATIONS>
PROJECTIONS
Fin Ind   Semiannually

Corporate Profits [Also called After-Tax Corporate Profits]
<DESCRIPTION>
Profits earned by U.S. corporations before taxes; data given for all domestic industries and for the financial, manufacturing, and wholesale and retail trade sectors; data include inventory valuation. Also presented as profits earned after taxes, showing the distribution among taxes, dividends, undistributed profits, and inventory.
<DERIVATION>
Annual tabulations by the Internal Revenue Service of corporate profits reported on unaudited tax returns are adjusted to make them comparable with other measures of income and extrapolated with quarterly data from the Federal Trade Commission, from federal regulatory agencies, and from surveys and miscellaneous sources. The resulting before-taxes estimated corporate profits are then seasonally adjusted. Dividends are estimated from a survey of publicly reported dividends. Other components of profit are estimated as residuals. Undistributed profits essentially equal the change in corporate net worth produced by current operations.
<USE>
In that it measures the contribution of corporate profits to the national income, this indicator is used to assess the state of health of a substantial part of the nation's business community.
<PUBLISHER>
U.S. Department of Commerce, Bureau of Economic Analysis

<ANNOUNCED IN>
Survey of Current Business
<ANNOUNCEMENT FREQUENCY>
Quarterly
<CUMULATIONS>
TABLES

NYT	Latest quarter and year ago, $
S&P Outlook	Latest quarter and year ago, $
EI	Quarterly and yearly, cum, $
FR Bull	Quarterly and yearly, cum, $
S&P Stats	Quarterly and yearly, cum, $
Bus Stats	Quarterly and yearly, cum, $
SCB	Quarterly and yearly, cum, $
BCD	Quarterly, cum, $
Stat Abstr	Yearly, cum, $
BW	Latest quarter, $
Q Fin Rept	Quarterly, cum, % change
Q Fin Rept	Quarterly, cum, $

GRAPHS

EI	Quarterly and yearly, cum, $
Stat Abstr	Yearly, cum, $
BCD	Yearly, cum, $
FR Bull	Quarterly and yearly, cum, $

PROJECTIONS

Bus Rev WF	Yearly, $
Value Line	Quarterly and yearly, $
Value Line	Quarterly and yearly, % change

<MORE INFORMATION>
   Joint Economic Committee, 1980 Supplement to Economic
Indicators, Historical and Descriptive Background, USGPO,
Washington, D.C., 1980.
   Readings in Concepts and Methods of National Income
Statistics, U.S. Department of Commerce, Bureau of Economic
Analysis, Washington, D.C., 1976.
   Gross National Product Data Improvement Project Report,
U.S. Department of Commerce, Office of Federal Statistical
Policy and Standards, Washington, D.C., 1977.

CRB (BLS-Formula) Spot Group Indices, Raw Industrials
[See Industrial Raw Materials Price Index]

**Current Assets and Liabilities of Nonfinancial
Corporations**
<DESCRIPTION>
A measure of the net working capital (cash, U.S. Government
securities, notes and accounts receivable, inventories, and
other current assets less notes and accounts payable and
other current liabilities) of a significant segment of U.S.
business.
<DERIVATION>
The data are derived primarily from the quarterly reports
from corporations required by the Federal Trade Commission
and various regulatory agencies. The data are directly
benchmarked to annual tabulations prepared by regulatory

agencies. Data on other industries are derived indirectly. The data are periodically benchmarked to the Statistics of Income prepared by the Internal Revenue Service.
<USE>
Used by business and industry for investment analysis and by the government to prepare the national economic and flow-of-funds accounts.
<PUBLISHER>
Federal Trade Commission and the Board of Governors of the Federal Reserve System
<ANNOUNCED IN>
Federal Reserve Bulletin
<ANNOUNCEMENT FREQUENCY>
Quarterly
<CUMULATIONS>
TABLES
EI   Quarterly and yearly, cum, $
FR Bull   Quarterly and yearly, cum, $
Stat Abstr Yearly, cum, $
<MORE INFORMATION>
   Joint Economic Committee, 1980 Supplement to Economic Indicators, Historical and Descriptive Background, USGPO, Washington, D.C., 1980.
   "Working Capital of Nonfinancial Corporations," Federal Reserve Bulletin, 533-537 (July 1978).

D

Deposit Turnover
<DESCRIPTION>
The ratio of bank debits to bank deposits
<DERIVATION>
The total debits and deposits are reported to the Federal
Reserve System by all member banks once a month. These
respective reported figures are totalled, and the total
deposits are divided into the total debits.
<USE>
As an indicator of the total velocity of money (a measure of
the number of times money circulates in one year) and as an
indicator of fluctuations of the business cycle.
<PUBLISHER>
Board of Governors of the Federal Reserve System
<ANNOUNCED IN>
Federal Reserve Bulletin
<ANNOUNCEMENT FREQUENCY>
Monthly
<CUMULATIONS>
TABLES
FR Bull   Monthly, yearly, cum, $
Stat Abstr   Yearly, cum, $
<MORE INFORMATION>
   G. Garvy, Debits and Clearings Statistics and Their Use,
Board of Governors of the Federal Reserve System, Washington,
D.C., 1959.

Diffusion Index [More properly referred to as the Principal
Diffusion Index]
<DESCRIPTION>
The frequency of rises in 20 component series during the 12
months ending with the month of reporting.
<DERIVATION>
Twenty indicators are followed; these are broken down into
industrial and nonindustrial indicators. The industrial
indicators are subdivided into production [(1) iron and
steel; (2) paper and printing; and (3)textiles, apparel, and
leather]; labor [(4) weekly hours of production of workers in

manufacturing, (5) help wanted, (6) unemployment rate, (7) layoff rate, and (8) accession rate]; and miscellaneous [(9) manufacturers' new orders for durables and (10) freightcar loadings]. The nonindustrial indicators are subdivided into prices [(11) industrial stocks and (12) spot commodities]; consumer [(13) retail trade of durable goods stores, (14) personal income, and (15) changes in installment credit outstanding]; construction [(16) commercial and industrial building contracts and (17) nonfarm housing starts]; and miscellaneous [(18) number of business failures, (19) change in manufacturing and trade inventories, and (20) bank debits outside New York]. Each of these components is assigned a weight. Each month, the indicators are determined to have risen, stayed the same, or fallen, and each is assigned a value: 1 if it has risen, 0.5 if it has stayed the same, or 0 if it has fallen. The order of assignment is reversed for indicators that have an inverted economic significance (such as unemployment). These assigned values are then multiplied by their respective weights, and the total calculated. A 12-month moving total of the number rising is computed with each indicator receiving equal weight and each month receiving a weight from 1 (the most distant month) to 12 (the most recent). This value, which can range from 0 to 1560, is then normalized to a range of 0 to 100 by division by 15.6. The resulting index is shown at the end of the 12-month period to which it applies.
<USE>
A means of rapidly identifying cyclical turning points; used to gage how widespread an expansion or contraction is.
<PUBLISHER>
The Conference Board
<ANNOUNCED IN>
Statistical Bulletin
<ANNOUNCEMENT FREQUENCY>
Monthly
<CUMULATIONS>
TABLES
Stat Bull   Monthly, cum, index nos.
GRAPHS
Stat Bull   Yearly, cum, index nos.
<MORE INFORMATION>
  M. Ehrlich, "Using the Conference Board's Diffusion Index," The Conference Board Record, 12-15 (July 1966).

Discomfort Index [See Misery Index in the Appendix Nonquantitative Indicators]

Discount Rate [See Federal Reserve Discount Rate]

Disposable Personal Income
<DESCRIPTION>
The income a person has after all financial obligations to governmental agencies (e.g., taxes, tuition, and hospital bills) have been deducted from the gross income.

\<DERIVATION\>
The quarterly estimate of personal tax and nontax payments to public agencies is subtracted from the quarterly estimate of the total personal income.
\<USE\>
Used to forecast consumption expenditures for goods and services and as a component in the measurement of the nation's standard of living.
\<PUBLISHER\>
U.S. Department of Commerce, Bureau of Economic Analysis
\<ANNOUNCED IN\>
Survey of Current Business
\<ANNOUNCEMENT FREQUENCY\>
Quarterly
\<CUMULATIONS\>
TABLES

EI	Quarterly and yearly, cum, $
Ind W	Quarterly and yearly, cum, $
Ind W	Quarterly and yearly, cum, % change
S&P Stats	Quarterly and yearly, cum, $
Pred Base	Yearly, cum, $
Pred Fore	Yearly, cum, $

GRAPHS

EI	Quarterly and yearly, cum, $

PROJECTIONS

Bus Rev WF	Yearly, $
Value Line	Quarterly and yearly, $
Pred Fore	Yearly, $

\<MORE INFORMATION\>
   Richard M. Snyder, Measuring Business Changes, Wiley, N.Y., 1955, p. 20 ff.
   John Kirk, "Economic Indicators: The How and the Why," Banking, 27-28 (Aug. 1964).

Disposition of Personal Income
\<DESCRIPTION\>
The uses to which individuals in the U.S. put their earnings.
\<DERIVATION\>
From the aggregate total personal income for the U.S. is subtracted the aggregate estimated personal taxes paid and nontax payments made to give the aggregate estimated disposable personal income of the U.S. From this personal disposable income is subtracted the estimated personal outlays (personal consumption expenditures, interest paid by consumers to business, and personal transfer payments to foreigners) to give the amount saved by indiduals, expressed both as an aggregate amout and as a percentage of disposable personal income. The personal consumption expenditures are derived for benchmark years by taking the producers' prices for goods produced and adding to them estimates of transportation charges, trade markups, and taxes. These benchmark data are updated quarterly with the Census Bureau's retail sales figures and other data. The aggregate disposable personal-income and personal-consumption-expenditure data are reduced to per capita figures by dividing them by the Census Bureau's estimate of total population of the U.S. These per

capita values are then deflated to constant 1972 dollars by
dividing them by an implicit deflator.
<USE>
Used as an indicator of income available for spending or
saving; of trends in consumer purchases; and of the division
of the national output among consumer demand, business
capital formation, and other expenditures.
<PUBLISHER>
U.S. Department of Commerce, Bureau of Economic Analysis and
Bureau of the Census
<ANNOUNCED IN>
Survey of Current Business
<ANNOUNCEMENT FREQUENCY>
Quarterly
<CUMULATIONS>
TABLES
Ind W   Latest quarter and year, % change
Ind W   Latest quarter and year, $
S&P Stats   Quarterly and yearly, cum, $
EI   Quarterly and yearly, cum, $
Bus Stats   Quarterly and yearly, cum, $
SCB   Quarterly and yearly, cum, $
Pred Base   Yearly, cum, $
Pred Fore   Yearly, cum, $
Stat Abstr   Yearly, cum, $
GRAPHS
EI   Quarterly and yearly, cum, $
PROJECTIONS
Value Line   Quarterly and yearly, % change
Pred Fore   Yearly, $
Bus Rev WF   Yearly, $
Ind W   Yearly, $
<MORE INFORMATION>
   Joint Economic Committee, 1980 Supplement to Economic
Indicators, Historical and Descriptive Background, USGPO,
Washington, D.C., 1980.

Dividend-Price Ratio [See Standard and Poor's 500
Dividend-Price Ratio]

Donoghue's Money Fund Averages
<DESCRIPTION>
The average yield of money-market mutual funds calculated for
the past week and the past 30 days.
<DERIVATION>
The yields of more than 300 money-market mutual funds are
tallied and averaged.
<USE>
An indicator of the current state of the capital markets.
<PUBLISHER>
Donoghue Organization, Inc.
<ANNOUNCED IN>
Donoghue's Money Letter

<ANNOUNCEMENT FREQUENCY>
Weekly
<CUMULATIONS>
TABLES
D Money   Latest week, month, year, %
Barron's   Latest week and month, %
NYT   Latest week, %
<MORE INFORMATION>
  W. E. Donoghue, William E. Donoghue's Complete Money Market
Guide, Harper and Row, New York, 1980.

Dow Jones Average [See Dow Jones 20-Bond Average, Dow Jones
Composite Average, Dow Jones Industrial Average, Dow Jones
Transportation Average, and Dow Jones Utilities Average]

Dow Jones 20-Bond Average
<DESCRIPTION>
A daily comparison of the closing prices of ten public
utilities and ten industrial issues.
<DERIVATION>
Dow Jones selects the common stocks of ten public utilities
and ten industrial corporations listed on the New York Stock
Exchange and sums the closing prices of those stocks each
day. These twenty issues are also among those included in the
utilities and industrials averages. This total is then
divided by a constant divisor to produce the average. This is
not a strict arithmetic average because the constant divisor
is not the number of listings being averaged. It is, instead,
a number derived from the previous day's average, taking into
account the effects of stock splits, dividends, or
substitutions. The constant divisor is revised by
recalculating the sum of the previous day's closing prices
with new values for affected stocks (e.g., with one-third of
the old price for a stock that split 3:1) and dividing that
new sum by the average that had originally been calculated
for that day. The resulting new constant divisor is used for
calculating subsequent days' averages. A new constant divisor
is calculated for the 20-Bond Average if stock splits or
other changes in individual component stocks cause an
appreciable distortion in the Average.
<USE>
Used as a yardstick to compare the yields of various
municipal bonds.
<PUBLISHER>
Dow Jones & Co.
<ANNOUNCED IN>
Wall Street Journal
<ANNOUNCEMENT FREQUENCY>
Daily
<CUMULATIONS>
TABLES
WSJ   Daily and last two years, averages
WSJ   Yearly high-low, cum, averages
Barron's   Daily, cum, averages

Barron's	Yearly high-low, last, averages
Barron's	Latest year to date, % change

Dow Jones Composite Average
<DESCRIPTION>
A daily comparison of the closing prices of about 65 selected securities.
<DERIVATION>
Dow Jones selects the common stocks of about 65 corporations listed on the New York Stock Exchange. These corporations are those included in the industrial, utilities, and transportation averages. It then sums the closing prices of those stocks each day. The total is then divided by a constant divisor to produce the average. This is not a strict arithmetic average because the constant divisor is not the number of listings being averaged. It is, instead, a number derived from the previous day's average, taking into account the effects of stock splits, dividends, or substitutions. The constant divisor is revised by recalculating the sum of the previous day's closing prices with new values for affected stocks (e.g., with one-third of the old price for a stock that split 3:1) and dividing that new sum by the average that had originally been calculated for that day. The resulting new constant divisor is used for calculating subsequent days' averages. A new constant divisor is calculated for the Composite Average if stock splits or other changes in individual component stocks cause an appreciable distortion in the Average.
<USE>
A technical indicator of stock-market cycles.
<PUBLISHER>
Dow Jones & Co.
<ANNOUNCED IN>
Wall Street Journal
<ANNOUNCEMENT FREQUENCY>
Daily
<CUMULATIONS>
TABLES

NYT	Daily, high-low-close, index nos.
Man Han	Latest week, index nos.
WSJ	Latest daily and year ago, index nos.
WSJ	Latest daily and year ago, % change
Bus Stats	Monthly and yearly, cum, index nos.
EI	Monthly and yearly, cum, index nos.
S&P Stats	Monthly and yearly, cum, index nos.
SCB	Monthly and yearly, cum, index nos.
Barron's	Hourly, cum, index nos.
Barron's	Daily, high-low, cum, index nos.
Hist Stats	Yearly, cum, index nos.
MG Fin Wkly	Daily, cum, index nos.
MG Fin Wkly	Latest week, high-low-close, % change
Stat Abstr	Yearly, cum, index nos.

GRAPHS

WSJ	Daily, cum, index nos.

<MORE INFORMATION>
  G. Munn, Encyclopedia of Banking and Finance, Bankers'
Publishing Co., Boston, 1983.

Dow Jones Industrial Average
<DESCRIPTION>
A daily comparison of the closing prices of the securities of
30 industrial corporations.
<DERIVATION>
Dow Jones selects 30 industrial common stocks listed on the
New York Stock Exchange and sums the closing prices of those
stocks each day. This total is then divided by a constant
divisor to produce the average. This is not a strict
arithmetic average because the constant divisor is not the
number of listings being averaged. It is, instead, a number
derived from the previous day's average, taking into account
the effects of stock splits, dividends, or substitutions. The
constant divisor is revised by recalculating the sum of the
previous day's closing prices with new values for affected
stocks (e.g., with one-third of the old price for a stock
that split 3:1) and dividing that new sum by the average that
had originally been calculated for that day. The resulting
new constant divisor is used for calculating subsequent days'
averages. A new constant divisor is calculated for the
Industrials Average if stock splits or other changes in
individual component stocks cause a change in the Average of
five or more points.
<USE>
The most important stock market indicator, it is used to
track stock-market cycles.
<PUBLISHER>
Dow Jones & Co.
<ANNOUNCED IN>
New York Stock Exchange ticker; Wall Street Journal
<ANNOUNCEMENT FREQUENCY>
Semihourly
<CUMULATIONS>
TABLES

Barron's	Daily and hourly, weekly, cum, avg
NYT	Latest week, high-low, % change
Barron's	Latest week-end, high-low, avg
Man Han	Latest week-end, avg
Man Han	Latest week-end and year ago, % change
MG Fin Wkly	Daily, cum, avg
Inc	Latest month and year ago, % change
Forbes	Latest month and year ago, % change
Value Line	Latest two weeks, avg
EI	Monthly, weekly, yearly, cum, avg
Value Line	Latest week, % change
Bus Stats	Monthly and yearly, cum, avg
SCB	Monthly and yearly, cum, avg
S&P Stats	Monthly and yearly, cum, avg
Barron's	Yearly, high-low, avg

GRAPHS

MG Fin Wkly	Daily, cum, avg

WSJ	Daily, cum, avg
NYT	Monthly, high-low, avg
Value Line	Yearly, cum, avg
Inc	Monthly, cum, % change
PROJECTIONS	
Fin Ind	Yearly, avg

<MORE INFORMATION>
   Michael Hayes, The Dow Jones - Irwin Guide to Stock Market Cycles, Dow Jones - Irwin, Homewood, Ill., 1977.
   Martin J. Pring, Technical Analysis Explained, An Illustrated Guide for the Investor, McGraw-Hill, New York, 1980, pp. 112-119.
   "Market Guides," Barron's, 9+ (Sept. 26, 1966).
   Keith V. Smith, "Stock Price and Economic Indexes for Generating Efficient Portfolios," Journal of Business, 326-336 (July 1969).

Dow Jones Transportation Average [Formerly Dow Jones Railroads Average]
<DESCRIPTION>
A daily comparison of the closing prices of the securities of about 20 corporations in the transportation industry.
<DERIVATION>
Dow Jones selects about 20 transportation-industry common stocks listed on the New York Stock Exchange and sums the closing prices of those stocks each day. This total is then divided by a constant divisor to produce the average. This is not a strict arithmetic average because the constant divisor is not the number of listings being averaged. It is, instead, a number derived from the previous day's average, taking into account the effects of stock splits, dividends, or substitutions. The constant divisor is revised by recalculating the sum of the previous day's closing prices with new values for affected stocks (e.g., with one-third of the old price for a stock that split 3:1) and dividing that new sum by the average that had originally been calculated for that day. The resulting new constant divisor is used for calculating subsequent days' averages. A new constant divisor is calculated for the Transportation Average if stock splits or other changes in individual component stocks cause a change in the Average of two or more points.
<USE>
A technical indicator of stock-market cycles.
<PUBLISHER>
Dow Jones & Co.
<ANNOUNCED IN>
Wall Street Journal
<ANNOUNCEMENT FREQUENCY>
Daily
<CUMULATIONS>
TABLES

NYT	Daily, high-low-close, index nos.
Man Han	Latest week, index nos.
WSJ	Latest daily and year ago, index nos.
WSJ	Latest daily and year ago, % change

Bus Stats	Monthly and yearly, cum, index nos.
EI	Monthly and yearly, cum, index nos.
S&P Stats	Monthly and yearly, cum, index nos.
SCB	Monthly and yearly, cum, index nos.
Barron's	Hourly, cum, index nos.
Barron's	Daily, high-low, cum, index nos.
Hist Stats	Yearly, cum, index nos.
MG Fin Wkly	Daily, cum, index nos.
MG Fin Wkly	Latest week, high-low-close, % change
Stat Abstr	Yearly, cum, index nos.
GRAPHS	
WSJ	Daily, cum, index nos.

<MORE INFORMATION>
   G. Munn, Encyclopedia of Banking and Finance, Bankers' Publishing Co., Boston, 1983.

Dow Jones Utilities Average
<DESCRIPTION>
A daily comparison of the closing prices of the securities of about 15 utility corporations.
<DERIVATION>
Dow Jones selects about 15 utilities' common stocks listed on the New York Stock Exchange and sums the closing prices of those stocks each day. This total is then divided by a constant divisor to produce the average. This is not a strict arithmetic average because the constant divisor is not the number of listings being averaged. It is, instead, a number derived from the previous day's average, taking into account the effects of stock splits, dividends, or substitutions. The constant divisor is revised by recalculating the sum of the previous day's closing prices with new values for affected stocks (e.g., with one-third of the old price for a stock that split 3:1) and dividing that new sum by the average that had originally been calculated for that day. The resulting new constant divisor is used for calculating subsequent days' averages. A new constant divisor is calculated for the Utilities Average if stock splits or other changes in individual component stocks cause a change in the Average of one or more points.
<USE>
A technical indicator of stock-market cycles.
<PUBLISHER>
Dow Jones & Co.
<ANNOUNCED IN>
Wall Street Journal
<ANNOUNCEMENT FREQUENCY>
Daily
<CUMULATIONS>
TABLES

NYT	Daily, high-low-close, index nos.
Man Han	Latest week, index nos.
WSJ	Latest daily and year ago, index nos.
WSJ	Latest daily and year ago, % change
Bus Stats	Monthly and yearly, cum, index nos.
EI	Monthly and yearly, cum, index nos.

```
S&P Stats      Monthly and yearly, cum, index nos.
SCB            Monthly and yearly, cum, index nos.
Barron's       Hourly, cum, index nos.
Barron's       Daily, high-low, cum, index nos.
Hist Stats     Yearly, cum, index nos.
MG Fin Wkly    Daily, cum, index nos.
MG Fin Wkly    Latest week, high-low-close, % change
Stat Abstr     Yearly, cum, index nos.
GRAPHS
WSJ            Daily, cum, index nos.
```
<MORE INFORMATION>
   G. Munn, Encyclopedia of Banking and Finance, Bankers' Publishing Co., Boston, 1983.

Drinking Couple Count [See Appendix A. Nonquantitative Indicators]

Dun & Bradstreet Businessmen's Expectations [See Dun & Bradstreet Profits Optimism Index and Dun & Bradstreet Sales Optimism Index]

Dun & Bradstreet Number of Business Failures [See Business Failures]

Dun & Bradstreet Profits Optimism Index
<DESCRIPTION>
The percentage of surveyed businessmen who expect their profits to increase minus the percentage who expect their profits to decrease.
<DERIVATION>
About 1500 executives are surveyed by Dun & Bradstreet with that firm's Survey of Business Expectations. Those executives are asked whether they expect their net sales, net profits, selling prices, level of inventories, number of employees, and new orders to increase or decrease during the ensuing quarter in comparison with that quarter in the previous year. The percentages expecting increasing and decreasing profits are calculated from the returns. The percentage expecting decreasing profits is subtracted from the number expecting increasing profits to give the index number.
<USE>
A leading indicator of overall future business activity.
<PUBLISHER>
Dun & Bradstreet, Inc.
<ANNOUNCED IN>
Press release
<ANNOUNCEMENT FREQUENCY>
Quarterly
<CUMULATIONS>
TABLES
Dun's Bus Mo Quarterly, %

Dun & Bradstreet Sales Optimism Index

<DESCRIPTION>
The percentage of surveyed businessmen who expect their sales to increase minus the percentage who expect their sales to decrease.

<DERIVATION>
About 1500 executives are surveyed by Dun & Bradstreet with that firm's Survey of Business Expectations. Those executives are asked whether they expect their net sales, net profits, selling prices, level of inventories, number of employees, and new orders to increase or decrease during the ensuing quarter in comparison with that quarter in the previous year. The percentages expecting increasing and decreasing sales are calculated from the returns. The percentage expecting decreasing sales is subtracted from the number expecting increasing sales to give the index number.

<USE>
A leading indicator of overall future business activity.

<PUBLISHER>
Dun & Bradstreet, Inc.

<ANNOUNCED IN>
Press release

<ANNOUNCEMENT FREQUENCY>
Quarterly

<CUMULATIONS>
TABLES
Dun's Bus Mo Quarterly, %

E

Earnings Index [See Hourly Earnings Index]

Earnings-Price Ratio [See American Stock Exchange Price-Earnings Ratio, New York Stock Exchange Price-Earnings Ratio, Price-Earnings Ratio for Over the Counter Stocks, and Standard & Poor's 500 Price-Earnings Ratio]

Electric Power Production

<DESCRIPTION>
The amount of electricity produced in the U.S. for public consumption during a given month expressed in watt-hours.
<DERIVATION>
All electric supply systems in the U.S. producing electricity for public use are surveyed monthly, and their reported production is totalled.
<USE>
A general indication of the health of the U.S. economy. To a certain degree, an early indicator of industrial production. A leading indicator of capital appropriations by the utilities industry.
<PUBLISHER>
U.S. Department of Energy, Energy Information Administration
<ANNOUNCED IN>
Electric Power Monthly
<ANNOUNCEMENT FREQUENCY>
Monthly
<CUMULATIONS>
TABLES

NYT	Latest month and year ago, kWhr
BW	Latest week, month, and year ago, kWhr
Barron's	Latest week and year ago, kWhr
Ind W	Latest week and year ago, kWhr
MG Fin Wkly	Latest week and year ago, kWhr
S&P Stats	Monthly, weekly, yearly, cum, kWhr
Bus Stats	Monthly and yearly, cum, kWhr
Mo En Rev	Monthly and yearly, cum, kWhr
SCB	Monthly and yearly, cum, kWhr

```
EP Mo        Monthly and yearly, cum, kWhr
Moody's Pub  Yearly, cum, kWhr
Pred Base    Yearly, cum, kWhr
Pred Fore    Yearly, cum, kWhr
PROJECTIONS
Pred Fore    Yearly, kWhr
Stat Abstr   Yearly, kWhr
```
<MORE INFORMATION>
Electric Power Quarterly, Energy Information Administration, Washington, D.C., quarterly.

Electric Power Annual, Energy Information Administration, Washington, D.C., annually.

Employment [See Agricultural Employment, Farm Employment, and Nonagricultural Employment]

Engineering News-Record Cost Index [See Building Cost Index and Construction Cost Index]

Equal Investment Indexes [See Media General American Stock Exchange Equal-Investment Index, Media General Composite Equal-Investment Index, and Media General New York Stock Exchange Equal-Investment Index]

Expenditures for New Plant and Equipment
<DESCRIPTION>
A measure of business expenditures (excluding current expenses) for new plant and equipment for actual outlays and for planned expenditures for two succeeding quarters and the current calendar year. Farming, real estate, the professions, and nonprofit institutions are excluded.
<DERIVATION>
Reports from a sample of incorporated and unincorporated companies are used to estimate the total expenditures of U.S. businesses for new plant and equipment. These totals, on an industry by industry basis, are used to update benchmarks derived from data supplied by the Bureau of the Census, the Internal Revenue Service, the Interstate Commerce Commission, and other government agencies. The resulting values are then adjusted for the season and for systematic biases of overestimation or underestimation.
<USE>
Because this indicator estimates planned events as well as assesses historical events, it finds wide use in the analysis of business conditions, indicating the overall trend of capital expenditures and reflecting cyclical turning points in the manufacturing and commercial sectors of the U.S. economy.
<PUBLISHER>
U.S. Department of Commerce, Bureau of Economic Analysis
<ANNOUNCED IN>
Department of Commerce press releases

```
<ANNOUNCEMENT FREQUENCY>
Quarterly
<CUMULATIONS>
TABLES
NYT          Latest quarter and year ago, $
BCD          Quarterly and yearly, cum, $
Bus Stats    Quarterly and yearly, cum, $
EI           Quarterly and yearly, cum, $
FR Bull      Quarterly and yearly, cum, $
SCB          Quarterly and yearly, cum, $
Pred Base    Yearly, cum, $
Pred Fore    Yearly, cum, $
GRAPHS
BCD          Yearly, cum, $
EI           Yearly, cum, $
PROJECTIONS
Pred Fore    Yearly, $
<MORE INFORMATION>
```

Joint Economic Committee, 1980 Supplement to Economic Indicators, Historical and Descriptive Background, USGPO, Washington, D.C., 1980.

John Kirk, "Economic Indicators: The How and the Why," Banking, 25-26 (July 1964).

Survey of Current Business, USGPO, Washington, D.C. (Jan. 1970).

Survey of Current Business, USGPO, Washington, D.C. (Feb. 1970).

Exports [See United States Merchandise Exports]

F

Failure Index [See Business Failures]

Farm Employment
<DESCRIPTION>
An estimate of the number of people who work on farms in the U.S. irrespective of whether they are paid or unpaid and whether farmwork is their principal employment.
<DERIVATION>
The farm employment data are gathered by the U.S. Department of Agriculture, which annually surveys a sample of farm operators, including a subset of farm operators that hire workers. Data are gathered once a year for actual employment during a specified week during July. From the results of this survey, farm employment is estimated based on the number of self-employed farmers, unpaid farm workers, and hired farm workers identified by the survey. Estimates are not adjusted for primary and secondary employment nor are they seasonally adjusted.
<USE>
These statistics are used by the Department of Agriculture for computing labor-productivity estimates. Wage data collected in association with the employment data are used by the U.S. Department of Labor in setting wages of foreign nationals employed in farm labor. The Bureau of Economic Analysis of the Department of Commerce also uses that wage data in its National Income Account series.
<PUBLISHER>
U.S. Department of Agriculture, Economic Research Service
<ANNOUNCED IN>
Farm Labor
<ANNOUNCEMENT FREQUENCY>
Annually
<CUMULATIONS>
TABLES

Ag Stats	Yearly, cum, nos.	
Farm L	Yearly, cum, nos.	
Farm Pop	Yearly, cum, nos.	
Hist Stats	Yearly, cum, nos.	
Stat Abstr	Yearly, cum, nos.	

<MORE INFORMATION>
    John Kirk, "Economic Indicators: The How and the Why," Banking, 27-28 (Aug. 1964).
    Geoffrey Moore, "Employment: The Neglected Indicator," Wall Street Journal, 10 (Feb. 3, 1972).
    G. H. Moore and J. Shiskin, "Why the Leading Indicators Really Do Lead," Across the Board, 71-75 (May 1978).
    Julius Shiskin, "Employment and Unemployment: The Doughnut or the Hole," Monthly Labor Review, 3-10 (Feb. 1976).

Farm Income
<DESCRIPTION>
A measure of the farming sector's value-added product and the income of farmer operators and operator landlords.
<DERIVATION>
A national gross farm income is derived by estimating the total cash marketing receipts, the value of physical changes in inventories of crops and livestock, direct government payments, other cash income, the value of farm products consumed in the farm households, and imputed rental value of farm dwellings. These estimates are based on market channel information, producer surveys, government records of payments, (including those for commodity price support loans), special surveys benchmarked to the quinquennial Census of Agriculture data, and surveys of farmers. Production expenses are estimated from benchmark data from the Census of Agriculture and subtracted from the gross farm income to give the net farm income. This net farm income is then adjusted to account for nonmoney income, the value of inventory changes, net capital investments, and the value of perquisites to hired workers to give the net cash income. Most of these components are not seasonally adjusted, and the quarterly estimates involve considerable interpretation of annual data. Several of the publishers of this indicator also publish monthly values derived by extrapolating recent trends and applying seasonal adjustment factors.
<USE>
Used by agriculture-related businesses and by governments as a general indicator of the economic activity of the farming sector of the U.S. economy.
<PUBLISHER>
U.S. Department of Agriculture, Economics, Statistics, and Cooperatives Service
<ANNOUNCED IN>
Farm Income Statistics
<ANNOUNCEMENT FREQUENCY>
Annually
<CUMULATIONS>
TABLES

Farm Ind	Monthly, cum, $
Bus Stats	Monthly and yearly, cum, $
S&P Stats	Monthly and yearly, cum, $
EI	Quarterly and yearly, cum, $
Ag Stats	Yearly, cum, $
Hist Stats	Yearly, cum, $
Stat Abstr	Yearly, cum, $

GRAPHS
```
Ag Stats      Yearly, cum, $
Ag Stats S    Yearly, cum, $
EI            Yearly, cum, $
```
<MORE INFORMATION>
Joint Economic Committee, 1980 Supplement to Economic Indicators, Historical and Descriptive Background, USGPO, Washington, D.C., 1980.
Major Statistical Series of the U.S. Department of Agriculture, Vol. 3, Gross and Net Farm Income, Agricultural Handbook No. 365, USDA, Washington, D.C., 1969.

Federal Budget Receipts by Source and Outlays by Function
<DESCRIPTION>
Monthly reports, cumulated for the current fiscal year, of the receipts (from individual income taxes, corporate income taxes, and other sources) and the outlays (for national defense, international affairs, health and income security, interest paid, and other payments) of the Federal Government.
<DERIVATION>
Data are derived from the accounts of the U.S. Treasury. These accounts tally the day-by-day inflows and outflows of the Treasury. Because of certain data difficulties, the reporting of the outlays by function is subject to error.
<USE>
These statistics are used to monitor how much money the government will probably have to borrow, thereby affecting future credit markets and interest rates. Also used to classify budget outlays and related data, to establish budget authority and total-outlay targets, to present a budget based on national needs and agency mission structure, and to ensure that total outlay targets are not exceeded.
<PUBLISHER>
U.S. Department of the Treasury and Office of Management and Budget
<ANNOUNCED IN>
Monthly Treasury Statement of Receipts and Outlays of the United States Government
<ANNOUNCEMENT FREQUENCY>
Monthly
<CUMULATIONS>
TABLES
```
US Budget     Latest, $
FR Bull       Monthly, semiannually, and yearly, cum, $
SCB           Monthly and yearly, cum, $
Treas Bull    Monthly and yearly, cum, $
BCD           Quarterly and yearly, cum, $
EI            Quarterly and yearly, cum, $
Budget Brief  Yearly, cum, $
Govt Fin      Yearly, cum, $
Hist Stats    Yearly, cum, $
Stat Abstr    Yearly, cum, $
```
GRAPHS
```
EI            Quarterly and yearly, cum, $
```

```
BCD          Yearly, cum, $
Stat Abstr   Yearly, cum, $
PROJECTIONS
Value Line   Quarterly and yearly, %
Budget Brief Yearly, $
```
<MORE INFORMATION>
   Joint Economic Committee, 1980 Supplement to Economic
Indicators, Historical and Descriptive Background, USGPO,
Washington, D.C., 1980.

Federal Budget Receipts, Outlays, and Debt

<DESCRIPTION>
Commonly called the Federal Budget; provides monthly data on
receipts, outlays, surpluses, deficits, and debt for the
current fiscal year and the corresponding months of the
previous fiscal year.
<DERIVATION>
Data are derived from the records of the U.S. Treasury kept
on a cash basis. Receipts include taxes, compulsory social
insurance, collections similar and closely related to
compulsory payments, fees, fines, deposits of earnings by the
Federal Reserve System, and other sources. Outlays include
all payments for budgeted programs, including offsetting
collections. The Gross Federal Debt is the public debt of
all federal agencies, some of which is in the form of
investment instruments held by the government itself. The
debt held by the public is the gross less that represented by
federally held securities.
<USE>
Used by the government and financial institutions to assess
the state of the government's finances, to determine
increases or decreases in the public debt, to guide executive
and legislative fiscal policy, and to assess the need and
appropriateness of tax and appropriation legislation.
<PUBLISHER>
U.S. Department of the Treasury
<ANNOUNCED IN>
Monthly Statement of Receipts and Expenditures of the United
States Government
<ANNOUNCEMENT FREQUENCY>
Monthly
<CUMULATIONS>
TABLES

```
US Budget    Latest, $
FR Bull      Monthly, semiannually, and yearly, cum, $
SCB          Monthly and yearly, cum, $
Treas Bull   Monthly and yearly, cum, $
BCD          Quarterly and yearly, cum, $
EI           Quarterly and yearly, cum, $
Budget Brief Yearly, cum, $
Govt Fin     Yearly, cum, $
Hist Stats   Yearly, cum, $
Stat Abstr   Yearly, cum, $
```
GRAPHS
```
EI           Quarterly and yearly, cum, $
```

BCD   Yearly, cum, $
Stat Abstr   Yearly, cum, $
PROJECTIONS
Value Line   Quarterly and yearly, %
Budget Brief Yearly, $
<MORE INFORMATION>
   Joint Economic Committee, 1980 Supplement to Economic
Indicators, Historical and Descriptive Background, USGPO,
Washington, D.C., 1980.

Federal Funds Rate
<DESCRIPTION>
The interest charged by one bank to another when the first
bank "loans" excess funds they have on deposit at a regional
Federal Reserve bank overnight to the second so the second
bank can maintain its legally required reserve with the
Federal Reserve System.
<DERIVATION>
The rates charged for each of the day's transactions are
weighted by the volume of transactions at each rate, and the
results are averaged to give the daily effective rate.
<USE>
Because these funds are banks' major source of funds to meet
reserve requirements, this measure is closely watched as an
indicator of future monetary policy. A leading indicator at
peaks, but a lagging indicator at troughs.
<PUBLISHER>
Board of Governors of the Federal Reserve System
<ANNOUNCED IN>
Federal Reserve System news release
<ANNOUNCEMENT FREQUENCY>
Daily
<CUMULATIONS>
TABLES
WSJ   Latest daily, %
Barron's   Latest daily and year ago, %
BCD   Monthly, cum, %
FR Bull   Monthly and quarterly, cum, %
GRAPHS
Stat Bull   Monthly, cum, %
BCD   Yearly, cum, %
<MORE INFORMATION>
   "The Federal Funds Market Revisited," Economic Review,
Federal Reserve Bank of Cleveland, 3-13 (Feb. 1970).
   P. B. Willis, The Federal Funds Market - Its Origin and
Development, 3rd ed., Federal Reserve Bank of Boston, Boston,
1968.

Federal Reserve Discount Rate
<DESCRIPTION>
The charge made by Federal Reserve banks on loans made to
member commercial banks for short-term (usually less than 15
days) adjustments in their reserves.

<DERIVATION>
Under the authority of the Federal Reserve Act, the various
Federal Reserve banks collectively set this rate every
fourteen days or more often, if needed. These discount rates
are subject to review by the Federal Reserve Board of
Governors.
<USE>
Used to estimate the basic cost of money.
<PUBLISHER>
Board of Governors of the Federal Reserve System
<ANNOUNCED IN>
Federal Reserve Board press release
<ANNOUNCEMENT FREQUENCY>
Daily
<CUMULATIONS>
TABLES
S&P Stats   Daily and yearly, cum, %
WSJ   Latest period, %
EI   Monthly, weekly, and yearly, cum, %
Bus Stats   Monthly and yearly, cum, %
SCB   Monthly and yearly, cum, %
Hist Stats   Yearly, cum, %
Int Fin Stat   Yearly, cum, %
Stat Abstr   Yearly, cum, %
FR Bull   Weekly, cum, %
GRAPHS
EI   Yearly, cum, %
Stat Abstr   Yearly, cum, %
<MORE INFORMATION>
   Joint Economic Committee, 1980 Supplement to Economic
Indicators, Historical and Descriptive Background, USGPO,
Washington, D.C., 1980.
   Board of Governors of the Federal Reserve System, Lending
Functions of the Federal Reserve Banks: A History, Federal
Reserve Board, Washington, D.C., 1973.
   Martin J. Pring, Technical Analysis Explained, An
Illustrated Guide for the Investor, McGraw-Hill, New York,
1980, pp. 196-198.

Federal Sector, National Income Accounts Basis
<DESCRIPTION>
Estimates of the receipts of the Federal Government (personal
tax and nontax receipts, corporate profits tax accruals,
indirect business tax and nontax accruals, and contributions
for social insurance) and of expenditures of the Federal
Government (purchases of goods and services, transfer
payments, grants in aid to state and local governments, net
interest paid, and subsidies less current surpluses of
government enterprises, all less wages owed).
<DERIVATION>
Data are based on the projections embodied in the federal
budget and on the reports of federal agencies, particularly
the Treasury Department. Quarterly data are presented in both
seasonally adjusted and nonadjusted forms. Seasonal
adjustment is accomplished by applying statistical factors to

individual components of the receipts and expenditures;
seasonal adjustment of the surplus or deficit results from
the adjustments to the receipts and expenditures.
<USE>
Used for the analysis of federal fiscal policy, specifically
for determining the effect of federal purchasing on private
capital and credit markets.
<PUBLISHER>
U.S. Department of Commerce, Bureau of Economic Analysis
<ANNOUNCED IN>
Survey of Current Business
<ANNOUNCEMENT FREQUENCY>
Quarterly
<CUMULATIONS>
TABLES
EI   Quarterly and yearly, cum, $
GRAPHS
EI   Quarterly and yearly, cum, $
<MORE INFORMATION>
   Joint Economic Committee, 1980 Supplement to Economic
Indicators, Historical and Descriptive Background, USGPO,
Washington, D.C., 1980.
   Special Analyses, The Budget of the United States
Government Fiscal Year 1972, USGPO, Washington, D.C., 1971,
pp. 7-21.

Fiscal Thrust
<DESCRIPTION>
Increases in discretionary federal budget expenditures plus
(minus) structural tax reductions (increases) expressed in
billions of dollars and percent of gross national product.
<DERIVATION>
Discretionary expenditures are defined as those outlays
called for in the federal budget that initiate or trigger
changes in economic activity and include defense purchases,
nondefense purchases, transfers to persons, grants in aid,
and other outlays. Quarterly changes in these discretionary
expenditures are totalled and amount to billions of dollars.
Structural changes (those caused by a change in either the
tax base or tax rate) in the quarterly tax receipts from
personal income taxes, corporate income taxes, social
security taxes, excise taxes and other taxes are also
totalled as billions of dollars. The sum of these two totals
is then calculated and designated the "fiscal thrust"; it is
expressed in billions of dollars and as a percentage of the
concurrent gross national product.
<USE>
Used to assess the initial, full, and autonomous effect of
the federal budget on the national economy.
<PUBLISHER>
The Conference Board
<ANNOUNCED IN>
Statistical Bulletin
<ANNOUNCEMENT FREQUENCY>
Quarterly

<CUMULATIONS>
GRAPHS
Stat Bull   Quarterly, cum, $
<MORE INFORMATION>
  M. E. Levy, Measuring the Fiscal Impact of the Federal
Budget, The Conference Board, New York, 1980.

Forbes Index
<DESCRIPTION>
A broad measure of U.S. economic activity derived from
various other economic indicators.
<DERIVATION>
The monthly values for total industrial production, new
unemployment claims, the consumer price index, manufacturers'
new orders and inventories, retail sales, new housing starts,
personal income, and consumer installment credit are
normalized and totalled, with each normalized value being
given equal weight. The resulting value is indexed to a value
of 100 for 1967.
<USE>
Presented as an assessment of the current performance of the
U.S. economy
<PUBLISHER>
Forbes, Inc.
<ANNOUNCED IN>
Forbes
<ANNOUNCEMENT FREQUENCY>
Monthly
<CUMULATIONS>
TABLES
Forbes   Latest and year ago, % change
GRAPHS
Forbes   Monthly, cum, index nos.

Free Credit Balance [See New York Stock Exchange Firms'
Free Credit Balance]

Freight Car Orders
<DESCRIPTION>
The monthly number of new orders placed for railroad freight
cars.
<DERIVATION>
Railroad equipment manufacturers, railroad shops, and
private-line shops report each month the number of new
freight cars ordered for domestic use by railroads,
private-car lines, industries, and the government. The
reported numbers are adjusted for cancellations by the
reporting institutions. End-of-period backlog figures are not
thus adjusted.
<USE>
A leading indicator of future transportation and general
economic activity.

<PUBLISHER>
Association of American Railroads and American Railway Car
Institute
<ANNOUNCED IN>
Rail News Update
<ANNOUNCEMENT FREQUENCY>
Monthly
<CUMULATIONS>
TABLES
Ind W   Latest month and year ago, units
Bus Stats   Monthly and yearly, cum, units
SCB   Monthly and yearly, cum, units

Freight-Car Loadings [See Carloadings]

G

Gold Prices
<DESCRIPTION>
The prices fixed for a troy ounce of gold on major gold
markets, such as Zurich, London, and New York, under the
influences of supply and demand.
<DERIVATION>
The members of a gold market commonly meet twice a day, once
in the morning and once in the afternoon. At those meetings,
a suggested price is put forward by the chairman. The
suggested price is determined by the previous fixing and
intervening events. Members then announce whether they wish
to buy or sell at the suggested price. The suggested price
can be adjusted until there are both willing buyers and
willing sellers. Quantities of gold to be sold at the
suggested price are offered by the members. The suggested
price is then adjusted again until the quantity desired for
purchase equals the quantity desired to be sold. The official
price is then fixed, the transactions are agreed to, and the
price is announced to the customers of the members. Payment
is made from one member to another within two days of the
transaction agreement.
<USE>
Used as a counter-indicator for inflationary trends and as an
indicator of economic stability.
<PUBLISHER>
Major gold exchanges
<ANNOUNCED IN>
News release
<ANNOUNCEMENT FREQUENCY>
Twice daily
<CUMULATIONS>
TABLES

NYT	Daily, $
WSJ	Daily, $
Inv Guide	Latest month, $
Barron's	Latest week's end, $
Comm Yr Bk	Monthly and yearly, cum, $
Min Ybk	Monthly and yearly, cum, $
S&P Stats	Monthly and yearly, cum, $
Stat Abstr	Yearly, cum, $

GRAPHS
Comm Chart   Monthly, cum, $
Min Ybk   Quarterly, cum, $
Comm Yr Bk   Yearly, cum, $
<MORE INFORMATION>
  Gold, Merrill, Lynch, Pierce, Fenner, & Smith, New York, 1974.
  James E. Sinclair and Harry D. Schultz, How You Can Profit from Gold, Arlington House, Westport, Conn., 1980.

Gross Business Product Fixed Weighted Price Index [See Gross Domestic Product]

Gross Domestic Product [Also called Gross Business Product Fixed Weighted Price Index]
<DESCRIPTION>
The prices of all goods and services that make up the gross domestic business product (the part of the gross national product held by the domestic business sector).
<DERIVATION>
The prices of all goods and services produced by private enterprises, farms, independent professions, lessors of real property, mutual financial institutions, private noninsured pension funds, cooperatives, nonprofit organizations serving businesses, Federal Reserve banks, federally sponsored credit agencies, and government enterprises are weighted together with 1972 constant-value dollars as weights.
<USE>
A broad, general barometer of overall business activity or lack of activity.
<PUBLISHER>
U.S. Department of Commerce, Bureau of Economic Analysis
<ANNOUNCED IN>
Survey of Current Business
<ANNOUNCEMENT FREQUENCY>
Quarterly
<CUMULATIONS>
TABLES
SCB   Quarterly and yearly, cum, $ (July)
BCD   Quarterly and yearly, cum, index nos.
BCD   Quarterly and yearly, cum, % change
Hist Stats   Yearly, cum, $
Stat Abstr   Yearly, cum, $
Pred Fore   Yearly, cum, $
GRAPHS
BCD   Yearly, cum, index nos.
PROJECTIONS
Pred Fore   Yearly, cum, $

Gross National Product
<DESCRIPTION>
The total national output of goods and services, expressed in both current and constant (1972) dollars.

<DERIVATION>
Hundreds of series of economic statistics are collected and evaluated. These statistics include those on personal consumption expenditures, gross private domestic investment, net exports of goods and services, and government purchases of goods and services. Most of these statistics are concerned with money transactions in the market economy, although some, like the imputed rental value of owner-occupied buildings, are not. Each of these series is appropriately and separately adjusted to eliminate seasonal variations. The detailed components of the GNP are then divided by appropriate price indexes to express them in "deflated" terms or dollars of constant purchasing power. The adjusted and deflated component values are then summed to obtain the GNP.

<USE>
The GNP is the most comprehensive measure of trends in the U.S. economy because movements in many sectors (including the sales of many industries and enterprises) are closely related to changes in the GNP. It is therefore a useful tool for assessing economic policy and for preparing economic projections.

<PUBLISHER>
U.S. Department of Commerce, Bureau of Economic Analysis

<ANNOUNCED IN>
Survey of Current Business

<ANNOUNCEMENT FREQUENCY>
Quarterly

<CUMULATIONS>
TABLES
Man Han	Latest quarter, $
Man Han	Latest quarter, % change
Barron's	Latest quarter and year ago, $
Ind W	Latest quarter and year ago, $
Ind W	Latest quarter and year ago, % change
NYT	Quarterly, cum, $
NYT	Quarterly, cum, % change
BCD	Quarterly and yearly, cum, $
Bus Stats	Quarterly and yearly, cum, $
EI	Quarterly and yearly, cum, $
Int Fin Stat	Quarterly and yearly, cum, $
S&P Stats	Quarterly and yearly, cum, $
Stat Bull	Quarterly and yearly, cum, $
FR Bull	Quarterly and yearly, cum, $
EI	Quarterly and yearly, cum, % change
Hist Stats	Yearly, cum, $
Int Fin Stat	Yearly, cum, $
Stat Abstr	Yearly, cum, $
Pred Base	Yearly, cum, index nos.
Pred Fore	Yearly, cum, index nos.

GRAPHS
BCD	Yearly, cum, $
EI	Yearly, cum, $
Stat Abstr	Yearly, cum, $

PROJECTIONS
Stat Bull	Quarterly and yearly, $

Value Line	Quarterly and yearly, $
Value Line	Quaretrly and yearly, % change
Ind W	Yearly, $
Bus Rev WF	Yearly, $
Pred Fore	Yearly, index nos.
Fin Ind	Yearly, % change.
S&P Outlook	Quarterly and yearly, $ (IRR)

<MORE INFORMATION>
"The National Income and Product Accounts of the United States: An Overview," Survey of Current Business, USGPO, Washington, D.C. (Oct. 1979).

Readings in Concepts and Methods of National Income Statistics, U.S. Department of Commerce, Bureau of Economic Analysis, Washington, D.C., 1976.

Gross National Product Data Improvement Project Report, U.S. Department of Commerce, Office of Federal Statistical Policy and Standards, Washington, D.C., 1977.

Joint Economic Committee, 1980 Supplement to Economic Indicators, Historical and Descriptive Background, USGPO, Washington, D.C., 1980.

Gross National Product Implicit Price Deflator

<DESCRIPTION>
The average price change of a given period's output in relation to the prices associated with a base year, a by-product of the process of deflating Gross National Product components on a disaggregated basis with detailed price indexes.

<DERIVATION>
The current-dollar Gross National Product is divided by the constant-dollar Gross National Product.

<USE>
This indicator is similar to the Consumer Price Index. Therefore, it is used as an inflation-adjusted measure of the overall economic activity of the country. However, it is a much broader measure because it uses the Gross National Product rather than a market basket of goods and because each item is weighted by its portion of the national output rather than of the portion of that mythical market basket.

<PUBLISHER>
U.S. Department of Commerce, Bureau of Economic Analysis

<ANNOUNCED IN>
Survey of Current Business

<ANNOUNCEMENT FREQUENCY>
Quarterly

<CUMULATIONS>
TABLES

BCD	Quarterly, cum, index nos.
BCD	Quarterly, cum, % change
EI	Quarterly and yearly, cum, index nos.
Econ Rept Pr	Quarterly and yearly, cum, index nos.
Econ Rept Pr	Quarterly and yearly, cum, % change
Natl Income	Quarterly and yearly, cum, index nos.
S&P Stats	Quarterly and yearly, cum, index nos.
Bus Stats	Yearly, cum, index nos.

```
Hist Stats      Yearly, cum, index nos.
Stat Abstr      Yearly, cum, index nos.
Stat Abstr      Yearly, cum, % change
GRAPHS
BCD             Yearly, cum, index nos.
BCD             Yearly, cum, % change
```
<MORE INFORMATION>
Readings in Concepts and Methods of National Income Statistics, U.S. Department of Commerce, Bureau of Economic Analysis, Washington, D.C., 1976.

Gross Private Domestic Investment
<DESCRIPTION>
The estimated total of (1) the net acquisitions of fixed capital goods by private business and nonprofit institutions; (2) the commissions arising in the sale and purchase of new and existing fixed assets, principally real estate; and (3) the value of the change in the volume of inventories held by businesses.
<DERIVATION>
Estimates of nine types of private domestic investment are obtained from Bureau of the Census surveys of manufacturers, from trade source data, and from the Bureau of Economic Analysis survey of plant and equipment expenditures. These estimates are of (1 and 2) fixed investment in nonresidential farm and nonfarm structures, (3 and 4) producers' fixed investment in nonresidential farm and nonfarm durable equipment, (5 and 6) fixed investment in residential farm and nonfarm structures, (7) producers' fixed investment in residential durable equipment, and (8 and 9) changes in farm and nonfarm business inventories. Because inventory calculation by different businesses varies widely, numerous adjustments are made to the reported data to make these calculations comparable. The estimates are then totalled into three categories: change in business inventories, residential fixed investment, and nonresidential fixed investment. These three categories are then summed to produce the Gross Private Domestic Investment.
<USE>
A major component of the Gross National Product; possibly the most important indicator of business conditions, past, present, and to be expected.
<PUBLISHER>
U.S. Department of Commerce, Bureau of Economic Analysis
<ANNOUNCED IN>
Survey of Current Business
<ANNOUNCEMENT FREQUENCY>
Quarterly
<CUMULATIONS>
TABLES
```
BCD             Quarterly and yearly, cum, $
EI              Quarterly and yearly, cum, $
FR Bull         Quarterly and yearly, cum, $
Bus Stats       Yearly, cum, $
```

```
Hist Stats    Yearly, cum, $
Stat Abstr    Yearly, cum, $
GRAPHS
BCD           Yearly, cum, $
EI            Yearly, cum, $
<MORE INFORMATION>
```

Business Statistics, U.S. Department of Commerce, Bureau of Economic Analysis, Washington, D.C., 1979.

Readings in Concepts and Methods of National Income Statistics, U.S. Department of Commerce, Bureau of Economic Analysis, Washington, D.C., 1976.

Gross National Product Data Improvement Project Report, U.S. Department of Commerce, Office of Federal Statistical Policy and Standards, Washington, D.C., 1977.

Joint Economic Committee, 1980 Supplement to Economic Indicators, Historical and Descriptive Background, USGPO, Washington, D.C., 1980.

H

Hambrecht & Quist Technology Stock Index
<DESCRIPTION>
A measure of long-term trends and daily fluctuations in the technolgy sector of the stock market.
<DERIVATION>
Equal investments are assumed to have been made in each of the stocks of more than 130 technological companies. The distribution of firms by size is representative of the distribution in the total technology sector. Because more small companies than large companies engage in technical enterprises, more small ones than large ones appear in the Hambrecht & Quist sample. Additional holdings produced by stock dividends and splits are considered to be reinvested in the stock. The value of the stocks is indexed to their value on Dec. 26, 1973 (base = 100).
<USE>
Used to measure performance of volatile high-technology securities against other market indicators.
<PUBLISHER>
Hambrecht & Quist, Inc.
<ANNOUNCED IN>
Business Wire
<ANNOUNCEMENT FREQUENCY>
Daily
<CUMULATIONS>
TABLES
Inc   Latest month, % change
GRAPHS
Inc   Monthly, cum, % change

Heller/Roper Small Business Barometer
<DESCRIPTION>
A measure of the attitudes and opinions of small-business executives about the present and future states of the economy as it affects their businesses.
<DERIVATION>
The chief executive officers of more than 1000 small to midsized businesses in manufacturing, mining, construction,

wholesale or retail trade, and nonfinancial services are surveyed by telephone. The businesses are selected from Dun & Bradstreet's listing on the basis of the number of employees (40 to 500) and annual sales volume ($1 million to $50 million). The CEOs are asked whether they expect their sales to be higher or lower in the next four months than during the same period last year; whether they expect their profits on sales to be higher or lower; whether they expect their profits as a percentage of sales to be higher or lower; whether they expected their level of borrowing to be higher or lower; whether they feel their inventories are higher or lower than they would like to see them; how long it takes to get paid money their firms are owed; whether they expect to have more or fewer employees four months hence; whether they see their own company or the economy as a whole in a period of economic recovery; and, if a recovery is sensed, how robust a recovery is occurring? The responses are averaged and the appropriate percentages calculated.
<USE>
Used as an indicator of present and future business activities.
<PUBLISHER>
Walter E. Heller International Corp. Institute for Small Business
<ANNOUNCED IN>
The Heller/Roper Small Business Barometer
<ANNOUNCEMENT FREQUENCY>
Triennial
<CUMULATIONS>
TABLES
Nation's Bus Triyearly, nos.

Help-Wanted Index
<DESCRIPTION>
A weighted counting of the help-wanted ads appearing in 51 newspapers across the U.S.
<DERIVATION>
The help-wanted advertisements (except display ads) in 51 newspapers in 51 cities across the U.S. are counted each month. These raw counts are adjusted to account for variations in the number of weekdays and Sundays in the month and to compensate for the seasonal variations normally exhibited in the data for each city. The adjusted data are divided by the adjusted number for 1967, and the resulting city indexes are then multiplied by a factor weighted to reflect the nonagricultural employment for that city. These weighted city indexes are summed to produce regional and national indexes.
<USE>
This index provides a measure of the labor-market activity and the economic conditions in cities, regions, and the nation as a whole. It has been shown to exhibit very pronounced cyclical movements, the peaks of which generally lead other business-cycle reference peaks but the troughs of which usually coincide with those of other business-cycle indicators.

\<PUBLISHER>
The Conference Board
845 Third Ave.
New York, N.Y. 10022
\<ANNOUNCED IN>
Statistical Bulletin
\<ANNOUNCEMENT FREQUENCY>
Monthly
\<CUMULATIONS>
TABLES

Bus W	Latest and year ago, index nos.
Ind W	Latest and year ago, index nos.
Stat Bull	Monthly, cum, index nos.
BCD	Monthly and yearly, cum, index nos.
Bus Stats	Monthly and yearly, cum, index nos.
S&P Stats	Monthly and yearly, cum, index nos.
SCB	Monthly and yearly, cum, index nos.

GRAPHS

BCD	Monthly and yearly, cum, index nos.
Stat Bull	Yearly, cum, index nos.

\<MORE INFORMATION>
   The Help-Wanted Index: Technical Description and Behavioral
Trends, Report 7161, The Conference Board, New York, 1977.

Hemline Index [See Short Skirt Index in Appendix A.
Nonquantitative Indicators]

High-Grade Municipal Bond Yields
\<DESCRIPTION>
A general measure of the performance in the market of the
best tax-exempt municipal bonds.
\<DERIVATION>
Fifteen high-grade, tax-exempt, general-obligation, domestic
municipal bonds with about 20 years to maturity are selected
on the basis of quality, trading activity, and geographic
representation, and their yields to maturity based on their
closing bid quotations on Wednesday are arithmetically
averaged.   Monthly values are the averages of the weekly
figures for each month.
\<USE>
Used as an inverse indicator of stock-market securities
prices.
\<PUBLISHER>
Standard & Poor's Corp.
\<ANNOUNCED IN>
Standard & Poor's Outlook
Bond Outlook (Standard & Poor)
\<ANNOUNCEMENT FREQUENCY>
Weekly
\<CUMULATIONS>
TABLES

S&P Outlook	Latest week and yearly high-low, %
EI	Monthly, weekly, yearly, cum, %

```
S&P Stats     Monthly, weekly, yearly, cum, %
Bus Stats     Monthly and yearly, cum, %
SCB           Monthly and yearly, cum, %
Stat Abstr    Yearly, cum, %
```
<MORE INFORMATION>
   David M. Darst, The Complete Bond Book, A Guide to All
Types of Fixed Income Securities, McGraw-Hill, New York,
1975.

High-Low Differential
<DESCRIPTION>
A chart of the net difference between the ten-day moving
average of the new yearly highs and new lows of either the
New York Stock Exchange or the America Stock Exchange.
<DERIVATION>
For any period (e.g., a day or week), the total number of new
high issues is added to an arbitrary number, and the total
number of new low issues is subtracted. The resulting
differential, which is normalized to the selected arbitrary
base, is then graphed.
<USE>
To forecast major turning points in stock market movements
and to determine the general strength or weakness of market
movements, often ahead of such indexes as the Standard & Poor
500 and the Dow Jones Industrials Average.
<PUBLISHER>
New York Stock Exchange
American Stock Exchange
<ANNOUNCED IN>
Stock exchange tickers
<ANNOUNCEMENT FREQUENCY>
Daily
<CUMULATIONS>
TABLES
```
NYT           Latest daily, nos.
WSJ           Latest daily, nos.
Barron's      Latest weekly, nos.
```
GRAPHS
```
MG Fin Wkly   Monthly, cum, nos.
```
<MORE INFORMATION>
   Martin J. Pring, Technical Analysis Explained, An
Illustrated Guide for the Investor, McGraw-Hill, New York,
1980, 178-182.
   Michael Hayes, The Dow Jones - Irwin Guide to Stock Market
Cycles, Dow Jones - Irwin, Homewood, Ill., 1977, pp. 110-114.

Hourly Earnings Index
<DESCRIPTION>
An indexed estimate of the hourly wages (in constant 1967
dollars) paid to production or nonsupervisory employees, both
full- and part-time.
<DERIVATION>
Business establishments are surveyed each month to determine
the average hourly earnings. The results of this survey are

adjusted to exclude the effects of fluctuations in overtime premiums in manufacturing establishments, employment shifts between low- and high-wage industries, and normal seasonal variations. They are also adjusted for the season and the value of the dollar. The index is then constructed by weighting the average hourly earnings in each industry at the three-digit SIC level. The weighted average is then indexed to a value of 100 for 1967.
<USE>
A precursor of cost-of-living indexes; used as a benchmark in labor-contract negotiations.
<PUBLISHER>
U.S. Department of Labor, Bureau of Labor Statistics
<ANNOUNCED IN>
Employment and Earnings
<ANNOUNCEMENT FREQUENCY>
Monthly
<CUMULATIONS>
TABLES

MLR	Monthly, cum, index nos.
Emp & Earn	Monthly, cum, index nos.
Bus Stats	Monthly and yearly, cum, index nos.
SCB	Monthly and yearly, cum, index nos.
EI	Monthly and yearly, cum, index nos.
EI	Monthly and yearly, cum, % change
Emp & Earn S	Yearly, cum, index nos.

<MORE INFORMATION>
   Norman J. Samuels, "New Hourly Earnings Index," Monthly Labor Review, 66 (Dec. 1971).
   Richard M. Snyder, Measuring Business Changes, Wiley, New York, 1955, pp. 47 and 64-65.

Housing Permits [Also called Index of New Private Housing Units Authorized by Local Building Permits]
<DESCRIPTION>
The month-to-month change in the number of housing units authorized by local permit-issuing places.
<DERIVATION>
About 15,000 locations around the country, including practically all large cities and about 85% of all new residential construction in the U.S., report the number of building permits issued monthly. This sample is extended to represent the entire country by applying a ratio of reporting to nonreporting locations, and the data are seasonally adjusted. The result is then converted to an index with a base of 1967 = 100. The method of constructing this index has varied over time, and the index values for before 1972 are therefore not directly comparable with those for after 1972.
<USE>
Used as one of the components of the Leading Indicators Composite Index. A leading indicator for peaks, troughs, and overall.
<PUBLISHER>
U.S. Department of Commerce, Bureau of the Census

<ANNOUNCED IN>
Construction Reports, Series C40
<ANNOUNCEMENT FREQUENCY>
Monthly
<CUMULATIONS>
TABLES

BCD	Monthly, cum, index nos.
S&P Stats	Monthly and yearly, cum, index nos.
Bus Stats	Monthly and yearly, cum, units
Const Rev	Monthly and yearly, cum, units
SCB	Monthly and yearly, cum, units
Stat Abstr	Yearly, cum, units

GRAPHS

BCD	Yearly, cum, index nos.

<MORE INFORMATION>
    "Residential   and   Nonresidential   Building   Permit
Authorization Data - Sources and Availability," Construction
Review, 4-15 (Aug. 1979).

Housing Starts
<DESCRIPTION>
An estimate of the number of new homes for which construction
began during a given month.
<DERIVATION>
Permit authorizations for the construction of new residential
housing issued by 3700 locations that grant such permits are
counted on the first working day of each month by a Bureau
interviewer. The results are then scaled up to estimate the
number of such permits granted by the 16,000 such locations
nationwide and the number of such starts made nationwide in
both permit-granting and non-permit-granting locations. The
totals are adjusted to reflect the time lag between permit
issuance and the actual start of construction and the number
of projects that are cancelled after permit issuance. The
factors used to perform these scalings and adjustments are
produced by surveys of sites, owners of sampled buildings,
and local panels of persons knowledgeable about new
construction.
<USE>
Taken as a major indicator of the health and strength of the
national economy.
<PUBLISHER>
U.S. Department of Commerce, Bureau of the Census
<ANNOUNCED IN>
Construction Reports, Series C-20
<ANNOUNCEMENT FREQUENCY>
Monthly
<CUMULATIONS>
TABLES

Ind W	Latest month, quarterly, yearly, units
Man Han	Latest month, units
Barron's	Latest month and year ago, units
BW	Latest month and year ago, units
NYT	Latest month and year ago, units
BCD	Monthly, cum, units

```
Bus Stats      Monthly and yearly, cum, units
Const Repts    Monthly and yearly, cum, units
Const Rev      Monthly and yearly, cum, units
EI             Monthly and yearly, cum, units
S&P Stats      Monthly and yearly, cum, units
SCB            Monthly and yearly, cum, units
Hist Stats     Yearly, cum, units
HUD Stats      Yearly, cum, units
Pred Base      Yearly, cum, units
Pred Fore      Yearly, cum, units
Stat Abstr     Yearly, cum, units
GRAPHS
Builder        Monthly, cum, units
BCD            Yearly, cum, units
Mo Econ Ind    Yearly, cum, units
PROJECTIONS
S&P Outlook    Quarterly and yearly, units (irr)
Value Line     Quarterly and yearly, % change
Ind W          Yearly, units
Pred Fore      Yearly, units
Bus Rev WF     Yearly, units
```
<MORE INFORMATION>

David Siskind, "Housing Starts: Background and Derivation of Estimates, 1945-82," Construction Review, 4-7 (May-June 1982).

I

Imports [See United States Merchandise Imports]

Index of Business Activity [See U.S. News and World Report Weekly Index of Business Activity]

Index of Industrial Materials Prices [See Industrial Raw Materials Price Index]

Index of Net Business Formation [See Net Business Formation]

Index of New Private Housing Units Authorized by Local Building Permits [See Housing Permits]

Index of Prices Paid by Farmers for Commodities and Services, Interest, Taxes, and Farm Wage Rates [Also referred to as the Index of Prices Paid by Farmers]
<DESCRIPTION>
A weighted indicator of the costs to farmers for items used in family living, for items used in farm production, for interest on indebtedness secured by farm real estate, and for wages paid to farm labor.
<DERIVATION>
Produced by combining the Index of Commodities and Services with the indexes of interest, taxes, and wage rates. Data for these indexes are gathered from reports by firms and organizations providing production inputs to agricultural producers, surveys of farmers, the Department of Agriculture Market News Service, trade publications, labor surveys, and surveys of financial institutions. Compilation of the first index is the most complicated. There, data are expressed in a state-by-state manner, and state weights based on the quantities of goods and services purchased by farmers are applied to the data. National averages are then calculated

for specified types of farm expenditures. These groups of
expenditures are then summed and combined with a family
living component to obtain the Index of Commodities and
Services.
<USE>
Used in market planning, negotiating marketing contracts,
comparing changes in farming prices with those in nonfarm
areas, and establishing commodity parity prices for
agricultural price-support programs.
<PUBLISHER>
U.S. Department of Agriculture, Economics, Statistics, and
Cooperatives Service
<ANNOUNCED IN>
Agricultural Prices
<ANNOUNCEMENT FREQUENCY>
Monthly
<CUMULATIONS>
TABLES
Ag Prices   Latest month and year ago, index nos.
Bus Stats   Monthly and yearly, cum, index nos.
EI   Monthly and yearly, cum, index nos.
SCB   Monthly and yearly, cum, index nos.
Bus Stats   Monthly and yearly, cum, ratio nos.
EI   Monthly and yearly, cum, ratio nos.
SCB   Monthly and yearly, cum, ratio nos.
Ag Charts   Yearly, cum, index nos.
Hist Stats   Yearly, cum, index nos.
Stat Abstr   Yearly, cum, index nos.
GRAPHS
Ag Charts   Yearly, cum, index nos.
Ag Charts S   Yearly, cum, index nos.
EI   Yearly, cum, index nos.
EI   Yearly, cum, ratio nos.
Ag Prices   Yearly, cum, % change
<MORE INFORMATION>
   Joint Economic Committee, 1980 Supplement to Economic
Indicators, Historical and Descriptive Background, USGPO,
Washington, D.C., 1980.
   Scope and Method of the Statistical Reporting Service,
Misc. Publ. 1308, USDA, Washington, D.C., 1975.
   Major Statistical Series of the U.S. Department of
Agriculture, How They Are Constructed and Used, Vol. 1,
Agricultural Prices and Parity, USDA, Washington, D.C., 1970.

**Index of New Private Housing Units Authorized by Local
Building Permits** [See Housing Permits]

Index of Prices Received by Farmers
<DESCRIPTION>
A measure of the change from month to month in the average
prices of farm products.
<DERIVATION>
Prices for 44 commodities are estimated from personal
interviews with and mail and telephone surveys of buyers of

farm products and of producers that sell directly to consumers. Commodities are grouped into 11 subgroups, five of which are seasonally adjusted. These subgroup indexes are weighted according to average quantities of the respective commodities sold during a base period (1971-1973) and combined. Values of the indicator in terms of other base periods (1910-1914 and 1967)` are also calculated and published.
<USE>
Used to measure changes in average prices received for farm commodities, to approximate the price component of receipts by farmers for the sale of their products, and to calculate the commodity parity prices of agricultural products.
<PUBLISHER>
U.S. Department of Agriculture, Economics, Statistics, and Cooperatives Service
<ANNOUNCED IN>
Agricultural Prices
<ANNOUNCEMENT FREQUENCY>
Monthly
<CUMULATIONS>
TABLES
Ag Prices   Latest month and year ago, index nos.
Bus Stats   Monthly and yearly, cum, index nos.
EI   Monthly and yearly, cum, index nos.
SCB   Monthly and yearly, cum, index nos.
Bus Stats   Monthly and yearly, cum, ratio nos.
EI   Monthly and yearly, cum, ratio nos.
SCB   Monthly and yearly, cum, ratio nos.
Ag Charts   Yearly, cum, index nos.
Hist Stats   Yearly, cum, index nos.
Stat Abstr   Yearly, cum, index nos.
GRAPHS
Ag Charts   Yearly, cum, index nos.
Ag Charts S   Yearly, cum, index nos.
EI   Yearly, cum, index nos.
EI   Yearly, cum, ratio nos.
Ag Prices   Yearly, % change
<MORE INFORMATION>
   Joint Economic Committee, 1980 Supplement to Economic Indicators, Historical and Descriptive Background, USGPO, Washington, D.C., 1980.
   Scope and Method of the Statistical Reporting Service, Misc. Publ. 1308, USDA, Washington, D.C., 1975.
   Major Statistical Series of the U.S. Department of Agriculture, How They Are Constructed and Used, Vol. 1, Agricultural Prices and Parity, USDA, Washington, D.C., 1970.

Index of Stock Prices [See Standard and Poor's Composite Index]

Industrial Loans Outstanding [See Commercial and Industrial Loans Outstanding]

Industrial Production Index [See Industrial Production, Major Market Groups and Selected Manufacturers]

Industrial Production, Major Industrial Countries

<DESCRIPTION>
The value of all goods produced by the industries of seven countries (United States, Canada, Japan, France, Germany, Italy, and United Kingdom) each indexed to the value of such output in 1967.

<DERIVATION>
Each country calculates its industrial production differently, but generally the method is a base-weighted arithmetic average type of index. The base years vary considerably, but are normalized to 1967 by the Department of Commerce before publication. The weights used to combine products into group indexes are typically based on value-added market prices that have been appropriately adjusted (e.g., to eliminate duplications of values resulting from combining products). Indicators such as physical output, deflated values of output, deflated turnover, quantity of materials used, and man-hours are often used in calculating the production index.

<USE>
Used to assess and indicate trends in the overall economic activity of the foreign nations surveyed and to compare them with economic activities in the U.S.

<PUBLISHER>
U.S. Department of Commerce, International Trade Administration, Office of Planning and Research

<ANNOUNCED IN>
International Economic Indicators

<ANNOUNCEMENT FREQUENCY>
Monthly

<CUMULATIONS>
TABLES
EI   Monthly and yearly, cum, index nos.
BCD   Quarterly and yearly, cum, index nos.
Int Econ Ind Quarterly and yearly, cum, index nos.
Mo Econ Ind Quarterly and yearly, cum, index nos.
Int Econ Ind Quarterly and yearly, cum, % change
Int Fin Stat Yearly, cum, index nos.
Stat Abstr   Yearly, cum, index nos.
GRAPHS
BCD   Yearly, cum, index nos.
Int Econ Ind Yearly, cum, % change
Stat Bull   Yearly, cum, % change

<MORE INFORMATION>
   Joint Economic Committee, 1980 Supplement to Economic Indicators, Historical and Descriptive Background, USGPO, Washington, D.C., 1980.
   Geoffrey H. Moore, "What the Leading Indicators Indicate about Industrial Production in Certain Key Countries," Across the Board, 84-85 (Apr. 1980).

Industrial Production, Major Market Groups and Selected Manufactures [Also referred to as the Index of Industrial Production and as the Industrial Production Index]
<DESCRIPTION>
A measure of the changes in the physical volume or quantity of output of manufacturing and mining establishments and electric and gas utilities in the U.S., about 30% of the Gross National Product.
<DERIVATION>
The production by 265 industries is estimated from physical product data, production-worker hours, and kilowatt-hour data gathered from government agencies, trade organizations, and trade publications. These data are adjusted for undercoverage and seasonal change and combined according to the relative value added in 1967. These values indexed to a 1967 base are linked to bases for earlier benchmark years dating back to 1925. Value added is defined as the difference between the value of production and the cost of material or supplies consumed. The combination of the industry data produces indexes for four market groupings (consumer goods, equipment, intermediate products, and materials) that are in turn combined for the total.
<USE>
Used as a coinciding indicator of general economic conditions. Used with related data on employment, inventories, trade, prices, and other economic variables to analyze short- and long-term developments in the national economy. Used to determine the areas in which important changes have occurred and in analyses of the performance of individual businesses in comparison with the performance of the entire corresponding industry to which that business belongs.
<PUBLISHER>
Board of Governors of the Federal Reserve System
<ANNOUNCED IN>
Industrial Production, Statistical Release G.12.3 (414)
<ANNOUNCEMENT FREQUENCY>
Monthly
<CUMULATIONS>
TABLES

Man Han	Latest month, index nos.
Barron's	Latest month and year ago, index nos.
BW	Latest month and year ago, index nos.
NYT	Latest month and year ago, index nos.
BCD	Monthly, cum, index nos.
Bus Stats	Monthly and yearly, cum, index nos.
EI	Monthly and yearly, cum, index nos.
FR Bull	Monthly and yearly, cum, index nos.
S&P Stats	Monthly and yearly, cum, index nos.
SCB	Monthly and yearly, cum, index nos.
Int Econ Ind	Quarterly and yearly, cum, index nos.
Ind W	Quarterly and yearly, cum, index nos.
Int Econ Ind	Quarterly and yearly, cum, % change
Hist Stats	Yearly, cum, index nos.
Int Fin Stat	Yearly, cum, index nos.
Pred Base	Yearly, cum, index nos.

```
Pred Fore     Yearly, cum, index nos.
Stat Abstr    Yearly, cum, index nos.
GRAPHS
BCD           Yearly, cum, index nos.
EI            Yearly, cum, index nos.
Mo Econ Ind   Yearly, cum, index nos.
Stat Bull     Yearly, cum, index nos.
Int Econ Ind  Yearly, cum, % change
PROJECTIONS
S&P Outlook   Quarterly and yearly, index nos. (irr)
Value Line    Quarterly and yearly, % changes
Ind W         Yearly, index nos.
Pred Fore     Yearly, index nos.
```

<MORE INFORMATION>

Joint Economic Committee, 1980 Supplement to Economic Indicators, Historical and Descriptive Background, USGPO, Washington, D.C., 1980.

Kenneth Armitage and Juan D. Hosley, "Revision of Industrial Production Index," Federal Reserve Bulletin, 603-605 (Aug. 1979).

"Revised Industrial Production Index," Federal Reserve Bulletin, 1451-1474 (Dec. 1959).

G. H. Moore and J. Shiskin, "Why the Leading Indicators Really Do Lead," Across the Board, 71-75 (May 1978).

John Kirk, "Economic Indicators: The How and the Why," Banking, 27-28 (Aug. 1964).

Industrial Raw Materials Price Index [Also called Index of Industrial Materials Prices and the CRB (BLS-Formula) Spot Group Indices, Raw Materials]

<DESCRIPTION>
A measure of the spot-market price movements of thirteen raw materials traded on commodity markets and organized exchanges.

<DERIVATION>
Spot-market prices (the prices for which commodities are selling for immediate delivery) are determined each Tuesday for particular grades of and on particular markets for thirteen commodities: burlap, copper scrap, cotton, hides, lead scrap, print cloth, rosin, rubber, steel scrap, tallow, tin, wool tops, and zinc. When spot prices are not available, bid or asked prices may be used. Unweighted geometric averages of the individual price relatives are calculated with 1967 as the base year to produce the index value for the week. The prices and index are published on the following Friday. Monthly values are geometric averages of the Tuesday prices during the month. Data are not adjusted for seasonal variation.

<USE>
With the index of foodstuffs prices, this index makes up the Bureau of Labor Statistics's index of spot-market prices for 22 sensitive basic commodities whose markets are assumed to be among the first to be influenced by changes in economic conditions. A leading indicator overall and at troughs; unclassified at peaks.

<PUBLISHER>
Commodity Research Bureau, Inc., and the U.S. Department of Labor, Bureau of Labor Statistics
<ANNOUNCED IN>
CRB Commodity Index Report
Business Conditions Digest
<ANNOUNCEMENT FREQUENCY>
Weekly
<CUMULATIONS>
TABLES
Stat Bull   Latest period and year ago, % change
BCD   Monthly, cum, index nos.
Stat Abstr   Yearly, cum, index nos.
Com Indx Rep Weekly, monthly, year ago, index nos.
GRAPHS
Com Indx Rep Weekly, cum, index nos.
Mo Econ Ind Yearly, cum, index nos.
BCD   Yearly, cum, index nos.
<MORE INFORMATION>
  Julius Baer and E. Olin Saxon, Commodity Exchanges and Futures Trading, Harper and Row, New York, 1949.
  Richard M. Snyder, Measuring Business Changes, Wiley, New York, 1955, p. 77 ff.

Initial Unemployment Claims [See Unemployment Insurance Programs, Initial Claims]

Inventory Change
<DESCRIPTION>
The increase or decrease during a given quarter in U.S. businesses' inventories valued at the average price for the period.
<DERIVATION>
A sample of businesses and industries throughout the U.S. is surveyed and asked to provide the change in the physical volume of their inventories valued at the average price for the current period. Both farm and nonfarm inventories are included. Nonfarm inventories include purchased materials, supplies, goods in process, and finished goods on hand. The responses for nonfarm industries are deflated in accord with composite price indexes for about 150 components of the wholesale price index and then reinflated to provide a current value of the change in nonfarm inventories. Valuations of farm inventories are not adjusted. The Farm and nonfarm business inventories are then summed and seasonally adjusted. Values are expressed in current dollars; values for constant 1972 dollars and for the change as a percentage of the Gross National Product are also available.
<USE>
Used in the estimation of the Gross National Product; also used to gage the severity of recessions. Used as one of the components of the Leading Indicators Composite Index.
<PUBLISHER>
U.S. Department of Commerce, Bureau of Economic Analysis

<ANNOUNCED IN>
Economic Indicators
<ANNOUNCEMENT FREQUENCY>
Quarterly
<CUMULATIONS>
TABLES
Barron's   Latest and year ago, $
Man Han   Latest month, $
BW   Latest month and year ago, $
Ind W   Latest month and year ago, $
Bus Stats   Monthly and yearly, cum, $
EI   Monthly and yearly, cum, $
S&P Stats   Monthly and yearly, cum, $
SCB   Monthly and yearly, cum, $
GRAPHS
EI   Yearly, cum, $
Mo Econ Ind   Yearly, cum, $
<MORE INFORMATION>
   Moses Abramowitz, Inventories and Business Cycles,
Princeton University Press, Princeton, N.J., 1950.
   "Official Indicators: What Are They? Can They Predict the
Future?" U.S. News and World Report, 66-67 (Aug. 16, 1976).

Inventory-Sales Ratio [Also called Business Inventory-Sales
Ratio]
<DESCRIPTION>
The ratio of the value of inventory on hand during a given
period to the sales actually recorded during that period.
<DERIVATION>
The end-of-month book values of inventories held by merchant
wholesalers and retail traders are divided by the total sales
during the month. The data for this arithmetic operation are
derived from the seasonally adjusted sales and inventory
series for manufacturing and trade [see Business Sales and
Inventories, Wholesale and Retail Trade]. The yearly data are
calculated by dividing the weighted average of seasonally
adjusted inventories by the monthly average of unadjusted
sales for the year. No adjustments are made to bring
inventory book values (which might be either actual cost or
market value) up to selling prices.
<USE>
Stock-sales ratios are inversely related to business
activity. That is, the ratios tend to rise as sales decline
and to fall as sales increase. They are therefore used to
evaluate the current position of inventory holdings and to
forecast production activity. If the ratio of stock to sales
rises, future production may need to be curtailed; if the
ratio declines, future production may need to be increased to
meet consumer demand.
<PUBLISHER>
U.S. Department of Commerce, Bureau of Economic Analysis and
Bureau of the Census
<ANNOUNCED IN>
Survey of Current Business
<ANNOUNCEMENT FREQUENCY>
Monthly

<CUMULATIONS>
TABLES
Barron's   Latest and year ago, ratio nos.
BCD   Monthly, cum, ratio nos.
Bus Stats   Monthly and yearly, cum, ratio nos.
EI   Monthly and yearly, cum, ratio nos.
S&P Stats   Monthly and yearly, cum, ratio nos.
SCB   Monthly and yearly, cum, ratio nos.
GRAPHS
BCD   Yearly, cum, ratio nos.
EI   Yearly, cum, ratio nos.
Mo Econ Ind   Yearly, cum, ratio nos.
Stat Bull   Yearly, cum, ratio nos.
<MORE INFORMATION>
   Moses Abramowitz, Inventories and Business Cycles,
Princeton University Press, Princeton, N.J., 1950.

Inventory-Shipments Ratio [Also called Manufacturers'
Inventory-Shipments Ratio]
<DESCRIPTION>
The ratio of the value of manufacturers' inventory on hand
during a given period to the selling value of the goods
shipped by them during that period.
<DERIVATION>
For the monthly ratio, the end-of-month book value,
seasonally adjusted, of the inventories that manufacturers of
durable and nondurable goods have on hand is divided by the
monthly average of shipments (sales) recorded by those
manufacturers during that month. The data for this
calculation are derived from the manufacturers' shipments and
manufacturers' inventories series [see Manufacturers'
Shipments, Inventories, and Orders]. The yearly data are
calculated by dividing the weighted average of seasonally
adjusted inventories by the monthly average of shipments for
the year.
<USE>
Indicative of the match-up of production with demand. If the
ratio rises, inventories (and therefore production) are
getting ahead of demand for the goods produced, and perhaps
future production should be reduced. If the ratio decreases,
inventories and production are falling behind demand, and
perhaps future production should be increased.
<PUBLISHER>
U.S. Department of Commerce, Bureau of the Census
<ANNOUNCED IN>
Economic Indicators
<ANNOUNCEMENT FREQUENCY>
Monthly
<CUMULATIONS>
TABLES
NYT   Latest month and year ago, ratio nos.
EI   Monthly and yearly, cum, ratio nos.
Stat Abstr   Yearly, cum, ratio nos.
GRAPHS
EI   Yearly, cum, ratio nos.

<MORE INFORMATION>
  Moses   Abramowitz,   Inventories   and   Business   Cycles,
Princeton University Press, Princeton, N.J., 1950.

Investments [See Loans and Investments]

L

Labor Turnover [See also Accession Rate, Manufacturing; Layoff Rate, Manufacturing; and Quit Rate, Manufacturing]
<DESCRIPTION>
The gross movement of wage and salary workers into and out of employment in individual establishments during a given month expressed as three rates: the accession rate, the layoff rate, and the quit rate.
<DERIVATION>
Cooperating manufacturers are surveyed by state employment security agencies; respondents provide the number of employees that have been entered onto the payroll or have been removed from the payroll by virtue of having been laid off or of having quit. These data are divided by the total number of the respondents' employees and multiplied by 100 to give the three components of labor turnover: the Accession Rate, Manufacturing; the Layoff Rate, Manufacturing; and the Quit Rate, Manufacturing. The data are seasonally adjusted by the ratio-to-moving-average method.
<USE>
Used to provide early indications of business-cycle turning points.
<PUBLISHER>
U.S. Department of Labor, Bureau of Labor Statistics
<ANNOUNCED IN>
Employment and Earnings
<ANNOUNCEMENT FREQUENCY>
Monthly
<CUMULATIONS>

BCD	Monthly, cum, rate
Bus Stats	Monthly and yearly, cum, rate
Emp & Earn	Monthly and yearly, cum, rate
SCB	Monthly and yearly, cum, rate
Emp & Earn	Yearly, cum, rate
Hist Stats	Yearly, cum, rate
Stat Abstr	Yearly, cum, rate

GRAPHS
BCD   Monthly, cum, rate
<MORE INFORMATION>
   U.S. Dept. of Commerce, Bureau of Economic Analysis, Handbook of Cyclical Indicators, USGPO, Washington, D.C., 1977.

R. C. Mendelssohn, "Three BLS Series as Business Cycle Turn Signals," Monthly Labor Review, 973-976 (Sept. 1959).

Bureau of Labor Statistics, How the Government Measures Unemployment, Rept. 505, U.S. Department of Labor, Washington, D.C., 1977.

National Bureau of Economic Research, The Measurement and Bevavior of Unemployment, Princeton Univ. Press, Princeton, N.J., 1957.

Julius Shiskin, Labor Force and Unemployment, BLS Rept. 486, U.S. Department of Labor, Washington, D.C., 1976.

Seymour L. Wolfbein, Employment and Unemployment in the United States, Science Research Assoc., Chicago, 1964.

John E. Bregger, "Unemployment Statistics and What They Mean," Monthly Labor Review (June 1971).

Gloria P. Green, "Measuring Total and State Insured Unemployment," Monthly Labor Review (June 1971).

Bureau of Labor Statistics, Workers, Jobs, and Statistics, Rept. 698, U.S. Department of Labor, Washington, D.C., 1983.

Lagging Indicators [See Lagging Indicators Composite Index]

Lagging Indicators Composite Index
<DESCRIPTION>
The average behavior of a group of economic indicators whose values have been noted to follow business cycle turns.
<DERIVATION>
Six economic indicators were selected because their values generally changed in a manner similar to changes in the business cycles but changed after those business-cycle changes were evident. Those indicators are the average duration of unemployment, the labor cost per unit of manufactured output, the manufacturing and trade inventories, the commercial and industrial loans outstanding, the average prime rate charged by banks, and the ratio of consumer installment debt to personal income. Month-to-month percent changes or differences are calculated for each component of the composite index. The percent changes (or differences) for each component are standardized to an absolute value of one by dividing each monthly change by the average of these changes. These standardized changes are then weighted according to the economic significance, statistical adequacy, cyclical timing, conformity to business cycles, smoothness, and currency of each component. A weighted average of the standardized changes is computed for all the components. This average is then modified so its long-run average is equal to that of the coincident indicators composite's by deriving a ratio of the two long-term averages and then dividing the lagging indicators' monthly change by that ratio.
<USE>
Indicates changes in the direction of aggregate economic activity; viewed by many as an indicator of current and future levels of economic activity.
<PUBLISHER>
U.S. Department of Commerce, Bureau of Economic Analysis

<ANNOUNCED IN>
Business Conditions Digest
<ANNOUNCEMENT FREQUENCY>
Monthly
<CUMULATIONS>
TABLES
BCD   Monthly, cum, index nos.
GRAPHS
BCD   Yearly, cum, index nos.
BCD   Yearly, cum, % change
<MORE INFORMATION>
  Geoffrey   H.   Moore,   Ed.,   Business   Cycle   Indicators,
Princeton University Press, Princeton, N.J., 1961.
  "Indicators That Lag Economy's Ups and Downs Denote Strain
That Often Leads to Recession," Wall Street Journal, 46 (Nov.
29, 1978).

Layoff Rate, Manufacturing [Also called Separation Rate.
See also Labor Turnover; Accession Rate, Manufacturing; and
Quit Rate, Manufacturing]
<DESCRIPTION>
The number of employer-initiated suspensions from pay per 100
employees during a given month.
<DERIVATION>
The state employment security agencies survey cooperating
manufacturers; respondents provide the number of employees
(temporary or permanent) that were suspended from the payroll
without prejudice to the worker for a period of seven or more
consecutive days during the month because of lack of orders,
model   changeover,   termination   of   seasonal   or   temporary
employment, inventory taking, introduction of labor-saving
devices, plant breakdown, transfer to other establishments in
the same company, etc. These data are divided by the total
number of employees of the surveyed manufacturers, multiplied
by 100, and seasonally adjusted by the ratio-to-moving
average method.
<USE>
One of the three components of Labor Turnover as analyzed by
the Bureau of Labor Statistics (the other two components are
Accession Rate and Quit Rate). Used as one of the components
of the Leading Indicators Composite Index.
<PUBLISHER>
U.S. Department of Labor, Bureau of Labor Statistics
<ANNOUNCED IN>
Employment and Earnings
<ANNOUNCEMENT FREQUENCY>
Monthly
<CUMULATIONS>
TABLES
BCD   Monthly, cum, rate
Bus Stats   Monthly and yearly, cum, rate
Emp & Earn   Monthly and yearly, cum, rate
SCB   Monthly and yearly, cum, rate
Emp & Earn   Yearly, cum, rate
Hist Stats   Yearly, cum, rate
Stat Abstr   Yearly, cum, rate

GRAPHS
BCD   Monthly, cum, rate
<MORE INFORMATION>
U.S. Dept. of Commerce, Bureau of Economic Analysis,
Handbook of Cyclical Indicators, USGPO, Washington, D.C.,
1977.
R. C. Mendelssohn, "Three BLS Series as Business Cycle Turn
Signals," Monthly Labor Review, 973-976 (Sept. 1959).
"Official Indicators: What Are They? Can They Predict the
Future?" U.S. News and World Report, 66-67 (Aug. 16, 1976).
Bureau of Labor Statistics, Workers, Jobs, and Statistics,
Rept. 698, U.S. Department of Labor, Washington, D.C., 1983.
John E. Bregger, "Unemployment Statistics and What They
Mean," Monthly Labor Review (June 1971).
Gloria P. Green, "Measuring Total and State Insured
Unemployment," Monthly Labor Review (June 1971).
Bureau of Labor Statistics, How the Government Measures
Unemployment, Rept. 505, U.S. Department of Labor,
Washington, D.C., 1977.
National Bureau of Economic Research, The Measurement and
Bevavior of Unemployment, Princeton Univ. Press, Princeton,
N.J., 1957.
Julius Shiskin, Labor Force and Unemployment, BLS Rept.
486, U.S. Department of Labor, Washington, D.C., 1976.
Seymour L. Wolfbein, Employment and Unemployment in the
United States, Science Research Assoc., Chicago, 1964.

Leading Indicators [See Leading Indicators Composite Index]

Leading Indicators Composite Index
<DESCRIPTION>
The average behavior of a group of economic indicators whose
values have been noted to precede business cycle turns.
<DERIVATION>
Twelve economic indicators were selected because their values
generally changed in a manner similar to changes in the
business cycles but changed before those business-cycle
changes were evident. Those indicators are the average
workweek of manufacturing production workers, the
manufacturing layoff rate, vendor performance, the smoothed
percent change in total liquid assets, the smoothed percent
change in sensitive prices, the plant and equipment contracts
and orders, the index of net business formation, the index of
stock prices, the money supply (M1), the new orders of
consumer goods and materials, the private housing building
permits, and the smoothed change in inventories on hand and
on order. Month-to-month percent changes or differences are
calculated for each component of the composite index. The
percent changes (or differences) for each component are
standardized to an absolute value of one by dividing each
monthly change by the average of these changes. These
standardized changes are then weighted according to the
economic significance, statistical adequacy, cyclical timing,
conformity to business cycles, smoothness, and currency of

each component. A weighted average of the standardized changes is computed for all the components. This average is then modified so its long-run average is equal to that of the coincident indicators composite's by deriving a ratio of the two long-term averages and then dividing the leading indicators' monthly change by that ratio.
<USE>
Indicates changes in the direction of aggregate economic activity; viewed by many as an indicator of current and future levels of economic activity.
<PUBLISHER>
U.S. Department of Commerce, Bureau of Economic Analysis
<ANNOUNCED IN>
Business Conditions Digest
<ANNOUNCEMENT FREQUENCY>
Monthly
<CUMULATIONS>
TABLES
Barron's	Latest month and year ago, index nos.
BW	Latest month and year ago, index nos.
Ind W	Latest month and year ago, index nos.
Man Han	Latest month and year ago, index nos.
NYT	Latest month and year ago, index nos.
Stat Bull	Latest quarter and year ago, % change
BCD	Monthly, cum, index nos.
BCD	Monthly, cum, % change
S&P Stats	Monthly and yearly, cum, index nos.
Stat Bull	Quarterly and yearly, cum, index nos.
BCD	Yearly, cum, index nos.
Mo Econ Ind	Yearly, cum, index nos.
BCD	Yearly, cum, % change

GRAPHS
BCD	Yearly, cum, index nos.
BCD	Yearly, cum, % change
Mo Econ Ind	Yearly, cum, index nos.
Stat Bull	Quarterly, cum, index nos.

<MORE INFORMATION>
  Geoffrey H. Moore, Ed., Business Cycle Indicators, Princeton University Press, Princeton, N.J., 1961, vol. 1.
  G. H. Moore and J. Shiskin, "Why the Leading Indicators Really Do Lead," Across the Board, 71-75 (May 1978).
  Maury N. Harris and Debrorah Jamroz, Evaluating the Leading Indicators, Federal Reserve Bank of New York, New York, 1976, pp. 165-171.
  Saul H. Hymans, "On the Use of Leading Indicators to Predict Cyclical Turning Points," Brooking Papers on Economic Activity, 339-375 (1973).
  "Are They Wrong Even When They're Right," Business Week, 90 (May 4, 1983).
  "Official Indicators: What Are They? Can They Predict the Future?" U.S. News and World Report, 66-67 (Aug. 16, 1976).

Liquid Assets [See Change in Total Liquid Assets]

Loan Demand [See Commercial and Industrial Loans Outstanding, Weekly Reporting Large Commercial Banks]

Loans and Investments
[Also referred to as Bank Loans, Investments, and Reserves]
<DESCRIPTION>
Technically a subset of the Bank Loans, Investments, and Reserves. Estimates the total loans outstanding from (1) all commercial banks (which excludes mutual savings banks, savings and loan associations, and other institutions that do not accept demand deposits) and (2) member banks of the Federal Reserve System. A subset, total commercial and industrial loans (all business loans except those secured by real estate, loans for purchasing or carrying securities, and loans to financial institutions), is also compiled. Also estimates securities held by these institutions, broken down into U.S. Treasury securities and other securities (principally issues of states, municipalities, and federal agencies).
<DERIVATION>
Prepared on the basis of selected weekly banking reports (the selection is stratified by size of reporting banks) and quarterly call report information. Heavy reliance is placed on the data from banks that are members of the Federal Reserve to estimate the activities of nonmember banks. To these data are added data from the monthly condition reports of foreign financial institutions operating in the U.S. Data are normally for the last Wednesday of the month.
<USE>
Used in current banking and monetary analysis, in discerning trends in bank credit and its components, and in evaluating the banking system's performance and response to change in monetary policy.
<PUBLISHER>
Board of Governors of the Federal Reserve System
<ANNOUNCED IN>
Loans and Investments at All Commercial Banks, Statistical Release G.7 (407)
<ANNOUNCEMENT FREQUENCY>
Monthly
<CUMULATIONS>
TABLES
BCD   Monthly, cum, $
FR Bull   Monthly, cum, $
EI   Monthly and yearly, cum, $
Stat Abstr   Yearly, cum, $
GRAPHS
BCD   Yearly, cum, $
EI   Yearly, cum, $
Moody's B&F Yearly, cum, $
<MORE INFORMATION>
   Joint Economic Committee, 1980 Supplement to Economic Indicators, Historical and Descriptive Background, USGPO, Washington, D.C., 1980.

Lumber Production

<DESCRIPTION>
An estimation of the amount of lumber in board feet that U.S. sawmills and planing mills have produced, have shipped, and have in stock during the given month.

<DERIVATION>
About half of the sawmills and planing mills in the U.S. are surveyed monthly to determine the amount of rough, dressed, and worked (matched, shiplapped, or patterned) lumber that has been produced, has been shipped, or is in stock. The output of flooring mills is not included. The data is then adjusted against annual production figures published by the Bureau of the Census. Current data are revised as more-relevant Census figures become available.

<USE>
A leading indicator of future business activity, especially in the paper and housing segments of the economy.

<PUBLISHER>
National Forest Products Association

<ANNOUNCED IN>
Survey of Current Business

<ANNOUNCEMENT FREQUENCY>
Monthly

<CUMULATIONS>
TABLES

Barron's	Latest and year ago, bd ft
Ind W	Latest and year ago, bd ft
NYT	Latest and year ago, bd ft
Bus Stats	Monthly and yearly, cum, bd ft
Const Rev	Monthly and yearly, cum, bd ft
S&P Stats	Monthly and yearly, cum, bd ft
SCB	Monthly and yearly, cum, bd ft
BW	Weekly, monthly, and year ago, bd ft
Hist Stats	Yearly, cum, bd ft
Stat Abstr	Yearly, cum, bd ft

GRAPHS

Stat Abstr	Yearly, cum, bd ft

M

M1 [See Money Stock Measures and Liquid Assets]

M2 [See Money Supply M2 Deflated]

M3 [See Money Stock Measures and Liquid Assets]

Machine Tool Orders
<DESCRIPTION>
A measure of the current sales level for metal cutting and metal forming machine tools.
<DERIVATION>
Respondents to a monthly survey of the industry provide their gross new orders, cancellations, shipments, and backlog of unfilled orders. From these data, a value for net new orders is derived by subtracting cancellations from gross orders. The result is multiplied by an expansion factor to estimate all machine-tool-industry activity. That factor is periodically determined by comparing the shipment total reported in the surveys to that reported by the Census Bureau.
<USE>
A leading indicator of the activity in the industrial sector of the U.S. economy.
<PUBLISHER>
National Machine Tool Builders Association
<ANNOUNCED IN>
Industry Estimates
<ANNOUNCEMENT FREQUENCY>
Monthly
<CUMULATIONS>
TABLES

Ind Est	Latest month, $
Ind Est	Latest month, backlog $
Barron's	Latest month and year ago, $
Ind W	Latest month and year ago, $
SCB	Monthly and yearly, cum, backlog $

Stat Abstr	Monthly and yearly, cum, backlog $
Bus Stats	Monthly and yearly, cum, $
S&P Stats	Monthly and yearly, cum, $
SCB	Monthly and yearly, cum, $
Stat Abstr	Monthly and yearly, cum, $

Major Industrial Countries' Industrial Production [See Industrial Production, Major Industrial Countries]

Major Market Groups and Selected Manufacturers' Industrial Production [See Industrial Production, Major Market Groups and Selected Manufacturers]

Manufacturing Accession Rate [See Accession Rate, Manufacturing]

Manufacturing Layoff Rate [See Layoff Rate, Manufacturing]

Manufacturers' Inventory-Shipments Ratio [See Inventory-Shipments Ratio]

Manufacturers' Capacity Utilization: Bureau of Economic Analysis [Also called Operating Rate]
<DESCRIPTION>
A measure of the percentage of the maximum practical capacity actually used by manufacturers during the final month of each calendar quarter. A ratio of the actual rate of utilization to the preferred rate is also calculated.
<DERIVATION>
Manufacturing companies are surveyed and asked to report their actual and preferred operating rates; capacity is not specifically defined but is left for each respondent to estimate. Responses are collected into industry groupings, weighted according to each group's gross depreciable assets, seasonally adjusted and combined.
<USE>
Used by industry and government in studies of investment patterns; output per man-hour; and costs, prices, and profits.
<PUBLISHER>
U.S. Department of Commerce, Bureau of Economic Analysis
<ANNOUNCED IN>
Bureau of Economic Analysis press release
<ANNOUNCEMENT FREQUENCY>
Quarterly
<CUMULATIONS>
TABLES

BW	Latest and year ago, %
EI	Quarterly and yearly, cum, %
BCD	Quarterly, cum, %
FR Bull	Quarterly and yearly,cum, %

GRAPHS
BCD   Yearly, cum, %
EI   Yearly, cum, %
<MORE INFORMATION>
   Joint Economic Committee, 1980 Supplement to Economic
Indicators, Historical and Descriptive Background, USGPO,
Washington, D.C., 1980.
   Board of Governors of the Federal Reserve System, Federal
Reserve Measures of Capacity and Capacity Utilization,
Federal Reserve System, Washington, D.C., 1978.
   Measures of Productive Capacity, Hearings Before the
Subcommittee on Economic Statistics of the U.S. Joint
Economic Committee, USGPO, Washington, D.C., 1962.

**Manufacturers' Capacity Utilization: Federal Reserve
Board** [Also called Capacity Utilization Rate]
<DESCRIPTION>
The ratio of industrial output to installed capacity
expressed as a percentage.
<DERIVATION>
The Federal Reserve estimates productive capacity by deriving
production indexes from the Census of Manufactures, dividing
those indexes by utilization rate data from various company
surveys, and smoothing that data to reflect long-term
production trends, business judgements about the degree of
facility use, and the pattern of real investment over the
course of the business cycle. Smoothed estimates from
several sources are averaged. This capacity index is then
divided into the Board's index of industrial production, and
the result is multiplied by 100.
<USE>
Used as important indicators of resource use; high
utilization rates are generally associated with increased
levels of investment and, in certain industries, with
bottlenecks and supply-side inflationary pressures.
<PUBLISHER>
Board of Governors of the Federal Reserve System
<ANNOUNCED IN>
Capacity Utilization: Manufacturing and Materials,
Statistical Release G.3 (402)
<ANNOUNCEMENT FREQUENCY>
Monthly
<CUMULATIONS>
TABLES
Cap Util   Quarterly and yearly, cum, %
EI   Quarterly and yearly, cum, %
FR Bull   Quarterly and yearly, cum, %
FR Bull   Quarterly and yearly, cum, index nos.
Stat Abstr   Yearly, cum, index nos.
Stat Abstr   Yearly, cum, %
GRAPHS
EI   Yearly, cum, %
<MORE INFORMATION>
   Joint Economic Committee, 1980 Supplement to Economic
Indicators, Historical and Descriptive Background, USGPO,
Washington, D.C., 1980.

Board of Governors of the Federal Reserve System, Federal Reserve Measures of Capacity and Capacity Utilization, Federal Reserve Board, Washington, D.C., 1978.
  Board of Governors of the Federal Reserve System, Industrial Production, rev. ed., Federal Reserve Board, Washington, D.C., 1977.

Manufacturers' Inventories
<DESCRIPTION>
Estimates of manufacturers' book values of raw materials and supplies, work in progress, and finished goods on hand at the end of the period.
<DERIVATION>
About 5000 companies or divisions of companies are surveyed monthly. Data are broken down into about 80 industry categories. The estimate for the previous month for each category is adjusted by the ratio of change indicated by the survey data. The estimates are benchmarked annually, are seasonally adjusted, and (where appropriate) adjusted for the number of trading days in the month.
<USE>
Used to discern trends in the difference between production and shipments of manufacturers, to predict the probable course of manufacturers' activity in selected industries in the near future, and to indicate future directions of the general business cycle. These data also allow the analysis of the impact of changes in demand in and on various sectors of the economy.
<PUBLISHER>
U.S. Department of Commerce, Bureau of the Census
<ANNOUNCED IN>
Current Industrial Report M3-1
<ANNOUNCEMENT FREQUENCY>
Monthly
<CUMULATIONS>
TABLES
Man Han	Lastest month, $
Barron's	Latest month and year ago, $
BW	Latest month and year ago, $
Ind W	Latest month and year ago, $
Stat Bull	Latest quarter and year ago, % change
BCD	Monthly, cum, $
Bus Stats	Monthly and yearly, cum, $
EI	Monthly and yearly, cum, $
S&P Stats	Monthly and yearly, cum, $
SCB	Monthly and yearly, cum, $
Hist Stats	Yearly, cum, $
Stat Abstr	Yearly, cum, $

GRAPHS
BCD	Yearly, cum, $
EI	Yearly, cum, $
Mo Econ Ind	Yearly, cum, $

<MORE INFORMATION>
  Joint Economic Committee, 1980 Supplement to Economic Indicators, Historical and Descriptive Background, USGPO, Washington, D.C., 1980.

Manufacturers' Shipments, Inventories, and Orders: 1967-1978, Bureau of the Census Report M3-1.8, Department of Commerce, Washington, D.C., 1979.

Manufacturers' Orders
<DESCRIPTION>
Estimates of net orders on hand to manufacturers after cancellations and contract changes.
<DERIVATION>
About 5000 companies or divisions of companies are surveyed monthly. Data are broken down into about 80 industry categories. The estimate for the previous month for each category is adjusted by the ratio of change indicated by the survey data. The estimates are benchmarked annually, are seasonally adjusted, and (where appropriate) adjusted for the number of trading days in the month.
<USE>
Used to discern trends in the difference between production and shipments of manufacturers, to predict the probable course of manufacturers' activity in selected industries in the near future, and to indicate future directions of the general business cycle. These data also allow the analysis of the impact of changes in demand in and on various sectors of the economy.
<PUBLISHER>
U.S. Department of Commerce, Bureau of the Census
<ANNOUNCED IN>
Current Industrial Report M3-1
<ANNOUNCEMENT FREQUENCY>
Monthly
<CUMULATIONS>
TABLES

Barron's	Latest month and year ago, $
NYT	
Stat Bull	Latest quarter and year ago, % change
BCD	Monthly, cum, $
Bus Stats	Monthly and yearly, cum, $
EI	Monthly and yearly, cum, $
SCB	Monthly and yearly, cum, $
Stat Abstr	Yearly, cum, $

GRAPHS

BCD	Yearly, cum, $
EI	Yearly, cum, $

<MORE INFORMATION>
Joint Economic Committee, 1980 Supplement to Economic Indicators, Historical and Descriptive Background, USGPO, Washington, D.C., 1980.

Manufacturers' Shipments, Inventories, and Orders: 1967-1978, Bureau of the Census Report M3-1.8, Department of Commerce, Washington, D.C., 1980.

"Official Indicators: What Are They? Can They Predict the Future?" U.S. News and World Report, 66-67 (Aug. 16, 1976).

Manufacturers' Shipments
<DESCRIPTION>
Estimates of shipments (foreign and domestic), expressed in net selling values.

<DERIVATION>
About 5000 companies or divisions of companies are surveyed
monthly. Data are broken down into about 80 industry
categories. The estimate for the previous month for each
category is adjusted by the ratio of change indicated by the
survey data. The estimates are benchmarked annually to the
most recent level of the Average Monthly Shipments, are
seasonally adjusted, and (where appropriate) adjusted for the
number of trading days in the month.
<USE>
Used to discern trends in the difference between production
and shipments of manufacturers, to predict the probable
course of manufacturers' activity in selected industries in
the near future, and to indicate future directions of the
general business cycle. These data also allow the analysis of
the impact of changes in demand in and on various sectors of
the economy.
<PUBLISHER>
U.S. Department of Commerce, Bureau of the Census
<ANNOUNCED IN>
Current Industrial Report M3-1
<ANNOUNCEMENT FREQUENCY>
Monthly
<CUMULATIONS>
TABLES
Ind W   Latest month and year ago, $
Bus Stats   Monthly and yearly, cum, $
EI   Monthly and yearly, cum, $
SCB   Monthly and yearly, cum, $
Hist Stats   Yearly, cum, $
Stat Abstr   Yearly, cum, $
GRAPHS
EI   Yearly, cum, $
<MORE INFORMATION>
   Joint Economic Committee, 1980 Supplement to Economic
Indicators, Historical and Descriptive Background, USGPO,
Washington, D.C., 1980.
   Manufacturers' Shipments, Inventories, and Orders:
1967-1978, Bureau of the Census Report M3-1.8, Department of
Commerce, Washington, D.C., 1980.

Margin Debt
<DESCRIPTION>
The total money borrowed from brokers and bankers by
brokerage customers with securities as collateral.
<DERIVATION>
The Federal Reserve Board and the Securities and Exchange
Commission regulate the percentage of the total portfolio
value that can be borrowed against securities to purchase
other securities. Brokerage houses are required by law to
report their total debt in dollars to the SEC and the FRB.
These reports are totalled to produce this indicator.
<USE>
Used as a sentiment indicator and as a flow-of-funds
indicator because as prices rise on the stock market, the

confidence of margin traders also grows. Thus, rising markets produce larger margin debts, pushing the market even higher. In a falling market, margin debtors must cover their losses by selling the securities that they had put up as collateral, thus causing the market to fall even faster.
<PUBLISHER>
Board of Governors of the Federal Reserve System
<ANNOUNCED IN>
Federal Reserve Bulletin
<ANNOUNCEMENT FREQUENCY>
Monthly
<CUMULATIONS>
FR Bull   Monthly and yearly, cum, $
<MORE INFORMATION>
   Frank G. Zarb and Gabriel T. Kerekes, Ed., The Stock Market Handbook, Dow Jones - Irwin, Homewood, Ill., 1970, pp. 316-324.
   Martin J. Pring, Technical Analysis Explained, An Illustrated Guide for the Investor, McGraw Hill, New York, 1980, pp. 216-220.
   Michael Hayes, The Dow Jones - Irwin Guide to Stock Market Cycles, Dow Jones - Irwin, Homewood, Ill., 1977, pp. 158-160.
   Sloan J. Wilson, "The Customers' Free Credit Balances and Margin Debt," pp. 19-1 to 19-22 in The Encyclopedia of Stock Market Techniques, Investors Intelligence, Larchmont, N.Y., 1983.

Market Value Index [See Media General Market Value Index]

McCann-Erickson National Advertising Index
<DESCRIPTION>
Measures of the monthly advertising revenues of the major national media.
<DERIVATION>
Large advertisers are surveyed. Expenditures by national advertisers are totalled for each month and for each medium: network television, spot television, weekly magazines, women's magazines, monthly magazines, and newspapers. These values are seasonally adjusted and indexed to a value of 100 for 1967. The general index is a composite (roughly an average) of the network television, spot television, total magazines, and newspaper values.
<USE>
Barometers of the month-to-month changes in national expenditures for advertising.
<PUBLISHER>
McCann-Erikson, Inc.
<ANNOUNCED IN>
Advertising Age
<ANNOUNCEMENT FREQUENCY>
Monthly
<CUMULATIONS>
TABLES
S&P Stats   Monthly and yearly, cum, index nos.
Bus Stats   Monthly and yearly, cum, index nos.

SCB   Monthly and yearly, cum, index nos.
Hist Stats   Yearly, cum, index nos.
Stat Abstr   Yearly, cum, index nos.

Measure of Business Confidence [Also called Business
Executives' Expectations]
<DESCRIPTION>
An assessment of the economic sentiment and expectations of
business executives.
<DERIVATION>
The chief executive officers of American business firms, both
large and small, are surveyed each quarter. About 1500 of
them reply. They are asked three questions about the current
prospects of the economy: How would you rate business
conditions for the economy as a whole, as compared with six
months ago? In looking ahead six months as compared to now,
how do you think general business conditions will be? In
appraising prospects for your own particular industry, how do
you think business over the next six months, as compared to
now, will be? (A fourth question is also asked but not used
in composing the Measure of Business Confidence: How would
you rate business conditions for your own industry, as
compared with those for six months ago?) Possible replies and
their assigned scores are: Substantially Better (100),
Moderately Better (75), Same (50), Moderately Worse (25), and
Substantially Worse (0). The replies are averaged to produce
the index and its subsets.
<USE>
Used as a leading sentiment indicator; an informed,
collective opinion of future movements in business activity.
<PUBLISHER>
The Conference Board
<ANNOUNCED IN>
Business Executives' Expectations
<ANNOUNCEMENT FREQUENCY>
Quarterly
<CUMULATIONS>
TABLES
Bus Exec Exp Monthly, cum, index nos.
Stat Bull   Monthly, cum, index nos.
GRAPHS
Bus Exec Exp Monthly, cum, index nos.

**Media General American Stock Exchange Equal-Investment
Index**
<DESCRIPTION>
A reflection of the total change in value of an investment in
securities listed on the American Stock Exchange.
<DERIVATION>
A $1000 investment was theoretically made in each common
stock listed on the American Stock Exchange as of the base
date of Jan. 11, 1973. Provisions are made for reflecting the
effects of splits, mergers, new listings, and delistings of
stocks. Dividends are not considered to be reinvested. To

calculate the current index value, the number of shares held are multiplied by their current stock prices, and the result is indexed to a value of 1000 for the base date.
<USE>
Used to show average change in value of all included issues.
<PUBLISHER>
Media General Financial Services, Inc.
<ANNOUNCED IN>
Media General Financial Weekly
<ANNOUNCEMENT FREQUENCY>
Weekly
<CUMULATIONS>
TABLES
MG Fin Wkly Monthly and weekly, cum, index nos.
<MORE INFORMATION>
   "The Media General Market Value Indexes," Media General Financial Services, Richmond, Va., nd.

Media General American Stock Exchange Market Value Index
<DESCRIPTION>
A measure of the change in aggregate market value of the outstanding common shares of stocks listed on the American Stock Exchange.
<DERIVATION>
The share price for common shares is multiplied by the number of shares outstanding for all corporations listed on the American Stock Exchange. Rights, preferred stocks, and when-issued stocks are not included. This calculation is then indexed to the value for Jan. 2, 1970, which was assigned an index value of 100.00. The effects on the index of new listings, delistings, splits, suspensions or halts of trading, or distributions of dividends are compensated for by recalculating the base market value. Proprietary subsidiary indexes for industry groups are also calculated.
<USE>
A measure of the overall market strength and of speculative activity.
<PUBLISHER>
Media General Financial Services, Inc.
<ANNOUNCED IN>
Media General Financial Weekly
<ANNOUNCEMENT FREQUENCY>
Weekly
<CUMULATIONS>
TABLES
MG Fin Wkly Monthly and weekly, cum, index nos.
<MORE INFORMATION>
   "The Media General Market Value Indexes," Media General Financial Services, Richmond, Va., nd.

Media General Composite Equal-Investment Index
<DESCRIPTION>
A reflection of the total change in value of an investment in

securities listed on the American Stock Exchange and the New York Stock Exchange.
<DERIVATION>
A $1000 investment was theoretically made in each common stock listed on the American Stock Exchange and the New York Stock Exchange as of the base date of Jan. 11, 1973. Provisions are made for reflecting the effects of splits, mergers, new listings, and delistings of stocks. Dividends are not considered to be reinvested. To calculate the current index value, the number of shares held are multiplied by their current stock prices, and the result is indexed to a value of 1000 for the base date.
<USE>
Used to show average change in value of all included issues.
<PUBLISHER>
Media General Financial Services, Inc.
<ANNOUNCED IN>
Media General Financial Weekly
<ANNOUNCEMENT FREQUENCY>
Weekly
<CUMULATIONS>
TABLES
MG Fin Wkly Monthly and weekly, cum, index nos.
<MORE INFORMATION>
  "The Media General Market Value Indexes," Media General Financial Services, Richmond, Va., nd.

Media General Composite Market Value Index
<DESCRIPTION>
A measure of the change in aggregate market value of the outstanding common shares of stocks traded on the American Stock Exchange, on the New York Stock Exchange, and over the counter.
<DERIVATION>
The share price for common shares is multiplied by the number of shares outstanding for all corporations traded on the American Stock Exchange, New York Stock Exchange, and the NASDAQ System. Rights, preferred stocks, and when-issued stocks are not included. This calculation is then indexed to the value for Jan. 2, 1970, which was assigned an index value of 100.00. The effects on the index of new listings, delistings, splits, suspensions or halts of trading, or distributions of dividends are compensated for by recalculating the base market value. Proprietary subsidiary indexes for industry groups are also calculated.
<USE>
A measure of the overall market strength and of speculative activity.
<PUBLISHER>
Media General Financial Services, Inc.
<ANNOUNCED IN>
Media General Financial Weekly
<ANNOUNCEMENT FREQUENCY>
Weekly

<CUMULATIONS>
TABLES
MG Fin Wkly   Latest two weeks, month ago, quarter ago,
              index nos.
MG Fin Wkly   Latest week, month, quarter, % change
MG Fin Wkly   Monthly and weekly, cum, index nos.
MG Fin Wkly   Latest year, moving average
<MORE INFORMATION>
  "The Media General Market Value Indexes," Media General
Financial Services, Richmond, Va., nd.

Media General New York Stock Exchange Equal-Investment Index

<DESCRIPTION>
A reflection of the total change in value of an investment in
securities listed on the New York Stock Exchange.
<DERIVATION>
A $1000 investment was theoretically made in each common
stock listed on the New York Stock Exchange as of the base
date of Jan. 11, 1973. Provisions are made for reflecting the
effects of splits, mergers, new listings, and delistings of
stocks. Dividends are not considered to be reinvested. To
calculate the current index value, the number of shares held
are multiplied by their current stock prices, and the result
is indexed to a value of 1000 for the base date.
<USE>
Used to show average change in value of all included issues.
<PUBLISHER>
Media General Financial Services, Inc.
<ANNOUNCED IN>
Media General Financial Weekly
<ANNOUNCEMENT FREQUENCY>
Weekly
<CUMULATIONS>
TABLES
MG Fin Wkly   Monthly and weekly, cum, index nos.
<MORE INFORMATION>
  "The Media General Market Value Indexes," Media General
Financial Services, Richmond, Va., nd.

Media General New York Stock Exchange Market Value Index

<DESCRIPTION>
A measure of the change in aggregate market value of the
outstanding common shares of stocks listed on the New York
Stock Exchange.
<DERIVATION>
The share price for common shares is multiplied by the number
of shares outstanding for all corporations listed on the New
York Stock Exchange. Rights, preferred stocks, and
when-issued stocks are not included. This calculation is then
indexed to the value for Jan. 2, 1970, which was assigned an
index value of 100.00. The effects on the index of new
listings, delistings, splits, suspensions or halts of
trading, or distributions of dividends are compensated for by

recalculating the base market value. Proprietary subsidiary indexes for industry groups are also calculated.
<USE>
A measure of the overall market strength and of speculative activity.
<PUBLISHER>
Media General Financial Services, Inc.
<ANNOUNCED IN>
Media General Financial Weekly
<ANNOUNCEMENT FREQUENCY>
Weekly
<CUMULATIONS>
TABLES
MG Fin Wkly   Monthly and weekly, cum, index nos.
<MORE INFORMATION>
  "The Media General Market Value Indexes," Media General Financial Services, Richmond, Va., nd.

Media General Over-the-Counter Market Value Index
<DESCRIPTION>
A measure of the change in aggregate market value of the outstanding common shares of stocks listed on the National Association of Securities Dealers Automated Quotation System, a computerized service instituted in 1971.
<DERIVATION>
The share price for common shares is multiplied by the number of shares outstanding for all corporations traded on the NASDAQ System. Rights, preferred stocks, and when-issued stocks are not included. This calculation is then indexed to the value for Jan. 2, 1970, which was assigned an index value of 100.00. The effects on the index of new listings, delistings, splits, suspensions or halts of trading, or distributions of dividends are compensated for by recalculating the base market value. Proprietary subsidiary indexes for industry groups are also calculated.
<USE>
A measure of the overall market strength and of speculative activity.
<PUBLISHER>
Media General Financial Services, Inc.
<ANNOUNCED IN>
Media General Financial Weekly
<ANNOUNCEMENT FREQUENCY>
Weekly
<CUMULATIONS>
TABLES
MG Fin Wkly   Monthly and weekly, cum, index nos.
<MORE INFORMATION>
  "The Media General Market Value Indexes," Media General Financial Services, Richmond, Va., nd.

Misery Index [Also called the Discomfort Index; see Appendix A. Nonquantitative Indicators]

Mobile Home Sales
<DESCRIPTION>
The number of mobile homes sold by manufacturers nationwide each month.
<DERIVATION>
The number of residential units sold by manufacturers to dealers is collected from all mobile-home manufacturers in the continental U.S. monthly. The total is seasonally adjusted. Mobile homes are defined as single, expandable, or double-wide dwelling units with undercarriages and wheels; a double-wide unit consisting of two single units joined together at the site is counted as a single unit.
<USE>
Used as a measure of the current state of the housing industry.
<PUBLISHER>
National Conference of States on Building Codes and Standards and U.S. Department of Commerce, Bureau of the Census
<ANNOUNCED IN>
Construction Review
<ANNOUNCEMENT FREQUENCY>
Monthly
<CUMULATIONS>
TABLES

Ind W	Latest month and year ago, units
Bus Stats	Monthly and yearly, cum, units
Const Rev	Monthly and yearly, cum, units
SCB	Monthly and yearly, cum, units
Pred Base	Yearly, cum, units
Pred Fore	Yearly, cum, units

PROJECTIONS

Pred Fore	Yearly, units

<MORE INFORMATION>
   "Mobile Homes - A Growing Force in the Housing Sector," Construction Review, 4-8 (Sept. 1972).

Monetary Stock [See Money Stock Measures and Liquid Assets]

Money Balance [See Money Supply M2 Deflated]

Money Stock Measures and Liquid Assets
<DESCRIPTION>
Five estimates of the amount of money and liquefiable assets held by the public are made on a monthly basis: (1) M-1A, the demand deposits at commercial banks and currency; (2) M-1B, demand deposits at commercial banks and mutual savings banks, interest-earning checking deposits, negotiable order of withdrawal and automatic transfer from savings accounts at banks and thrift institutions, and share draft accounts at credit unions; (3) M-2, the deposits covered by M-1B plus savings and time deposits of less than $100,000 at all depository institutions, money market mutual fund shares, overnight repurchase agreements at commercial banks, and

certain overnight Eurodollars; M-3, the amounts covered by M-2 plus large-denomination time deposits and term repurchase agreements at banks and savings and loan associations; and L, the assets covered by M-3 plus term Eurodollars held by nonbanks, bankers' acceptances, commercial paper, savings bonds, and 18-month or less Treasury securities.

<DERIVATION>
Derived from daily Treasury figures for money in circulation less vault cash holdings of commercial banks as reported by the Federal Reserve; daily and weekly deposit data from the Federal Reserve and the Federal Deposit Insurance Corporation; demand-deposit reports less items in the process of collection; data collected from thrift institutions by the Federal Home Loan Bank Board; and samples of large banks; weekly data of the Investment Company Institute. Adjustments are made to avoid double counting, and individual components are seasonally adjusted.

<USE>
Money Supply (M1) is used as one of the components of the Leading Indicators Composite Index. Because aggregate money-stock measures are affected by financial innovations, regulatory changes, and other factors, these data about the public's money holdings and the relationships between the money supply and ultimate economic variables are often used in analyzing economic change and in setting monetary policy.

<PUBLISHER>
Board of Governors of the Federal Reserve System

<ANNOUNCED IN>
Money Stock Measures, Statistical Release H.6

<ANNOUNCEMENT FREQUENCY>
Weekly

<CUMULATIONS>

TABLES

NYT	Latest quarter and year ago, % change
Man Han	Latest week, $
Man Han	Latest week, % change
BW	Latest week and year ago, $
BCD	Monthly, cum, $
BCD	Monthly, cum, % change
FR Bull	Monthly and quarterly, cum, % change
Bus Stats	Monthly and yearly, cum, $
EI	Monthly and yearly, cum, $
S&P Stats	Monthly and yearly, cum, $
SCB	Monthly and yearly, cum, $
EI	Monthly and yearly, cum, % change
Int Econ Ind	Quarterly and yearly, cum, index nos.
S&P Cred Wk	Weekly, cum, $
S&P Cred Wk	Weekly, cum, % change
Hist Stats	Yearly, cum, $
Int Fin Stat	Yearly, cum, $
Stat Abstr	Yearly, cum, $
Stat Abstr	Yearly, cum, % change

GRAPHS

MG Fin Wkly	Monthly, cum, % change
BCD	Yearly, cum, $
EI	Yearly, cum, $

```
MG Fin Wkly   Yearly, cum, $
Stat Bull     Yearly, cum, $
BCD           Yearly, cum, % change
```
PROJECTIONS
```
Value Line    Quarterly and yearly, % change
```
<MORE INFORMATION>
   Board of Governors of the Federal Reserve System, Improving
the Monetary Aggregates: Staff Papers, Federal Reserve
System, Washington, D.C., 1978.
   Joint Economic Committee, 1980 Supplement to Economic
Indicators, Historical and Descriptive Background, USGPO,
Washington, D.C., 1980.
   Beryl W. Sprinkel, "Monetary Growth as a Cyclical
Predictor," The Journal of Finance, 333-346 (Sept. 1959).

Money Supply [See Money Supply M2 Deflated and Money Stock
Measures and Liquid Assets]

Money Supply M1 [See Money Stock Measures and Liquid
Assets]

Money Supply M2 Deflated [See also Money Stock Measures and
Liquid Assets; also called Money Balance]
<DESCRIPTION>
A measure of real money supply.
<DERIVATION>
To the calculated value of M1, the Ferderal Reserve System
adds the estimated total amounts for savings deposits at
commercial banks, small-denomination time deposits, and time
certificates of deposit of less than $100,000. The resulting
total is seasonally adjusted and deflated with the Consumer
Price Index.
<USE>
Considered to be a leading indicator of all portions of the
business cycle.
<PUBLISHER>
Board of Governors of the Federal Reserve System
<ANNOUNCED IN>
Federal Reserve Bulletin
<ANNOUNCEMENT FREQUENCY>
Weekly
<CUMULATIONS>
TABLES
```
NYT          Latest quarter and year ago, % change
Man Han      Latest week, $
Man Han      Latest week, % change
BW           Latest week and year ago, $
BCD          Monthly, cum, $
BCD          Monthly, cum, % change
FR Bull      Monthly and quarterly, cum, % change
Bus Stats    Monthly and yearly, cum, $
EI           Monthly and yearly, cum, $
S&P Stats    Monthly and yearly, cum, $
SCB          Monthly and yearly, cum, $
```

EI	Monthly and yearly, cum, % change
S&P Cred Wk	Weekly, cum, $
S&P Cred Wk	Weekly, cum, % change
Hist Stats	Yearly, cum, $
Stat Abstr	Yearly, cum, $
Stat Abstr	Yearly, cum, % change
GRAPHS	
BCD	Yearly, cum, $
EI	Yearly, cum, $
MG Fin Wkly	Yearly, cum, $
Stat Bull	Yearly, cum, $
BCD	Yearly, cum, % change
PROJECTIONS	
Value Line	Quarterly and yearly, % change

<MORE INFORMATION>
   Michael Hayes, The Dow Jones – Irwin Guide to Stock Market Cycles, Dow Jones – Irwin, Homewood, Ill., 1977, pp. 120-127.
   "Official Indicators: What Are They? Can They Predict the Future?" U.S. News and World Report, 66-67 (Aug. 16, 1976).

Money Supply M3 [See Money Stock Measures and Liquid Assets]

Moody's Corporate Aaa Bond Yield Averages
<DESCRIPTION>
The currently prevailing maturity yield on seasoned, long-term corporate bonds of the highest quality.
<DERIVATION>
A standard list of corporate-bond issues is selected, and the daily yield for each selected bond is computed on the basis of closing price, as reported in the dealer's asked quotation, adjusted occasionally for temporarily distorting factors. These yields are then averaged.
<USE>
Used to indicate the level and movement of average yields of selected seasoned bonds with sufficiently long maturities and other features to allow them to indicate long-term interest rates.
<PUBLISHER>
Moody's Investors Service
<ANNOUNCED IN>
News release
<ANNOUNCEMENT FREQUENCY>
Daily
<CUMULATIONS>
TABLES

EI	Weekly, monthly, yearly, cum, % yield
Bus Stats	Monthly and yearly, cum, % yield
Moody's Bond	Monthly and yearly, cum, % yield
Moody's Ind	Monthly and yearly, cum, % yield
SCB	Monthly and yearly, cum, % yield
FR Bull	Monthly, weekly, yearly, cum, % yield
Stat Abstr	Yearly, cum, % yield

GRAPHS
Moody's Bond Yearly, cum, % yield
Moody's Ind Yearly, cum, % yield
EI   Monthly and yearly, cum, % yield
PROJECTIONS
Fin Ind   Quarterly, % yield
<MORE INFORMATION>
  Martin J. Pring, Technical Analysis Explained, An
Illustrated Guide for the Investor, McGraw-Hill, New York,
1980, pp. 185-189.

N

NASDAQ Over the Counter Indexes [See Over the Counter Index]

National Advertising Index [See McCann-Erikson National Advertising Index]

National Income
<DESCRIPTION>
The aggregate earnings by labor and property that arise from the production of goods and services in the U.S. economy, consisting of compensation of employees, proprietors' income, rental income of individuals, net interest, and corporate profits.
<DERIVATION>
Compensation is estimated from monthly reports by employers to the Bureau of Labor Statistics on employment and earnings; these estimates are benchmarked to annual data from the unemployment insurance system. Other income is estimated from Internal Revenue Service data, which is supplemented with information from surveys and data from the Census Bureau and the Federal Reserve System. Seasonal adjustments are not available for these data, and quarterly data for proprietors' income and net interest are not available and must be interpolated.
<USE>
Because this index measures the rate of flow of earnings from current output, its movements correspond with movements in production and show the relative contribution of wages and profits to those movements. It is also used as an indicator of the future availability of disposable income and, therefore, of near-term growth or decline of consumer purchases.
<PUBLISHER>
U.S. Department of Commerce, Bureau of Economic Analysis
<ANNOUNCED IN>
Survey of Current Business
<ANNOUNCEMENT FREQUENCY>
Quarterly

```
<CUMULATIONS>
TABLES
BCD          Quarterly, cum, $
EI           Quarterly and yearly, cum, $
FR Bull      Quarterly and yearly, cum, $
S&P Stats    Quarterly and yearly, cum, $
Bus Stats    Yearly, cum, $
Hist Stats   Yearly, cum, $
Int Fin Stat Yearly, cum, $
Natl Income  Yearly, cum, $
Stat Abstr   Yearly, cum, $
GRAPHS
BCD          Yearly, cum, $
<MORE INFORMATION>
```
   Joint Economic Committee, 1980 Supplement to Economic Indicators, Historical and Descriptive Background, USGPO, Washington, D.C., 1980.
   Office of Federal Statistical Policy and Standards, Gross National Product Data Improvement Project Report, Department of Commerce, Washington, D.C., 1977.
   John Kirk, "Economic Indicators: The How and the Why," Banking, 27-28 (Aug. 1964).

National Product [See Net National Product]

Net Business Formation
```
<DESCRIPTION>
```
A monthly estimate of the net formation of business enterprises; a representation of the short-term movement of new entries into and departures from the total business population.
```
<DERIVATION>
```
The number of new business incorporations for the month is received from Dun & Bradstreet. The number of business failures for the month (also received from Dun & Bradstreet) is subtracted from the new incorporations. The result is adjusted with confidential data on telephones installed. The data are seasonally adjusted and indexed to a value of 100 for 1967.
```
<USE>
```
Used as one of the components of the Leading Indicators Composite Index. Considered to be a leading indicator at peaks, troughs, and the entirety of the business cycle.
```
<PUBLISHER>
```
U.S. Department of Commerce, Bureau of Economic Analysis
```
<ANNOUNCED IN>
```
Monthly New Business Incorporation Report
```
<ANNOUNCEMENT FREQUENCY>
```
Monthly
```
<CUMULATIONS>
TABLES
Stat Bull    Latest month and year ago, % change
BCD          Monthly, cum, index nos.
S&P Stats    Monthly and yearly, cum, index nos.
Stat Abstr   Yearly, cum, index nos.
```

GRAPHS
BCD   Yearly, cum, index nos.
<MORE INFORMATION>
   G. H. Moore, Ed., Business Cycle Indicators, vol. II,
Princeton University Press, Princeton, N.J., 1961, p. 17.
   "Official Indicators: What Are They? Can They Predict the
Future?" U.S. News and World Report, 66-67 (Aug. 16, 1976).

Net Generation [See Electric Power Production]

Net National Product
<DESCRIPTION>
An estimate of the total value of all of the country's goods
and services produced and provided during the year after the
costs of production have been deducted.
<DERIVATION>
Two forms of the Net National Product are calculated, that at
market prices and that at factor cost. The Net National
Product at Market Prices is derived from the Gross National
Product by deducting the depreciation on capital plant and
equipment expenditures. This deduction is an effort to
account for the capital that has been used in producing the
gross output. Total depreciation allowances (both actual and
imputed) are used. That is to say, the total financial
allowances calculated by producers is counted along with
imputed depreciation allowances for those sectors of the
economy where no data exist (e.g., for farmers' tools and for
the houses of homeowners). The Net National Product at Factor
Cost goes beyond that for market cost by deducting additional
costs introduced by the factors of production (indirect
taxes, such as excise and property taxes; business transfer
payments; the current surpluses of government enterprises;
and the statistical discrepancy) and by adding any subsidies
received by producers.
<USE>
The Net National Product at Factor Cost is used to estimate
the total factor income of the nation in the same manner that
the Gross National Product is used to estimate the Gross
National Income. The total factor income is referred to as
the National Income.
<PUBLISHER>
U.S. Department of Commerce, Bureau of Economic Analysis
<ANNOUNCED IN>
Survey of Current Business
<ANNOUNCEMENT FREQUENCY>
Quarterly
<CUMULATIONS>
TABLES
Bus Stats   Quarterly and yearly, cum, $
SCB   Quarterly and yearly, cum, $
Stat Abstr   Yearly, cum, $
<MORE INFORMATION>
   Richard Ruggles and Nancy D. Ruggles, National Income
Accounts and Income Analysis, 2nd ed., McGraw-Hill, New York,
1956.

Lora S. Collins, "What NNP - not GNP - Tells Us," Across the Board, 25-29 (June 1981).
Richard M. Snyder, Measuring Business Changes, Wiley, New York, 1955, p. 16 ff.

New Business Incorporations
<DESCRIPTION>
The total number of stock corporations issued charters under the general business incorporation laws of the 50 states and the District of Columbia for a given month.
<DERIVATION>
Data for each state are collected from the secretaries of state at the end of each month and totalled. New incorporations are defined as completely new businesses that are incorporated, existing businesses that change from unincorporated to incorporated businesses, existing corporations that have been given certificates of authority to operate in an additional state, and existing corporations that have transferred to a new state. The data are seasonally adjusted with census data by the Bureau of Economic Analysis and the National Bureau of Economic Research.
<USE>
Considered to be a leading indicator at peaks, troughs, and the entirety of the business cycle.
<PUBLISHER>
Dun & Bradstreet, Inc.
<ANNOUNCED IN>
Monthly New Incorporations
<ANNOUNCEMENT FREQUENCY>
Monthly
<CUMULATIONS>
TABLES

Mo New Inc	Monthly, cum, nos.
SCB	Monthly and yearly, cum, nos.
Barron's	Latest and year ago, nos.
S&P Stats	Monthly and yearly, cum, nos.

<MORE INFORMATION>
Victor Zarnowitz, "Cyclical Aspects of Incorporations and the Formation of New Business Enterprises," Chap. 13 in Geoffrey H. Moore, Ed., Business Cycle Indicators, vol. 1, Princeton University Press, Princeton, N.J., 1961.

New Construction
<DESCRIPTION>
An estimate of the dollar value of the construction work done on residential and nonresidential new buildings and of renovations to existing structures. Includes erection of new structures; additions and alterations to existing buildings; mechanical installations to upgrade existing structures; outside improvements; installation of specific major components of industrial buildings; certain appliances, when installed as part of the construction; all fixed, mainly site-fabricated equipment; land development; and structural changes made to a building to accommodate new equipment.

<DERIVATION>
The construction cost of new one-unit houses is estimated each month by taking the data from the Census Bureau's surveys of housing authorized by building permits and of housing units started, adjusting it to compensate for construction not covered by permits, adjusting for undervaluation and fees not covered in permit valuations, and distributing the computed values over the coming months by applying fixed patterns of monthly construction progress. The value of new multiple-unit private residential buildings is directly measured from monthly progress reports from a sample of such projects started each month. The value of additions and alterations is obtained from a quarterly survey of owners of homes and rental properties by the Census Bureau; monthly values are interpolated from the quarterly data. Nonresidential, nonfarm building values are estimated from data gathered by the Bureau of the Census from a sample of project contractors who are asked to report the value of work done each month until the project is completed. Nonresidential farm construction expenditures are obtained annually by the U.S. Department of Agriculture through its Farm Production Expenditures Survey; monthly values are imputed by smoothing the data over the years and linking it with seasonal factors. Values for the construction by public utilities are derived by interpolating annual data gathered by the Census Bureau for communications utilities and by regulatory agencies (such as the Interstate Commerce Commission) for electric, gas, railroad, and pipeline utilities. All other private construction is estimated by adjusting the data reported by the F. W. Dodge Division of the McGraw-Hill Information Systems Company for additional costs not covered by the Dodge estimates, projects not covered by the survey, and geographical areas not covered. Federal construction expenditures are estimated from data reported to the Bureau of the Census by each federal agency for the fiscal year; these are prorated for each month. State and local governments' expenditures are estimated from progress reports solicited from a sample of such projects. The monthly values derived are converted to constant 1972 dollars by applying different cost indexes that have been derived for each category of construction.
<USE>
Used in short-term cyclical and long-term growth analyses; used to estimate the current volume of the economic activity in this segment of the U.S. economy, which has an important impact on employment in the construction and building-materials industries and on additions to capital stocks of structures in the private and public sectors.
<PUBLISHER>
U.S. Department of Commerce, Bureau of the Census
<ANNOUNCED IN>
Construction Report C30
<ANNOUNCEMENT FREQUENCY>
Monthly
<CUMULATIONS>
TABLES
Man Han   Latest month, $

```
Bus Stats      Monthly and yearly, cum, $
Const Repts    Monthly and yearly, cum, $
Const Rev      Monthly and yearly, cum, $
EI             Monthly and yearly, cum, $
SCB            Monthly and yearly, cum, $
HUD Stats      Yearly, cum, $
Stat Abstr     Yearly, cum, $
GRAPHS
Stat Abstr     Yearly, cum, $
```

<MORE INFORMATION>
   Joint Economic Committee, 1980 Supplement to Economic Indicators, Historical and Descriptive Background, USGPO, Washington, D.C., 1980.
   "New Construction, Housing and Mobile Homes - A Look Ahead," Construction Review, 4 (Sept. 1971).

New Construction Planning

<DESCRIPTION>
An estimation of the dollar value of new construction plans for public and private projects in the U.S.

<DERIVATION>
Field reporters in all 50 states review the results of competitive bids for construction projects and report the dollar value of federal, state, municipal, and private-sector construction projects involving nonindustrial buildings costing more than $500,000 or other items costing more than $100,000. The values reported from the first of the month to the last Thursday of the month are totalled. Thus monthly totals are not strictly comparable. Data are broken down by type of construction and by geographic area.

<USE>
A leading indicator of construction activity.

<PUBLISHER>
McGraw-Hill Information Systems Co.

<ANNOUNCED IN>
Engineering News-Record

<ANNOUNCEMENT FREQUENCY>
Monthly

<CUMULATIONS>
TABLES

```
Eng News-Rec Latest Week, $
Eng News-Rec Latest week, % change
Bus Stats      Monthly and yearly, cum, $
SCB            Monthly and yearly, cum, $
GRAPHS
Eng News-Rec Monthly, cum, $
```

<MORE INFORMATION>
   "Construction Costs Tracked for U.S.," Engineering News-Record 210 (12), 114-121 (Mar. 24, 1983).

New Home Mortgage Yield

<DESCRIPTION>
Measures average effective yields on fully amortized conventional first-mortgage loans that are secured both by

and for the purchase of newly built single-family nonfarm
residential properties.
<DERIVATION>
The Federal Home Loan Bank Board in cooperation with the
Federal Deposit Insurance Corporation surveys a sample of
major mortgage lenders, including   savings and loan
associations, mortgage bankers, commercial banks, and mutual
savings banks. The sample is stratified by size and by
geographic location of the lender. Data received from each
respondent is weighted according to the value   of that
institution's single-family conventional-mortgage holdings as
compared with the holdings of other institutions in the same
stratum.
<USE>
An indicator of future construction activity, affecting
housing-start statistics and new building permits.
<PUBLISHER>
Federal Home Loan Bank Board
<ANNOUNCED IN>
Federal Home Loan Bank Board Journal
<ANNOUNCEMENT FREQUENCY>
Monthly
<CUMULATIONS>
TABLES
EI   Monthly and yearly, cum, %
FHLBBJ   Monthly and yearly, cum, %
FR Bull   Monthly and yearly, cum, %
Stat Abstr Yearly, cum, %
<MORE INFORMATION>
  Saul B. Klaman, The Postwar Residential Mortgage Market,
Princeton University Press, Princeton, N.J., 1961.

New Incorporations [See New Business Incorporations]

New Orders, Aircraft [See Aircraft, New Orders]

New Orders, Consumer Goods and Materials [See New Orders,
Nondefense Capital Goods]

New Orders, Nondefense Capital Goods
<DESCRIPTION>
An estimate of the new orders received during a given month
less cancellations by manufacturers of durable goods that
fall in the categories of nonelectrical machinery; electrical
machinery; and the nondefense portions of communications
equipment, ships, tanks, aircraft, and ordnance.
<DERIVATION>
Manufacturers are surveyed monthly and asked to report the
sales value of orders for goods to be delivered at some
future date, the sales value of orders filled immediately
during the month, and the net sales value of contract changes
that have resulted in increases or decreases in order values.

New orders are defined as orders supported by binding legal documents. The value of any cancellations is to be deducted from the totals. Because some companies report only backlogs of unfilled orders and in order to maintain the distiction between orders and shipments, orders remaining unfilled at the end of the monthly reporting period are estimated directly and separately and they are then combined with shipments data to produce the new orders data. Although the new orders data are not independently seasonally adjusted, they are derived from data that are seasonally adjusted. The totals are presented in current dollars and in 1972 dollars.
<USE>
Used as one of the components of the Leading Indicators Composite Index and as a gage of future buying commitment (and hence of future business activity).
<PUBLISHER>
U.S. Department of Commerce, Bureau of the Census
<ANNOUNCED IN>
Survey of Current Business
<ANNOUNCEMENT FREQUENCY>
Monthly
<CUMULATIONS>
TABLES

Stat Bull	Latest period, % change
Barron's	Latest period and year ago, $
BCD	Monthly, cum, $
S&P Stats	Monthly and yearly, cum, $
Bus Stats	Monthly and yearly, cum, $
SCB	Monthly and yearly, cum, $

GRAPHS

BCD	Yearly, cum, $

<MORE INFORMATION>
   Victor Zarnowitz, "Cyclical Aspects of Incorporations and the Formation of New Business Enterprises," Chap. 13 in Geoffrey H. Moore, Ed., Business Cycle Indicators, vol. 1, Princeton University Press, Princeton, N.J., 1961.

New Plant and Equipment Expenditures [See Expenditures for New Plant and Equipment]

New Private Housing: Units Authorized by Permit Places
<DESCRIPTION>
The number of new private housing units authorized by local building permits presented by region of the country, type of structure, and inclusion (or noninclusion) in Standard Metropolitan Statistical Areas.
<DERIVATION>
Monthly data are accumulated from a sample of the 16,000 places in the U.S. that require building permits. Any place located in 101 selected SMSAs is chosen to be included in the sample; the rest of the sample is stratified by state and, within each state, by number of housing units authorized per year. All locations within a state having a large number of units authorized are included and one-tenth of all locations

having a small number are included. The data are adjusted for seasonal variation and for trading-day variation.
<USE>
These general indicators of the available inventory of new homes are used as advance indicators of the need for new construction, of demand for money, of employment in the construction industry, and of demand for building materials. The geographic detail of the building-permit data allows analyses of and comparisons between specific and narrowly defined areas and regions.
<PUBLISHER>
U.S. Department of Commerce, Bureau of the Census
<ANNOUNCED IN>
Construction Reports, Series C40
<ANNOUNCEMENT FREQUENCY>
Monthly
<CUMULATIONS>
Bus Stats   Monthly and yearly, cum, nos.
Const Rev   Monthly and yearly, cum, nos.
EI   Monthly and yearly, cum, nos.
Econ Rept Pr   Monthly and yearly, cum, nos.
SCB   Monthly and yearly, cum, nos.
Const Repts   Yearly, cum, nos.
Stat Abstr   Yearly, cum, nos.
<MORE INFORMATION>
   G. H. Moore and J. Shiskin, "Why the Leading Indicators Really Do Lead," Across the Board, 71-75 (May 1978).
   "Official Indicators: What Are They? Can They Predict the Future?" U.S. News and World Report, 66-67 (Aug. 16, 1976).

New York Stock Exchange Advance-Decline Line
<DESCRIPTION>
An indication of how many stock prices have increased during a given period on the New York Stock Exchange versus the number of prices that have decreased.
<DERIVATION>
Daily or weekly issues data for all of the issues on the Exchange are analyzed to determine the numbers of advances and of declines; the number of declines is subtracted from the number of advances; the resulting value is added to an arbitrary base reference number appropriate for the Exchange.
<USE>
Considered to. be an accurate leading indicator for market turns and directions. Used to forecast peaks and troughs in the stock market and to measure price trends.
<PUBLISHER>
New York Stock Exchange
<ANNOUNCED IN>
New York Stock Exchange news release
<ANNOUNCEMENT FREQUENCY>
Daily
<CUMULATIONS>
TABLES
MG Fin Wkly   Daily, cum, nos.
S&P Stats   Daily, cum, nos.

```
NYT           Latest daily, nos.
WSJ           Latest daily, nos.
Barron's      Latest week, nos.
GRAPHS
MG Fin Wkly   Daily, cum, nos.
S&P Outlook   Monthly, cum, nos.
```
<MORE INFORMATION>
   William Gordon, The Stock Market Indicators as a Guide to Market Timing, Investors Press, Palisades Park, N. J., 1968, pp. 45-65.
   Michael Hayes, The Dow Jones - Irwin Guide to Stock Market Cycles, Dow Jones - Irwin, Homewood, Ill., 1977, pp. 101-106.
   Martin J. Pring, Technical Analysis Explained, An Illustrated Guide for the Investor, McGraw-Hill, New York, 1980, pp. 164-169.

New York Stock Exchange Average Daily Volume [See New York Stock Exchange Volume]

New York Stock Exchange Big Block Activity
<DESCRIPTION>
The number of transactions during a month on the New York Stock Exchange that exceed 10,000 shares.
<DERIVATION>
New York Stock Exchange members report all large-block buy and sell orders electronically via the Block Automation System. The orders are transmitted to the Exchange floor where they are matched and executed. A tally of these trades is made daily.
<USE>
Because such large transactions are almost always the actions of institutions, these statistics are taken to indicate the gross market activity of traders with large and sophisticated analytical resources. This statistic is a coincident indicator that generally confirms movements in other stock-market indicators.
<PUBLISHER>
New York Stock Exchange
<ANNOUNCED IN>
New York Stock Exchange news release
<ANNOUNCEMENT FREQUENCY>
Daily
<CUMULATIONS>
TABLES
```
Barron's      Daily, cum, no. of transactions
NYSE Facts    Monthly and yearly, cum, daily average
NYSE Facts    Monthly and yearly, cum, no. of shares
NYSE Facts    Monthly and yearly, cum, no. of transactions
NYSE Facts    Monthly and yearly, cum, % of total volume
GRAPHS
MG Fin Wkly   Monthly and yearly, cum, no. of transactions
```
<MORE INFORMATION>
   Dudley R. Bohlen, "Large Block Transactions: A Premier Contrary Indicator," pp. 42-1 to 42-5 in The Encyclopedia of

Stock Market Techniques, Investors Intelligence, Larchmont, N.Y., 1983.

Martin J. Pring, Technical Analysis Explained, An Illustrated Guide for the Investor, McGraw-Hill, New York, 1980, pp. 158-159.

Martin E. Zweig, "Trusty Market Indicator, Bring the Record of the Big-Block Index up to Date," Barron's, 11-12 (Jan. 24, 1983).

New York Stock Exchange Composite Index

<DESCRIPTION>
A measure of the change in aggregate market value of common shares of all stocks listed on the New York Stock Exchange adjusted to eliminate the nonprice effects of changes in firm capitalization and exchange listings and delistings. Indexes are also prepared for four subgroups of stocks: industrial, transportation, utility, and financial. The data are compiled hourly and reported daily.

<DERIVATION>
The price per share of each listed stock is multiplied by its number of shares listed to give its market value. The market values of all listed stocks are summed, and the total is divided by the market value on a base date (Dec. 31, 1965). This quotient is multiplied by 50.00 (the base value of the index). Nonprice effects are eliminated by adjustments to the base-date market value.

<USE>
An indicator of general market conditions.

<PUBLISHER>
New York Stock Exchange

<ANNOUNCED IN>
News release

<ANNOUNCEMENT FREQUENCY>
Daily

<CUMULATIONS>
TABLES

Barron's	Daily, index nos.
MG Fin Wkly	Daily, index nos.
WSJ	Daily, index nos.
Forbes	Latest and year ago, % change
NYT	Latest week, index nos.
NYT	Latest week, % change
Man Han	Latest wekend, index nos.
Man Han	Latest weekend and year ago, % change
Value Line	Latest weekly, index nos.
Value Line	Latest weekly, % change
EI	Monthly, weekly, yearly, cum, index nos.
FR Bull	Monthly and yearly, cum, index nos.

GRAPHS

MG Fin Wkly	Daily, index nos.
NYT	Monthly, high-lows, index nos.
Moody's Ind	Monthly and yearly, high-lows, cum, index nos.
EI	Yearly, cum, index nos.

<MORE INFORMATION>
  Joint Economic Committee, 1980 Supplement to Economic

Indicators, Historical and Descriptive Background, USGPO, Washington, D.C., 1980.

Lawrence Fisher, "Some New Stock-Market Indexes," The Journal of Business, 191-225 (Jan. 1966).

Douglas K. Pearce, "Stock Prices and the Economy," Economic Review of the Federal Reserve Bank of Kansas City, 7-22 (Nov. 1983).

Keith V. Smith, "Stock Price and Economic Indexes for Generating Efficient Portfolios," Journal of Business, 326-336 (July 1969).

"Market Guides," Barron's, 9+ (Sept. 26, 1966).

John Kirk, "N.Y. Stock Exchange Launches Its Market Indicator," Banking, 4-5 (Aug. 1966).

New York Stock Exchange Firms' Free Credit Balance
<DESCRIPTION>
The proceeds of sales going to individual brokers and left by them in their accounts rather than being immediately reinvested or withdrawn as cash; the aggregate total of the account balances of NYSE members.
<DERIVATION>
The amount of cash held in individual accounts of NYSE firms is totalled.
<USE>
Used to forecast market trends. The theory has it that investors will tend to use this excess cash at the wrong time, usually during a rising market and not during a falling one. Therefore credit balances are expected to decline at the beginning of bull markets and to rise in bear markets.
<PUBLISHER>
New York Stock Exchange
<ANNOUNCED IN>
NYSE press release
<ANNOUNCEMENT FREQUENCY>
Monthly
<CUMULATIONS>
TABLES
Barron's   Latest month and year ago, $
NYSE Facts   Monthly, quarterly, yearly, cum, $
FR Bull   Monthly and yearly, cum, $
GRAPHS
MG Fin Wkly   Yearly, cum, $
<MORE INFORMATION>
Michael Hayes, The Dow Jones - Irwin Guide to Stock Market Cycles, Dow Jones - Irwin, Homewood, Ill., 1977, pp. 161-167.

M. Zweig, "New Sell Signal," Barron's, Oct. 13, 1975.

J. Cohen, A. Zinbarg, and A. Zeikel, Investment Analysis and Portfolio Managment, 3rd ed., Irwin, Homewood, Ill., 1977.

William Gordon, The Stock Market Indicators as a Guide to Market Timing, Investors Press, Palisades Park, N. J., 1968, p. 113.

Sloan J. Wilson, "The Customers' Free Credit Balances and Margin Debt," pp. 19-1 to 19-22 in The Encyclopedia of Stock Market Techniques, Investors Intelligence, Larchmont, N.Y., 1983.

New York Stock Exchange Firms' Margin Accounts
<DESCRIPTION>
The amount of cash owed to NYSE brokerage houses; also known as their debit balances.
<DERIVATION>
All of the funds owed to NYSE brokerage houses by their clients are totalled each month by each brokerage house. These totals are reported to the Exchange, and it totals all of the reported figures for the month. All debt is included.
<USE>
To predict short-term highs and lows in stock-market activity. A market decline is expected when there is a low use of margin purchases. During an expansion of the market, margin purchases increase because investors expect to recoup the cost of the loans through the increases of the market value of their purchases.
<PUBLISHER>
New York Stock Exchange
<ANNOUNCED IN>
NYSE press release
<ANNOUNCEMENT FREQUENCY>
Monthly
<CUMULATIONS>
TABLES
Barron's   Latest month and year ago, $
NYSE Facts   Monthly, quarterly, yearly, cum, $
FR Bull   Monthly and yearly, cum, $
MG Fin Wkly   Yearly, cum, $
<MORE INFORMATION>
   Michael Hayes, The Dow Jones - Irwin Guide to Stock Market Cycles, Dow Jones - Irwin, Homewood, Ill., 1977, pp. 158-160.

New York Stock Exchange Members' Short Sells Ratio
<DESCRIPTION>
The fraction of the weekly activity by NYSE members that is made up of short sells.
<DERIVATION>
The number of shares sold short by members of the NYSE during a week is divided by the total number of shares sold by them during that week.
<USE>
To predict peaks and troughs in stock-market activity. The theory is that when the ratio is high, members are selling short anticipating a decline in the market; when the ratio is low, they are collectively anticipating an upturn in the market in the near term.
<PUBLISHER>
New York Stock Exchange
<ANNOUNCED IN>
News release
<ANNOUNCEMENT FREQUENCY>
Weekly
<CUMULATIONS>
TABLES
NYSE Facts   Monthly and yearly, cum, ratio
Barron's   Weekly and year ago, ratio

GRAPHS
MG Fin Wkly Monthly, cum, ratio
<MORE INFORMATION>
  Martin   J.   Pring,   Technical   Analysis   Explained,   An
Illustrated Guide for the Investor, McGraw-Hill, New York,
1980, pp. 210-212.

New York Stock Exchange Nonmembers' Short Sells Ratio
<DESCRIPTION>
The portion of the total NYSE weekly volume made up of
selling-short transactions by traders that are not members of
the NYSE.
<DERIVATION>
The total nonmembers' round lot short sales for the week is
divided by the total weekly NYSE volume.
<USE>
As a contrary indicator of general market direction. Theory
has it that nonmembers will sell short at the wrong time; the
higher the percentage of nonmember short selling, the higher
the market is expected to go.
<PUBLISHER>
New York Stock Exchange
<ANNOUNCED IN>
NYSE press release
<ANNOUNCEMENT FREQUENCY>
Weekly
<CUMULATIONS>
TABLES
NYSE Facts   Monthly and yearly, cum, ratio
Barron's   Weekly and year ago, ratiio
GRAPHS
MG Fin Wkly Monthly, cum, ratio

New York Stock Exchange Odd-Lot Index
<DESCRIPTION>
A measure of the portion of the daily or weekly sales on the
New York Stock Exchange that are made up of 100 shares or
less.
<DERIVATION>
The daily or weekly total transactions that were made up of
odd-lot sales on the Exchange are divided by the total number
of transactions occurring on the Exchange during the same
period.
<USE>
To predict future movements in stock market activity; a
contrary indicator of market activity.
<PUBLISHER>
New York Stock Exchange
<ANNOUNCED IN>
New York Stock Exchange news release
<ANNOUNCEMENT FREQUENCY>
Daily
<CUMULATIONS>
TABLES
Barron's   Latest week's end, nos.

MG Fin Wkly   Weekly and daily, cum, nos.
S&P Stats   Monthly and yearly, cum, nos.
<MORE INFORMATION>
   Michael Hayes, The Dow Jones - Irwin Guide to Stock Market
Cycles, Dow Jones - Irwin, Homewood, Ill., 1977, pp. 168-172.
   William Gordon, The Stock Market Indicators as a Guide to
Market Timing, Investors Press, Palisades Park, N. J., 1968,
pp. 61-71.

New York Stock Exchange Odd-Lot Sales and Purchase Index
<DESCRIPTION>
The ratio of odd-lot sales to odd-lot purchases for a given
week, month, or year.
<DERIVATION>
The number of shares sold in odd-lots (less than 100 shares
transferred) is divided by the number of shares purchased in
odd lots.
<USE>
Used to determine the sentiment of the smaller investors.
<PUBLISHER>
New York Stock Exchange
<ANNOUNCED IN>
NYSE press release
<ANNOUNCEMENT FREQUENCY>
Weekly
<CUMULATIONS>
TABLES
Barron's   Latest week, nos.
WSJ   Latest week, nos.
NYSE Facts   Monthly and yearly, cum, nos.
GRAPHS
MG Fin Wkly   Monthly, cum, index nos.
<MORE INFORMATION>
   Michael Hayes, The Dow Jones - Irwin Guide to Stock Market
Cycles, Dow Jones - Irwin, Homewood, Ill., 1977.

New York Stock Exchange Odd-Lot Short Sales
<DESCRIPTION>
The total number of shares sold short on the NYSE in
transactions of less than 100 shares during a given period.
<DERIVATION>
The number of odd-lot short sales in shares is totalled for a
given week.
<USE>
To predict market activity in the near term; considered to be
a contrary indicator; when odd-lot short sales rise, the
market is expected to continue rising.
<PUBLISHER>
New York Stock Exchange
<ANNOUNCED IN>
NYSE News Release
<ANNOUNCEMENT FREQUENCY>
Weekly

<CUMULATIONS>
TABLES
Barron's   Latest week, nos.
WSJ   Latest week, nos.
NYSE Facts   Monthly and yearly, cum, nos.
GRAPHS
MG Fin Wkly Monthly, cum, nos.
<MORE INFORMATION>
   Carroll A. Aby, Jr., "The Odd Lot Short Sales Index and
Market Bottoms, 1960-1973," University of Michigan Business
Review, 10-13 (Nov. 1974).
   William Gordon, The Stock Market Indicators as a Guide to
Market Timing, Investors Press, Palisades Park, N. J., 1968,
pp. 71-75.
   Michael Hayes, The Dow Jones - Irwin Guide to Stock Market
Cycles, Dow Jones - Irwin, Homewood, Ill., 1977, pp. 171-172.

New York Stock Exchange Price-Earnings Ratio
<DESCRIPTION>
A measure of the value of the stocks purchased on the New
York Stock Exchange; more accurately, a measure of the
speculative nature of the purchases on that exchange.
<DERIVATION>
The average price for all of the stocks listed on the New
York Stock Exchange divided by the average earnings reported
for those stocks.
<USE>
As a gage of speculative activity in the market and to
assess turning points of the market in the near term. The
higher the ratio, the more speculative the market is
considered to be because increased investment is not being
reflected in increased returns (earnings) from the
corporations' performances. Conversely, a lower ratio
indicates better value of purchases in the market.
<PUBLISHER>
New York Stock Exchange
<ANNOUNCED IN>
New York Stock Exchange news release
<ANNOUNCEMENT FREQUENCY>
Daily
<CUMULATIONS>
TABLES
MG Fin Wkly Latest week and year ago, nos.
<MORE INFORMATION>
   Michael Hayes, The Dow Jones - Irwin Guide to Stock Market
Cycles, Dow Jones - Irwin, Homewood, Ill., 1977, p. 54.

New York Stock Exchange Seat Sales
<DESCRIPTION>
The price paid in dollars for one seat on or membership in
the New York Stock Exchange; such membership is required to
actively trade on the exchange, and the number of seats is
limited (currently to 1366). Prices paid are determined by
supply and demand, and the sales are private ones between
individuals.

<DERIVATION>
Seats on the New York Stock Exchange can be transferred by an auction system. The price paid for a seat is determined by prevailing stock-market conditions and by supply and demand. Brokers involved in these sales report them and the prices to the Exchange.
<USE>
An indicator of expected future profitability of the exchange; used mostly for historical comparisons of stock-market activity and current strength of the market.
<PUBLISHER>
New York Stock Exchange
<ANNOUNCED IN>
New York Stock Exchange news release
<ANNOUNCEMENT FREQUENCY>
Monthly
<CUMULATIONS>
TABLES
NYSE Facts   Monthly, cum, $
NYSE Facts   Yearly, high-low, cum, $
GRAPHS
MG Fin Wkly   Yearly, cum, $
<MORE INFORMATION>
   F. G. Zarb and G. Kerekes (Eds.), The Stock Market Handbook Reference Manual for the Securities Industry, Dow Jones - Irwin, Homewood, Ill., 1970.

New York Stock Exchange Short Interest Ratio
<DESCRIPTION>
The portion of the New York Stock Exchange's volume that is made up of short selling.
<DERIVATION>
The monthly uncovered short positions on the New York Stock Exchange expressed in shares are divided by the average daily volume for each day of the preceding month.
<USE>
A buy or sell signal; a measure of the demand for future trading. Short sellers eventually have to cover their positions. In a rising market, this necessity increases the demand for the shorted stocks, increasing their prices. In a declining market, no such immediate demand for the stocks exists, and their values are likely to decline.
<PUBLISHER>
New York Stock Exchange
<ANNOUNCED IN>
New York Stock Exchange news release
<ANNOUNCEMENT FREQUENCY>
Monthly (midmonth)
<CUMULATIONS>
TABLES
NYSE Facts   Monthly and yearly, cum, nos.
GRAPHS
MG Fin Wkly   Monthly, cum, nos.
<MORE INFORMATION>
   Michael Hayes, The Dow Jones - Irwin Guide to Stock Market Cycles, Dow Jones - Irwin, Homewood, Ill., 1977, pp. 147-150.

Thomas J. Kerrigan, "The Short Interest Ratio and Its Component Parts," Financial Analysts Journal, 45-49 (Nov./Dec. 1974).

Randall O. Smith, "Short Interest and Stock Market Prices," Financial Analysts Journal, 151-154 (Nov./Dec, 1968).

J. B. Cohen, E. D. Zinbarg, and Arthur Zeikel, Investment Analysis and Portfolio Management, Irwin, Homewood, Ill., 1977.

William Gordon, The Stock Market Indicators as a Guide to Market Timing, Investors Press, Palisades Park, N. J., 1968, pp. 93-110.

New York Stock Exchange Volume

<DESCRIPTION>
The number of shares traded on the New York Stock Exchange on a given day.
<DERIVATION>
The number of shares traded in each transaction are tallied and then totalled.
<USE>
Used to judge market breadth and, in concert with other indicators, the attitudes of investors.
<PUBLISHER>
New York Stock Exchange.
<ANNOUNCED IN>
News release
<ANNOUNCEMENT FREQUENCY>
Daily
<CUMULATIONS>
TABLES

MG Fin Wkly	Daily, cum, nos.
Man Han	Latest week, nos.
Man Han	Latest week, % change
Barron's	Latest week-end and month, nos.
NYT	Latest week and year to date, nos.
FR Bull	Monthly and yearly, cum, average nos.
S&P Stats	Daily, monthly, and yearly, cum, average nos.

GRAPHS

NYT	Monthly, high-lows, nos.
MG Fin Wkly	Daily, cum, nos.
WSJ	Weekly, cum, nos.
S&P Outlook	Weekly, cum, nos.

<MORE INFORMATION>
Donald E. Fischer and Ronald A. Jordan, Security Analysis and Portfolio Management, 3rd ed., Prentice Hall, Englewood Cliffs, N.J., 1983.

New York Stock Exchange Volume Momentum

<DESCRIPTION>
A measure of the current performance of the New York Stock Exchange in comparison with its performance during the recent past.
<DERIVATION>
The average volume per day of shares bought and sold on the New York Stock Exchange for the past month is divided by the

monthly volume of shares on that exchange averaged over the past six months.
<USE>
To determine trends in market activity; used in conjunction with the Price Momentum. Total volume usually falls in advance of declines and rises before advances.
<PUBLISHER>
New York Stock Exchange
<ANNOUNCED IN>
Media General Financial Weekly
<ANNOUNCEMENT FREQUENCY>
Monthly
<CUMULATIONS>
GRAPHS
MG Fin Wkly Monthly, cum, ratio nos.

Nonagricultural Employment
<DESCRIPTION>
Estimates of the total number of persons employed in nonagricultural establishments in the U.S. during a specified payroll period; includes all those who worked during, received wages for, or were sick or on strike during any part of the payroll period as full-time, part-time, or temporary employees. Proprietors, the self employed, unpaid family workers, and domestic workers in households are not included.
<DERIVATION>
Data are collected each month from a sample of establishments in the private sector and in state and local governments by cooperating state agencies that mail questionnaires to about 165,000 reporting establishments and edit them when returned before passing the information on to the Bureau of Labor Statistics. These data are supplemented with monthly data on federal civilian employment obtained from the Office of Personnel Management. The sampling is proportionate to the average size of the establishment; all large establishments are included in the sample, but coverage is much lower for small establishments. The data are benchmarked to a reasonably complete count prepared annually from a number of sources and adjusted with a ratio of the current month's employment to the previous month's employment computed from the sample establishments reporting for both months. The data are then seasonally adjusted.
<USE>
Widely used as a timely indicator of changes in economic activity in the manufacturing, transportation, public utilities, wholesale and retail trade, finance, insurance, real estate, and governmental sectors of the U.S. economy. It is used to follow business trends in nearly 260 labor markets across the country. It is frequently factored into other economic indicators dealing with production, productivity, and national income.
<PUBLISHER>
U.S. Department of Labor, Bureau of Labor Statistics
<ANNOUNCED IN>
Bureau of Labor Statistics press release.

Employment and Earnings
<ANNOUNCEMENT FREQUENCY>
Monthly
<CUMULATIONS>
TABLES

Man Han	Latest month, nos.
Barron's	Latest month and year ago, nos.
BW	Latest month and year ago, nos.
Ind W	Latest month and year ago, nos.
NYT	Latest month and year ago, nos.
Bus Stats	Monthly and yearly, cum, nos.
EI	Monthly and yearly, cum, nos.
Emp & Earn	Monthly and yearly, cum, nos.
FR Bull	Monthly and yearly, cum, nos.
S&P Stats	Monthly and yearly, cum, nos.
SCB	Monthly and yearly, cum, nos.
Hist Stats	Yearly, cum, nos.
Hbk Lbr Stat	Yearly, cum, nos.
MLR	Yearly, cum, nos.
Pred Base	Yearly, cum, nos.
Pred Fore	Yearly, cum, nos.
Stat Abstr	Yearly, cum, nos.
Ybk Labor	Yearly, cum, nos.

GRAPHS

EI	Yearly, cum, nos.

PROJECTIONS

Pred Fore	Yearly, nos.

<MORE INFORMATION>

Joint Economic Committee, 1980 Supplement to Economic Indicators, Historical and Descriptive Background, USGPO, Washington, D.C., 1980.

Bureau of Labor Statistics, Handbook of Methods, Bull. 1910, Department of Labor, Washington, D.C., 1976.

Abba A. Lerner, Economics of Employment, McGraw-Hill, New York, 1951.

S. A. Levitan and R. Taggert, "The Hardship Index," Across the Board, 55-60 (Nov. 1976).

John Kirk, "Economic Indicators: The How and the Why," Banking, 27-28 (Aug. 1964).

G. H. Moore and J. Shiskin, "Why the Leading Indicators Really Do Lead," Across the Board, 71-75 (May 1978).

Geoffrey Moore, "Employment: The Neglected Indicator," Wall Street Journal, 10 (Feb. 3, 1972).

Julius Shiskin, "Employment and Unemployment: The Doughnut or the Hole," Monthly Labor Review, 3-10 (Feb. 1976).

Bureau of Labor Statistics, A Guide to Seasonal Adjustment of Labor Force Data, Bull. 2114, U.S. Department of Labor, Washington, D.C., 1982.

Bureau of Labor Statistics and Bureau of the Census, Concepts and Methods Used in Labor Force Statistics Derived from the Current Population Survey, BLS Rept. 463 and Current Pop. Rept. (Ser. P-23) 62, U.S. Department of Labor and U.S. Department of Commerce, Washington, D.C., 1976.

Bureau of Labor Statistics, Workers, Jobs, and Statistics, Rept. 698, U.S. Department of Labor, Washington, D.C., 1983.

Number of Business Failures [see Business Failures]

O

Odd-Lot Index [See American Stock Exchange Odd-Lot Index and New York Stock Exchange Odd-Lot Index]

Odd-Lot Sales and Purchase Index [See New York Stock Exchange Odd-Lot Sales and Purchase Index]

Odd-Lot Short Sales [See New York Stock Exchange Odd-Lot Short Sales]

Operating Rate [See Manufacturers' Capacity Utilization: Bureau of Economic Analysis]

Over the Counter Average [See Over the Counter Index]

Over the Counter Index
<DESCRIPTION>
A descriptor of the ups and downs of the securities that are not listed on the major exchanges.
<DERIVATION>
The 35 over-the-counter securities that have the largest number of shareholders and the greatest market value are selected. Because no accurate measure of volume is possible, the highest bid price of each of the 35 stocks is tallied each day, and those prices are totalled. That sum is divided by a factor that is adjusted for stock dividends and splits. Moreover, the factor is changed with every substitution in the 35 selected securities. Such substitutions are fairly common because selected stocks become listed on a major exchange, merge, or become inactive. Because of the nature of the selection process, the index is heavily weighted toward industrial firms.
<USE>
The only indicator of the trends of unlisted securities' prices; provides a general comparison of the performances of

stocks that are listed on the major exchanges with those of
stocks that are not. Generally moves in concert with the
Dow-Jones Industrials during times of intense investment
activity, but trails the trend of the Dow-Jones Industrials
by several weeks or even months during periods of slower
trading.
<PUBLISHER>
National Association of Securities Dealers
<ANNOUNCED IN>
News release
<ANNOUNCEMENT FREQUENCY>
Daily
<CUMULATIONS>
TABLES
MG Fin Wkly Daily, index nos.
Barron's   Latest week-end, index nos.
Barron's   Latest week-end, % change
WSJ   Latest and week ago, index nos.
WSJ   Latest and week ago, % change
Forbes   Latest month and year ago, % change
Inc   Monthly, cum, %change
NYT   Weekly high-low, % change
GRAPHS
Inc   Monthly, cum, % change
<MORE INFORMATION>
   "What's in an Index?" Barron's, Nov. 11, 1965, pp. 5+.

P

Paperboard Production

<DESCRIPTION>
Estimated national total of new and unfilled orders for and production of paperboard.

<DERIVATION>
Approximately 90% of the paperboard mills report their totals to the American Paper Institute. These reports are supplemented with and extrapolated with estimates for the other ~10% based on annual reports on the entire industry. For new orders and production, the weekly data are averaged to produce the monthly data and the yearly data. Because of the manner in which new orders are received, new-order data and production data are not for the same weeks. For unfilled orders, the data are those for the end of the month.

<USE>
A reliable leading indicator of overall industrial activity. Its reliability is commonly attributed to the need of manufacturers for paperboard to ship their products in. When business is slow, less paperboard is needed. When an upturn in business is anticipated, orders for paperboard are increased.

<PUBLISHER>
American Paper Institute, Paperboard Group

<ANNOUNCED IN>
American Paper Institute Weekly Report

<ANNOUNCEMENT FREQUENCY>
Weekly

<CUMULATIONS>
TABLES

BW	Latest month and week, year ago, tons
Barron's	Latest week and year ago, tons
Ind W	Latest week and year ago, tons
NYT	Latest week and year ago, tons
Bus Stats	Monthly and yearly, cum, tons
S&P Stats	Monthly and yearly, cum, tons
SCB	Monthly and yearly, cum, tons
Stat Paper	Monthly and yearly, cum, tonnage
Hist Stats	Yearly, cum, tons
Stat Abstr	Yearly, cum, tons

<MORE INFORMATION>
"The Rage for Faster Forecasts," Business Week, 135-136
(Oct. 18, 1982).

Parity Index
<DESCRIPTION>
The Index of Prices Paid by Farmers for Commodities and
Services, Interest, Taxes, and Farm Wage Rates expressed on a
1910-1914 base. A weighted indicator of the costs to farmers
for items used in family living, for items used in farm
production, for interest on indebtedness secured by farm real
estate, and for wages paid to farm labor.
<DERIVATION>
Produced by combining the Index of Commodities and Services
with the indexes of interest, taxes, and wage rates, all
indexed to 1910-1914 as the base year and all for the costs
to farmers. These data are gathered from reports by firms and
organizations providing production inputs to agricultural
producers, surveys of farmers, the Department of Agriculture
Market News Service, trade publications, labor surveys, and
surveys of financial institutions. Compilation of the first
index is the most complicated. There, data are expressed in a
state-by-state manner, and state weights (based on the
quantities of goods and services purchased by farmers) are
applied to the data. National averages are then calculated
for specified types of farm expenditures. These groups of
expenditures are then summed and combined with a family
living component to obtain the Index of Commodities and
Services.
<USE>
Used in market planning, negotiating marketing contracts,
comparing changes in farming prices with those in nonfarm
areas, and establishing commodity parity prices for
agricultural price-support programs.
<PUBLISHER>
U.S. Department of Agriculture, Economics, Statistics, and
Cooperatives Service
<ANNOUNCED IN>
Agricultural Prices
<ANNOUNCEMENT FREQUENCY>
Monthly
<CUMULATIONS>
TABLES
Ag Prices   Latest month and year ago, index nos.
Bus Stats   Monthly and yearly, cum, index nos.
EI   Monthly and yearly, cum, index nos.
SCB   Monthly and yearly, cum, index nos.
Bus Stats   Monthly and yearly, cum, ratio nos.
EI   Monthly and yearly, cum, ratio nos.
SCB   Monthly and yearly, cum, ratio nos.
Ag Charts   Yearly, cum, index nos.
Hist Stats   Yearly, cum, index nos.
Stat Abstr   Yearly, cum, index nos.
GRAPHS
Ag Chrts   Yearly, cum, index nos.

```
Ag Charts S  Yearly, cum, index nos.
EI           Yearly, cum, index nos.
EI           Yearly, cum, ratio nos.
Ag Prices    Yearly, cum, % change
```
<MORE INFORMATION>
   Joint Economic Committee, 1980 Supplement to Economic Indicators, Historical and Descriptive Background, USGPO, Washington, D.C., 1980, p. 92.
   Scope and Method of the Statistical Reporting Service, Misc. Publ. 1308, USDA, Washington, D.C., 1975.
   Major Statistical Series of the U.S. Department of Agriculture, How They Are Constructed and Used, Vol. 1, Agricultural Prices and Parity, USDA, Washington, D.C., 1970.

Parity Ratio
<DESCRIPTION>
A measure of the purchasing power of the products sold by farmers in terms of the the goods and services they buy compared with the comparable purchasing power in a base period. The ratio of the income of farmers to the costs of operation paid by farmers indexed to a particular base time.
<DERIVATION>
The Index of Prices Received by Farmers and the Index of Prices Paid by Farmers are both expressed on a base of 1910-1914. The Index of Prices received by Farmers is then divided by the Index of Prices Paid by Farmers and multiplied by 100. When this Parity Ratio is less than 100, prices paid have increased at a faster rate than the prices the farmers received for their goods since the 1910-1914 base period. Conversely, when the Ratio is more than 100, prices paid have increased at a slower rate than the prices farmers received for their goods since the base period.
<USE>
Actuates Department of Agriculture price support programs to farmers, which guard against sharp fluctuations in price. These actions, in turn, affect food prices and farm purchasing power.
<PUBLISHER>
U.S. Department of Agriculture, Statistical Reporting Service
<ANNOUNCED IN>
Agricultural Prices
<ANNOUNCEMENT FREQUENCY>
Monthly
<CUMULATIONS>
TABLES
```
Ag Prices     Monthly, cum, ratio
Ag Prices An  Monthly and yearly, cum, ratio
Bus Stats     Monthly and yearly, cum, ratio
SCB           Monthly and yearly, cum, ratio
Ag Stats      Yearly, cum, ratio
Hist Stats    Yearly, cum, ratio
Stat Abstr    Yearly, cum, ratio
```
<MORE INFORMATION>
   Joint Economic Committee, 1980 Supplement to Economic Indicators, Historical and Descriptive Background, USGPO, Washington, D.C., 1980.

Personal Consumption Expenditures
<DESCRIPTION>
An estimate of the total expenditures made by individuals, nonprofit institutions, etc. for goods and services.
<DERIVATION>
Estimates for benchmark years are made from census data. Estimates for years between benchmarks and for quarters are derived chiefly from trends shown by the Census Bureau's retail sales figures by kind of store and other source data. The data are seasonally adjusted.
<USE>
Used in the calculation of Disposition of Personal Income. Data trends will closely follow the trends of total retail sales.
<PUBLISHER>
U.S. Department of Commerce, Bureau of Economic Analysis
<ANNOUNCED IN>
Survey of Current Business
<ANNOUNCEMENT FREQUENCY>
Quarterly
<CUMULATIONS>
TABLES
EI   Quarterly and yearly, cum, $
Pred Base   Yearly, cum, $
Pred Fore   Yearly, cum, $
GRAPHS
Mo Econ Ind   Yearly, cum, $
PROJECTIONS
Pred Fore   Yearly, $
Pred Fore   Yearly, % change
<MORE INFORMATION>
   Richard M. Snyder, Measuring Business Changes, Wiley, New York, 1955.
   Joint Economic Committee, 1980 Supplement to Economic Indicators, Historical and Descriptive Background, USGPO, Washington, D.C., 1980.
   John Kirk, "Economic Indicators: The How and the Why," Banking, 25-26 (July 1964).

Personal Income [See Sources of Personal Income and Disposition of Personal Income]

Personal Saving [See also Savings Rate]
<DESCRIPTION>
An estimation of the current saving of individuals (including the owners of unincorporated businesses); nonprofit institutions; and private health, welfare, and trust funds.
<DERIVATION>
A number of available statistical series are used to estimate personal savings. Disposable personal income is the starting point. From it is subtracted personal consumption expenditures, interest paid by consumers, and net personal transfer payments to foreigners (cash, goods, or services sent or donated abroad less any remittances from abroad). The remainder is assumed to be what is saved.

<USE>
Used to judge long-term trends in income, expenditures, and
economic growth.
<PUBLISHER>
U.S. Department of Commerce, Bureau of Economic Analysis
<ANNOUNCED IN>
Survey of Current Business
<ANNOUNCEMENT FREQUENCY>
Quarterly
<CUMULATIONS>
TABLES
BCD   Quarterly, cum, $
FR Bull   Quarterly and yearly, cum, $
SCB   Quarterly and yearly, cum, $
Bus Stats   Yearly, cum, $
Hist Stats   Yearly, cum, $
Stat Abstr   Yearly, cum, $
GRAPHS
BCD   Yearly, cum, $
<MORE INFORMATION>
   Raymond W. Goldsmith, A Study of Saving in the United
States, Princeton University Press, Princeton, N.J., 1955.
   Richard M. Snyder, Measuring Business Changes, Wiley, New
York, 1955, p. 21 ff.
   Stanley Schor, "Who Saves," Review of Economics and
Statistics 41 (2), 213-248 (1959).

Personal Saving Rate [See Savings Rate]

Petroleum Production
<DESCRIPTION>
The sum of crude oil production (including lease condensate),
natural gas processing plant liquid production, and field
production of other liquids used by refineries, expressed in
thousands of barrels per day.
<DERIVATION>
Crude oil production is estimated monthly from data reported
to the Department of Energy (DOE) by each of the state
conservation agencies, which collect crude oil production
values for tax purposes. Ten states do not report such
monthly data, and the values for those states are estimated
from linear extrapolations of the trends in their historical
production values. The U.S. Geological Survey (USGS) reports
the volume of crude oil that is produced offshore in
federally controlled waters. At the end of each calendar
year, these monthly numbers are updated with data from the
annual reports of the state conservation agencies and the
USGS. Because the reporting of these monthly data lags about
four months behind, estimates of production during the most
recent months are made from historical production patterns,
and these estimates are later updated with reported values.
In some cases, adjustments are made to any of these estimates
based on additional information supplied by a state agency, a
trade association, or an individual field operator. Field

production of natural gas liquids (including finished petroleum products) is reported monthly to DOE by all operators of such facilities (approximately 1000 respondents). Nonrespondents are contacted by telephone, and imputed values are calculated for nonresponding companies that submitted reports the previous month. Values obtained through all of these collection methods are summed.
<USE>
Indicates the near-term availability of oil and therefore presages the costs of petroleum-derived fuels, and those prices are important contributors to the costs of industrial production and to the cost of living. Moreover, shortages of these fuels could severely impair industrial production on a national scale.
<PUBLISHER>
U.S. Department of Energy, Energy Information Administration
<ANNOUNCED IN>
Monthly Energy Review
<ANNOUNCEMENT FREQUENCY>
Monthly
<CUMULATIONS>
TABLES
Bus Stats   Monthly and yearly, cum, barrels
Mo En Rev   Monthly and yearly, cum, barrels
SCB   Monthly and yearly, cum, barrels
Pred Base   Yearly, cum, barrels
Pred Fore   Yearly, cum, barrels
Stat Abstr   Yearly, cum, barrels
PROJECTIONS
Pred Fore   Yearly, cum, barrels
<MORE INFORMATION>
  Richard M. Snyder, Measuring Business Changes, Wiley, 1955.
  Energy Information Administration, "Explanatory Notes," Petroleum Supply Monthly, USGPO, Washington, D.C., monthly.

Plant and Equipment Contracts and Orders [See Contracts and Orders for Plant and Equipment]

Plant and Equipment Expenditures [See Expenditures for New Plant and Equipment]

Price-Dividend Ratio [See Standard & Poor's 500 Dividend-Price Ratio]

Price-Earnings Ratio [See American Stock Exchange Price-Earnings Ratio, New York Stock Exchange Price-Earnings Ratio, and Price-Earnings Ratio for Over the Counter Stocks]

Price-Earnings Ratio for Over the Counter Stocks
<DESCRIPTION>
A measure of the value of the stocks purchased over the

counter; more accurately, a measure of the speculative nature of those types of purchases.
<DERIVATION>
The average price for all of the stocks included in the NASDAQ system is divided by the average earnings reported for those stocks.
<USE>
As a gage of speculative activity in the market and to assess turning points of the market in the near term. The higher the ratio, the more speculative the market is considered to be because increased investment is not being reflected in increased returns (earnings) from the corporations' performances. Conversely, a lower ratio indicates better value of purchases in the market.
<PUBLISHER>
National Association of Securties Dealers
<ANNOUNCED IN>
National Association of Securities Dealers news release
<ANNOUNCEMENT FREQUENCY>
Daily
<CUMULATIONS>
TABLES
MG Fin Wkly   Latest week and year ago, nos.

Price Momentum
<DESCRIPTION>
A measure of the general movement of prices on a stock exchange.
<DERIVATION>
The average price of the stocks traded by a stock exchange is calculated for the past month. This value is then divided by the average price of the stocks traded by that exchange for the past six months. A value >1 for this indicator means that the stocks, in aggregate, have performed better during the past month than they have in recent months.
<USE>
To gage the performance of a market as a whole in recent months. and to forecast performance in the near term.
<PUBLISHER>
Media General Financial Services, Inc.
<ANNOUNCED IN>
Media General Financial Weekly
<ANNOUNCEMENT FREQUENCY>
Monthly
<CUMULATIONS>
TABLES
MG Fin Wkly   Monthly, cum, ratio nos.
<MORE INFORMATION>
  G. Appel and F. Hitschler, Stock Market Trading System, Dow Jones - Irwin, Homewood, Ill., 1980.

Prices Paid Index [See Index of Prices Paid by Farmers for Commodities and Services, Interest, Taxes, and Farm Wage Rates]

Prices Received Index [See Index of Prices Received by Farmers]

Prime Commercial Paper
<DESCRIPTION>
The prevailing rate on prime four- to six-months commercial paper.
<DERIVATION>
The Federal Reserve Bank of New York daily determines the prevailing selling quotation of inventory commercial paper from information provided by dealers in such paper in New York City; this information is periodically augmented with reports concerning rates outside New York. Daily offering rates are averaged to produce weekly and monthly figures.
<USE>
Used to measure the cost of open-market short-term credit available to large business borrowers of the highest credit standing.
<PUBLISHER>
Board of Governors of the Federal Reserve System
<ANNOUNCED IN>
Selected Interest Rates, Statistical Release H.15 (519)
<ANNOUNCEMENT FREQUENCY>
Weekly
<CUMULATIONS>
TABLES
WSJ   Latest week, %
Barron's   Latest week and year ago, %
Bus Stats   Monthly and yearly, cum, %
EI   Weekly, monthly, and yearly, cum, %
FR Bull   Weekly, monthly, and yearly, cum, %
<MORE INFORMATION>
  Richard T. Selden, Trends and Cycles in the Commercial Paper Market, Occasional Paper 85, National Bureau of Economic Research, New York, 1963.

Prime Rate [See Average Prime Rate Charged by Banks]

Principal Diffusion Index [See Diffusion Index]

Profits Optimism Index [See Dun & Bradstreet Profits Optimism Index]

Producer Price Indexes [Formerly called Wholesale Price Index]
<DESCRIPTION>
Measures of the average changes in prices received in primary markets of the U.S. by producers of commodities in all stages of processing. The indexes are designed to measure real price changes, not changes in quality, quantity, or terms of sale; moreover, they do not measure changes in manufacturers'

average realized prices. Producer Price Indexes can be organized by stage of processing (degree of fabrication: from crude materials to finished goods) or by commodity (similarity in end use or material composition).
<DERIVATION>
The Bureau of Labor Statistics surveys a sample of approximately 2,800 commodities, receiving approximately 10,000 quotations from producers in the manufacturing, agriculture, forestry, fishing, mining, gas, electricity, and public utility sectors about the prices received for their goods. The responses provide the average net prices (with all applicable discounts) received by the producers for their products on a given day. Each reporter usually has equal weight with all the other reporters. List or book prices are used if transaction prices are not available. Some prices are taken from trade publications or received from other government agencies. Insofar as possible, identical qualities of the commodities are priced from period to period. For each commodity, the ratio of the current month's average price to the previous month's average price is then multiplied with the previous month's index to derive the current month's index. To derive indexes for commodity groupings, the sequential months' price ratio for each commodity in the group is first weighted, and then they are summed and divided by the corresponding weighted value for the index base period. Most producer price indexes are computed on a reference base of 1967 = 100. Price changes for the various commodities are averaged together with weights representing their importance in the total net selling value of all commodities. Weights are revised periodically with data from the industrial census.
<USE>
Frequently used in escalation clauses of long-term sales contracts, to determine pricing policies that are congruous with the prices charged for similar products in national trade, to measure inflation at the primary market level, to analyze the sources and transmission of price changes through the American economy, to formulate and evaluate the fiscal and monetary policies and activities of the government and specific industries, to make or review budgets, to deflate time series so they can be reported in constant dollars, to establish replacement cost estimates, to appraise the value of inventories, and to research and predict business cycles.
<PUBLISHER>
U.S. Department of Labor, Bureau of Labor Statistics
<ANNOUNCED IN>
Bureau of Labor Statistics news release
<ANNOUNCEMENT FREQUENCY>
Monthly
<CUMULATIONS>
TABLES

FR Bull	Latest month, index nos.
Man Han	Latest month, % change
Barron's	Latest month and year ago, index nos.
BW	Latest month and year ago, index nos.
NYT	Latest month and year ago, index nos.

Ind W	Latest quarter and year ago, index nos.
Ind W	Latest quarter and year ago, % change
Bus Stats	Monthly and yearly, cum, index nos.
EI	Monthly and yearly, cum, index nos.
PPI	Monthly and yearly, cum, index nos.
S&P Stats	Monthly and yearly, cum, index nos.
SCB	Monthly and yearly, cum, index nos.
EI	Monthly and yearly, cum, % change
FR Bull	Monthly and yearly, cum, % change
Hist Stats	Yearly, cum, index nos.
Pred Base	Yearly, cum, index nos.
Pred Fore	Yearly, cum, index nos.
Stat Abstr	Yearly, cum, index nos.
GRAPHS	
EI	Yearly, cum, index nos.
PROJECTIONS	
Value Line	Quarterly and yearly, % change
Ind W	Yearly, % change
Pred Fore	Yearly, index nos.

<MORE INFORMATION>
   Joint Economic Committee, 1980 Supplement to Economic Indicators, Historical and Descriptive Background, USGPO, Washington, D.C., 1980.
   Bureau of Labor Statistics, Handbook of Methods for Surveys and Studies, Bull. 1910, Department of Labor, Washington, D.C., 1976.

Productivity and Related Data, Private Business Sector
<DESCRIPTION>
Estimates of the gross domestic product of the private business sector, the hours of all persons engaged in producing that output, the computed output per hour of those persons, their compensation per hour, the computed unit labor costs, and the resulting implicit price. All estimates are divided into contributions from the nonfarm business sector and the total private business sector and expressed as indexes to the base year (1976).
<DERIVATION>
Private-business and nonfarm business output is measured in constant dollars by the Bureau of Economic Analysis each quarter (see entry for Gross National Product). An output index is constructed by the Bureau of Labor Statistics by subtracting from the BEA data the areas for which productivity cannot be meaningfully measured. In this index, output is composed of employee compensation, profits, depreciation, indirect business taxes, and other income; it does not include intermediate purchases of goods and services. Employment is multiplied by average weekly hours (collected monthly in the BLS survey of establishments) to produce the hours of all persons; for proprietors, unpaid family workers, and farmworkers, data from the BLS monthly survey of households are used. The output per hour is derived by dividing the measured output by the hours worked. Compensation-per-hour data are again taken from the national accounts of the BEA but are adjusted by the BLS to include an

estimate of the wages, salaries, and supplements of
proprietors. This last measure is then divided by the output
per hour to calculate the unit labor cost. The implicit price
deflator is then computed as the ratio of output in current
dollars to the output in constant dollars in the sector.
<USE>
Used in the forecasting and analysis of prices, wages, and
effects of technological changes.
<PUBLISHER>
U.S. Department of Labor, Bureau of Labor Statistics
<ANNOUNCED IN>
Monthly Labor Review
<ANNOUNCEMENT FREQUENCY>
Quarterly
<CUMULATIONS>
TABLES
BCD   Quarterly and yearly, cum, index nos.
EI   Quarterly and yearly, cum, index nos.
MLR   Quarterly and yearly, cum, index nos.
BCD   Quarterly and yearly, cum, % change
EI   Quarterly and yearly, cum, % change
MLR   Quarterly and yearly, cum, % change
Hbk Lbr Stat Yearly, cum, index nos.
Hist Stats   Yearly, cum, index nos.
Pred Base   Yearly, cum, index nos.
Pred Fore   Yearly, cum, index nos.
Stat Abstr   Yearly, cum, index nos.
GRAPHS
BCD   Yearly, cum, index nos.
BCD   Yearly, cum, % change
Stat Abstr   Yearly, cum, % change
PROJECTIONS
Pred Fore   Yearly, index nos.
<MORE INFORMATION>
   Joint Economic Committee, 1980 Supplement to Economic
Indicators, Historical and Descriptive Background, USGPO,
Washington, D.C., 1980.
   Bureau of Labor Statistics, Meaning and Measurement of
Productivity, Bull. 1714, Department of Labor, Washington,
D.C., 1971.
   S. Fabricant, Basic Facts on Productivity Change,
Occasional Paper 63, National Bureau of Economic Research,
New York, 1959.

Q

Quit Rate, Manufacturing
<DESCRIPTION>
The number of employees that have left the workforce under
their own volition during a given month per hundred extant
employees.
<DERIVATION>
Cooperating manufacturers are surveyed by state employment
security agencies; respondents provide the number of
employees that have been removed from the payroll at their
own request because of a new job, dissatisfaction, return to
school, marriage, maternity, ill health, voluntary
retirement, unauthorized absence, or failure to report after
being hired. These data are divided by the total number of
the respondents' employees and multiplied by 100. The data
are seasonally adjusted.
<USE>
Used to predict business-cycle movements, especially in the
manufacturing sector.
<PUBLISHER>
U.S. Department of Labor, Bureau of Labor Statistics
<ANNOUNCED IN>
Employment and Earnings
<ANNOUNCEMENT FREQUENCY>
Monthly
<CUMULATIONS>

BCD	Monthly, cum, rate
Bus Stats	Monthly and yearly, cum, rate
Emp & Earn	Monthly and yearly, cum, rate
SCB	Monthly and yearly, cum, rate
Emp & Earn	Yearly, cum, rate
Hist Stats	Yearly, cum, rate
Stat Abstr	Yearly, cum, rate
GRAPHS	
BCD	Monthly, cum, rate

<MORE INFORMATION>
  U.S. Dept. of Commerce, Bureau of Economic Analysis,
Handbook of Cyclical Indicators, USGPO, Washington, D.C.,
1977.
  Bureau of Labor Statistics, How the Government Measures

Unemployment, Rept. 505, U.S. Department of Labor, Washington, D.C., 1977.

National Bureau of Economic Research, The Measurement and Bevavior of Unemployment, Princeton Univ. Press, Princeton, N.J., 1957.

Julius Shiskin, Labor Force and Unemployment, BLS Rept. 486, U.S. Department of Labor, Washington, D.C., 1976.

Seymour L. Wolfbein, Employment and Unemployment in the United States, Science Research Assoc., Chicago, 1964.

John E. Bregger, "Unemployment Statistics and What They Mean," Monthly Labor Review (June 1971).

Gloria P. Green, "Measuring Total and State Insured Unemployment," Monthly Labor Review (June 1971).

Bureau of Labor Statistics, Workers, Jobs, and Statistics, Rept. 698, U.S. Department of Labor, Washington, D.C., 1983.

R

Raw Materials Price Index [See Industrial Raw Materials Price Index]

Reserves and Borrowing [A portion of and also referred to as Bank Loans, Investments, and Reserves]
<DESCRIPTION>
The total reserves and borrowings of the nationally chartered and state-chartered banks that are members of the Federal Reserve System. The total reserves are the sum of reserve balances of member banks (each is required to maintain a specific minimum balance determined by the type, maturity, and size of its deposit liabilities) held at Federal Reserve Banks in the current week, the average of member-bank vault cash held two weeks earlier, and a minor amount of waivers of penalties for reserve deficiencies. The total borrowings include all member-bank seasonal and regular borrowings on Federal Reserve credit. Reserves are reported as required, nonborrowed, and total; borrowings are reported as seasonal and total.
<DERIVATION>
Each member bank reports its assets and liabilities to the Federal Reserve System. From these reports, the minimum reserve balance for that bank is computed. The required reserves are tabulated weekly by the Federal Reserve System and seasonally adjusted. To this aggregate reserve are added excess reserves (deposits with the Federal Reserve above and beyond the minimum required); these excess reserves are not seasonally adjusted. The borrowings by member banks are totalled and (without being seasonally adjusted) are subtracted from the seasonally adjusted total reserves to give the seasonally adjusted nonborrowed reserves. Monthly data are derived as prorations of the weekly data.
<USE>
The rates of growth of reserve aggregates are used by some analysts as indicators of monetary policy.
<PUBLISHER>
Board of Governors of the Federal Reserve System
<ANNOUNCED IN>
Aggregate Reserves and Member Bank Deposits, Statistical Release H.3 (502)

<ANNOUNCEMENT FREQUENCY>
Weekly
<CUMULATIONS>
TABLES
FR Bull   Monthly and yearly, cum, $
EI   Monthly and yearly, cum, $
GRAPHS
EI   Yearly, cum, $
<MORE INFORMATION>
   Joint Economic Committee, 1980 Supplement to Economic
Indicators, Historical and Descriptive Background, USGPO,
Washington, D.C., 1980.

Retail Price Index [See Consumer Price Index]

Retail Trade
<DESCRIPTION>
Estimates of retail sales and inventories by establishments
primarily engaged in retail trade to individuals, industrial
users, and other retailers; net sales include merchandise and
services sold for cash or credit after deductions for refunds
and allowances and before carrying charges, taxes,
commissions, and nonoperating income are factored in;
inventories represent stocks of merchandise on hand at the
end of the month valued at cost. Both sales and inventories
are reported in durable- and nondurable-goods categories.
<DERIVATION>
A sample representing all sizes of firms and types of
businesses in retail trade throughout the nation are surveyed
by mail monthly by the Bureau of the Census. The data
received are periodically benchmarked to the results of
censuses of retail trade and the Annual Retail Trade Survey.
Both the sales and inventories data are adjusted for seasonal
variations, and the sales data are also adjusted for holiday
and trading-day differences.
<USE>
Used to indicate probable future economic activity at the
manufacturing and other, earlier stages of production and
distribution. Also used in determining the gross national
product.
<PUBLISHER>
U.S. Department of Commerce, Bureau of the Census
<ANNOUNCED IN>
Bureau of the Census press release
<ANNOUNCEMENT FREQUENCY>
Monthly
<CUMULATIONS>
TABLES
EI   Monthly and yearly, cum, $
Ind W   Latest month, quarter, and year, $
Barron's   Latest month and year ago, $
NYT   Latest month and year ago, $
Ann Retail   Monthly and yearly, cum, $
BCD   Monthly and yearly, cum, $
Bus Stats   Monthly and yearly, cum, $

```
Mo Retail      Monthly and yearly, cum, $
S&P Stats      Monthly and yearly, cum, $
SCB            Monthly and yearly, cum, $
Hist Stats     Yearly, cum, $
Stat Abstr     Yearly, cum, $
GRAPHS
EI             Yearly, cum, $
BCD            Yearly, cum, $
Stat Bull      Yearly, cum, $
PROJECTIONS
Ind W          Yearly, $
```
<MORE INFORMATION>
   Joint Economic Committee, 1980 Supplement to Economic Indicators, Historical and Descriptive Background, USGPO, Washington, D.C., 1980.
   Bureau of the Census, Revised Monthly Retail Sales and Inventories: January 1967-December 1979, Department of Commerce, Washington, D.C., 1980.
   Monthly Retail Trade Reports for 1979, U.S. Department of Commerce, Washington, D.C., 1980.

Revenue Passenger Miles
<DESCRIPTION>
The number of miles flown by paying passengers on flights within the U.S.
<DERIVATION>
Airlines calculate the number of miles flown on their aircraft by each ticketed customer, total these "revenue passenger miles" each month, and report that total each month to the Civil Aeronautics Board. The Board sums the revenue passenger miles of all U.S. scheduled airlines.
<USE>
Besides being an obvious indicator of the health of the airline industry, the number of passenger miles flown is also an indicator of the current intensity of business activity because most air travel is made by businessmen.
<PUBLISHER>
Air Transport Association of America
<ANNOUNCED IN>
Air Transport Facts and Figures
<ANNOUNCEMENT FREQUENCY>
Yearly
<CUMULATIONS>
TABLES
```
Air Trans      Yearly, cum, miles
Stat Abstr     Yearly, cum, miles
Travel Ybk     Yearly, cum, miles
Travel Ybk     Latest year, % change
```

S

Sales-Inventory Ratio [See Inventory-Sales Ratio]

Sales Optimism Index [See Dun & Bradstreet Sales Optimism Index]

Savings Rate [Also called Savings Ratio and Personal Saving Rate]
<DESCRIPTION>
The percentage of current disposable personal income that is made up of current personal savings.
<DERIVATION>
The total personal saving is divided by disposable personal income and the resulting ratio is converted into a percentage.
<USE>
Used to judge long-term trends in income, expenditures, and economic growth.
<PUBLISHER>
U.S. Department of Commerce, Bureau of Economic Analysis
<ANNOUNCED IN>
Survey of Current Business
<ANNOUNCEMENT FREQUENCY>
Monthly
<CUMULATIONS>
TABLES

Ind W	Latest quarter and year, %
BCD	Quarterly, cum, %
EI	Quarterly and yearly, cum, %
Econ Rept Pr	Quarterly and yearly, cum, %
FR Bull	Quarterly and yearly, cum, %
Hist Stats	Yearly, cum, %
Pred Base	Yearly, cum, %
Pred Fore	Yearly, cum, %
Stat Abstr	Yearly, cum, %
Bus Stats	Monthly and yearly, cum, %
SCB	Monthly and yearly, cum, %

GRAPHS

BCD	Yearly, cum, %

PROJECTIONS
Ind W   Yearly, %
Value Line   Yearly, %
Pred Fore   Yearly, %
<MORE INFORMATION>
  Handbook of Cyclical Indicators, U.S. Department of
Commerce, Washington, D.C., 1977, p. 58.

Savings Ratio [See Savings Rate]

Seat Sales [See American Stock Exchange Seat Sales and New
York Stock Exchange Seat Sales]

**Selected Measures of Unemployment and Unemployment
Insurance Programs, Initial Claims** [See Unemployment
Insurance Programs, Initial Claims]

**Selected Measures of Unemployment and Unemployment
Insurance, Total Unemployment** [See Total Unemployment]

Sensitive Prices [See Changes in Sensitive Prices]

Sentiment Index of the Leading Services [See Advisory
Service Index]

Separation Rate [See Layoff Rate, Manufacturing]

Shipments-Inventory Ratio [See Inventory-Shipments Ratio]

Short Interest Ratio [See American Stock Exchange Short
Interest Ratio and New York Stock Exchange Short Interest
Ratio]

Short Sells Ratio [See New York Stock Exchange Members'
Short Sells Ratio and New York Stock Exchange Nonmembers'
Short Sells Ratio]

Short-Skirt Index [Also called the Hemline Index; see
Appendix A. Nonquantitative Indicators]

Short-Term Trading Index [Also called the Arms Index and
TRIN]
<DESCRIPTION>
An hour-by-hour measure of the activity on the New York Stock
Exchange.

<DERIVATION>
Each hour, the Advance-Decline Ratio is calculated for the
day's trading. The ratio of up volume (the total volume of
all stocks that have risen during the day) to down volume is
also calculated. The Advance-Decline Ratio is then divided by
the ratio of up volume to down volume to give the Short-Term
Trading Index.
<USE>
Used as an indicator of what the market is currently doing
and of what it might do in the very short, near, and
intermediate terms. The Index will be below 1 on days when
the market rises a lot and above 1 on days when it falls a
lot. These values indicate bullish and bearish markets,
respectively, on the very short and near terms. Some analysts
use values of the Index smoothed with a moving average in an
attempt to gain insight into intermediate and major trends.
<PUBLISHER>
New York Stock Exchange
<ANNOUNCED IN>
Quotron
<ANNOUNCEMENT FREQUENCY>
Hourly
<CUMULATIONS>
None
<MORE INFORMATION>
   John R. McGinley, Jr., "The Short Term Trading Index," pp.
38-1 to 38-6 in The Encyclopedia of Stock Market Techniques,
Investors Intelligence, Larchmont, N.Y., 1983.
   Martin E. Zweig, "Handy Trader's Tool, A Long Look at a
Short-Term Indicator," Barron's, 34+ (May 24, 1982).

Six-Month Treasury Bills
<DESCRIPTION>
An average interest rate expressed on a bank discount basis
computed for issuances of U.S. securities auctioned weekly.
<DERIVATION>
Bids are accepted by the Treasury, and securities are
auctioned weekly, usually on Tuesdays. Payment for the
securities must accompany the bids; the securities are
discounted (i.e., the interest for the full term is paid
immediately; the principle is repaid at maturity). The
computed average is based on varying prices at which portions
of the issue are awarded to the highest bidders. Monthly
cumulations are simple averages of the auction average rates
for the issues sold during the month.
<USE>
Used as a measure of the availability of money and of
short-term rates for default-free borrowing; several rates
for borrowing are pegged to this rate.
<PUBLISHER>
Board of Governors of the Federal Reserve System
<ANNOUNCED IN>
Federal Reserve press release
<ANNOUNCEMENT FREQUENCY>
Weekly

```
<CUMULATIONS>
TABLES
MG Fin Wkly  Latest week, %
WSJ          Latest week, %
Wkly Econ    Latest week and month, %
Barron's     Latest week and year ago, %
WSJ          Latest week and week ago, %
Treas Bull   Monthly, cum, %
FR Bull      Monthly and quarterly, cum, %
Bus Stats    Monthly and yearly, cum, %
Econ Rept    Monthly and yearly, cum, %
FHLBBJ       Monthly and yearly, cum, %
S&P Stats    Monthly and yearly, cum, %
SCB          Monthly and yearly, cum, %
Moody's B&F  Quarterly and yearly, cum, %
GRAPHS
MG Fin Wkly  Monthly, cum, %
EI           Yearly, cum, %
Moody's Bond Yearly, cum, %
PROJECTIONS
Wkly Econ    Monthly, %
<MORE INFORMATION>
```
  Handbook of Securities of the United States Government and Federal Agencies and Related Money Market Instruments, First Boston Corp., Boston, 1982.

Sotheby's Art Index

```
<DESCRIPTION>
```
A guide to general movements in the art and antiques markets.
```
<DERIVATION>
```
Sotheby's Auction House's experts select a market basket of specific art and antique items in 12 categories and determine a value for each item based on sales prices. These items are chosen to represent the types of things that come on the market frequently. When a comparable object is sold in the marketplace, a market-basket item is revalued according to what happened in the market. About 95% of the revaluations are based on auction sales, an open market. These revisions are used to recalculate the index number for the appropriate category. The category index numbers are weighted according to their dollar-volume portion of Sotheby's business, and a single-figure aggregate number is calculated. This aggregate number is then indexed to a 1972 value of 100.
```
<USE>
```
Used to follow trends in the art and antiques markets and to determine the value of assets composed of art or antique pieces.
```
<PUBLISHER>
```
Sotheby's
```
<ANNOUNCED IN>
```
Barron's
```
<ANNOUNCEMENT FREQUENCY>
```
Weekly

CUMULATIONS
TABLES
Barron's   Latest month and week and year ago, index nos.
<MORE INFORMATION>
  Gigi Mahon, "Unveiling Sotheby's Art Index," Barron's, Nov. 9, 1981, pp 4+.

Sources and Uses of Funds, Nonfarm Nonfinancial Corporate Business

<DESCRIPTION>
A comprehensive picture of the financial lending and borrowing transactions of the U.S. economy. The sources of funds are apportioned into internal sources (undistributed profits, capital consumption allowances, and foreign branch profits) and external (long- and short-term credit-market funds and other sources). The uses are apportioned into the purchase of physical assets (plant and equipment, residential structures, inventory investment, and mineral rights from the U.S. Government) and the increase in financial assets.
<DERIVATION>
Data for the internal sources and for the purchase of physical assets come from National Income and Products Accounts of the Department of Commerce [see the entries under National Income and Gross National Product]. Data for the external sources and financial assets are compiled from the Federal Trade Commission's Quarterly Report for Manufacturing, Mining, and Trade Corporations, the quarterly U.S. International Transactions in the Survey of Current Business, New Security Issues of Corporations published monthly in the Federal Reserve Bulletin, and the Federal Reserve.
<USE>
Used for developing projections of capital financing that are both realistic and consistent with projections of gross national product, in establishing targets for monetary policy associated with employment and inflation, and for projecting the probable trend of interest rates.
<PUBLISHER>
Board of Governors of the Federal Reserve System
<ANNOUNCED IN>
Flow of Funds Accounts
<ANNOUNCEMENT FREQUENCY>
Quarterly
<CUMULATIONS>
TABLES
EI   Quarterly and yearly, cum, $
Econ Rept Pr Quarterly and yearly, cum, $
FR Bull   Yearly, cum, $
Stat Abstr   Yearly, cum, $
<MORE INFORMATION>
  Joint Economic Committee, 1980 Supplement to Economic Indicators, Historical and Descriptive Background, USGPO, Washington, D.C., 1980.
  Board of Governors of the Federal Reserve System, Introduction to Flow of Funds, Federal Reserve System, Washington, D.C., 1975.

Sources of Personal Income
<DESCRIPTION>
An estimate of the current income received before taxes by individuals, nonprofit institutions, private trust funds, and private health and welfare funds from all sources except transfers among themselves; income is broken down into labor income, farm and nonfarm proprietors' income, rental income, dividends, personal interest income, and transfer payments (such as social security benefits and military pensions).
<DERIVATION>
Monthly, the Bureau of Economic Analysis totals the following types of income, which it estimates from the results of surveys: wage and salary disbursements, other labor income, farm and nonfarm proprietors' income, rental income of individuals, dividend and interest income of individuals, and transfer payments (e.g., Social Security benefits, direct-relief payments, and veterans' benefits). From this total are subtracted contributions to social insurance programs.
<USE>
Used to measure trends in the spending power of individuals and to predict future consumer spending.
<PUBLISHER>
U.S. Department of Commerce, Bureau of Economic Analysis
<ANNOUNCED IN>
Survey of Current Business
<ANNOUNCEMENT FREQUENCY>
Monthly
<CUMULATIONS>
TABLES

Man Han	Latest month, $
Moody's Mun	Latest year, $ by states
Moody's Mun	Latest year, $ per capita
BCD	Monthly and yearly, cum, $
Bus Stats	Monthly and yearly, cum, $
EI	Monthly and yearly, cum, $
SCB	Monthly and yearly, cum, $
FR Bull	Quarterly and yearly, cum, $
S&P Stats	Quarterly and yearly, cum, $
Govt Fin	Yearly, cum, $
Hist Stats	Yearly, cum, $
Stat Abstr	Yearly, cum, $

GRAPHS

BCD	Yearly, cum, $
EI	Yearly, cum, $
Mo Econ Ind	Yearly, cum, $

PROJECTIONS

Value Line	Quarterly and yearly, $

<MORE INFORMATION>
  D. Creamer, Personal Income During Business Cycles, Princeton University Press, Princeton, N.J., 1956.
  Joint Economic Committee, 1980 Supplement to Economic Indicators, Historical and Descriptive Background, USGPO, Washington, D.C., 1980.
  Richard M. Snyder, Measuring Business Changes, Wiley, 1955, p. 18 ff.

John Kirk, "Economic Indicators: The How and the Why," Banking, 27-28 (Aug. 1964).

Speculation Index
<DESCRIPTION>
A measure of the amount of speculative stock buying, expressed in the form of a ratio of the American Stock Exchange prices to the New York Stock Exchange prices. Because the American Stock Exchange is loaded with lower-priced issues (associated with risk and speculation), speculators are expected to favor that exchange. More staid and institutional investors looking for long-term investments are expected to favor the offerings on the NYSE. Price is used as an indicator of market activity, and a rise in activity on the American Stock Exchange relative to the activity of the NYSE is taken to indicate an increase in speculation.
<DERIVATION>
The average price of all of the stocks listed on the American Stock Exchange is divided by the average price of all of the stocks listed on the New York Stock Exchange on a monthly basis.
<USE>
To determine the speculative activity of the market and, therefore, the stability of the market in the near to intermediate term.
<PUBLISHER>
Media General Financial Services, Inc.
<ANNOUNCED IN>
Media General Financial Weekly
<ANNOUNCEMENT FREQUENCY>
Monthly
<CUMULATIONS>
GRAPHS
MG Fin Wkly Monthly, cum, index nos.
<MORE INFORMATION>
  J. B. Cohen, E. D. Zinbarg, and Arthur Zeikel, Investment Analysis and Portfolio Management, Irwin, Homewood, Ill., 1977.
  Directory of Indicators, Indicator Digest, Palisades Park, N.J., 1983.
  William Gordon, The Stock Market Indicators as a Guide to Market Timing, Investors Press, Palisades Park, N. J., 1968, pp. 133-139.

Spot Market Price Index [See Industrial Raw Materials Price Index]

Standard & Poor's 20 Transportation Index
<DESCRIPTION>
A measure of the change in aggregate market value of 20 common stocks of corporations in the transportation industry, primarily (but not entirely) stocks traded on the New York Stock Exchange.

<DERIVATION>
The Standard & Poor's Corporation selects 20 stocks of transportation companies and calculates their aggregate market value hourly. The aggregate market value is calculated by multiplying the price per share of each selected stock by the number of shares listed for that stock; these values are then totalled for all of the selected stocks, and the sum divided by the market value on a base date (1941-1943). Appropriate adjustments are made for stock dividends, splits, consolidations, and similar events to ensure that the index will reflect only price movements.
<USE>
Used as a leading indicator because it anticipates business-cycle rises and declines.
<PUBLISHER>
Standard & Poor's Corporation
<ANNOUNCED IN>
Standard & Poor's Outlook
<ANNOUNCEMENT FREQUENCY>
Daily
<CUMULATIONS>
TABLES

Bus Stats   Monthly and yearly, cum, index nos.
SCB   Monthly and yearly, cum, index nos.
S&P Stock   Weekly, cum, index nos.
S&P Outlook   Weekly high-low-close, cum, index nos.
<MORE INFORMATION>
  "Market Guides," Barron's, 9+ (Sept. 26, 1966).

Standard & Poor's 40 Financial Index

<DESCRIPTION>
A measure of the change in aggregate market value of 40 common stocks of financial institutions, primarily (but not entirely) stocks traded on the New York Stock Exchange.
<DERIVATION>
The Standard & Poor's Corporation selects 40 stocks of financial institutions and calculates their aggregate market value hourly. The aggregate market value is calculated by multiplying the price per share of each selected stock by the number of shares listed for that stock; these values are then totalled for all of the selected stocks, and the sum divided by the market value on a base date (1941-1943). Appropriate adjustments are made for stock dividends, splits, consolidations, and similar events to ensure that the index will reflect only price movements.
<USE>
Used as a leading indicator because it anticipates business-cycle rises and declines.
<PUBLISHER>
Standard & Poor's Corporation
<ANNOUNCED IN>
Standard & Poor's Outlook
<ANNOUNCEMENT FREQUENCY>
Daily

<CUMULATIONS>
TABLES
Bus Stats   Monthly and yearly, cum, index nos.
SCB   Monthly and yearly, cum, index nos.
S&P Stock   Weekly, cum, index nos.
S&P Outlook Weekly high-low-close, cum, index nos.
<MORE INFORMATION>
  "Market Guides," Barron's, 9+ (Sept. 26, 1966).

Standard & Poor's 40 Utility Index

<DESCRIPTION>
A measure of the change in aggregate market value of 40
common stocks of private utilities, primarily (but not
entirely) stocks traded on the New York Stock Exchange.
<DERIVATION>
The Standard & Poor's Corporation selects 40 stocks of
private utilities and calculates their aggregate market value
hourly. The aggregate market value is calculated by
multiplying the price per share of each selected stock by the
number of shares listed for that stock; these values are then
totalled for all of the selected stocks, and the sum divided
by the market value on a base date (1941-1943). Appropriate
adjustments are made for stock dividends, splits,
consolidations, and similar events to ensure that the index
will reflect only price movements.
<USE>
Used as a leading indicator because it anticipates
business-cycle rises and declines.
<PUBLISHER>
Standard & Poor's Corporation
<ANNOUNCED IN>
Standard & Poor's Outlook
<ANNOUNCEMENT FREQUENCY>
Daily
<CUMULATIONS>
TABLES
Bus Stats   Monthly and yearly, cum, index nos.
SCB   Monthly and yearly, cum, index nos.
S&P Stock   Weekly, cum, index nos.
S&P Outlook Weekly high-low-close, cum, index nos.
<MORE INFORMATION>
  "Market Guides," Barron's, 9+ (Sept. 26, 1966).

Standard & Poor's 400 Industrial Index

<DESCRIPTION>
A measure of the change in aggregate market value of 400
common stocks of industrial corporations, primarily (but not
entirely) stocks traded on the New York Stock Exchange.
<DERIVATION>
The Standard & Poor's Corporation selects 400 stocks of
industrial companies and calculates their aggregate market
value hourly. The aggregate market value is calculated by
multiplying the price per share of each selected stock by the
number of shares listed for that stock; these values are then

totalled for all of the selected stocks, and the sum divided
by the market value on a base date (1941-1943). Appropriate
adjustments are made for stock dividends, splits,
consolidations, and similar events to ensure that the index
will reflect only price movements.
<USE>
Used as a leading indicator because it anticipates
business-cycle rises and declines.
<PUBLISHER>
Standard & Poor's Corporation
<ANNOUNCED IN>
Standard & Poor's Outlook
<ANNOUNCEMENT FREQUENCY>
Daily
<CUMULATIONS>
TABLES
Barron's   Daily, index nos.
S&P Outlook   Daily and weekly, cum, index nos.
WSJ   Latest and year ago, index nos.
Inc   Latest period, % change
WSJ   Latest and year ago, % change
S&P Outlook   Daily and weekly, cum, % change
S&P Corp Rec   Hourly, daily, weekly, yearly, index nos.
Bus Stats   Monthly and yearly, cum, index nos.
SCB   Monthly and yearly, cum, index nos.
S&P Stats   Daily, monthly, yearly, cum, index nos.
GRAPHS
Inc   Monthly, cum, % change
<MORE INFORMATION>
  "Market Guides," Barron's, 9+ (Sept. 26, 1966).

Standard & Poor's 500 [See Standard & Poor's Composite
Index]

Standard & Poor's 500 Dividend-Price Ratio
<DESCRIPTION>
A comparison of the cash dividends earned by 500 selected
stocks with their market value at the end of a quarter.
<DERIVATION>
Five hundred stocks are selected by Standard & Poor. The
cash dividends they pay are totalled at the end of a quarter,
and this sum is divided by the aggregate market value of
those stocks at the end of the same quarter. Annual data are
averages of the four calculated quarterly ratios.
<USE>
Used to forecast future movements of the market. Higher
ratios are taken as an indication that the market is at or
near a peak; lower ratios are taken to indicate that the
market is due for an upswing.
<PUBLISHER>
Standard & Poor's Corporation
<ANNOUNCED IN>
Standard & Poor's Outlook
<ANNOUNCEMENT FREQUENCY>
Quarterly

<CUMULATIONS>
TABLES
EI   Weekly, monthly, yearly, cum, %
S&P Stats   Weekly, monthly, yearly, cum, %
FR Bull   Monthly, weekly, yearly, %
Bus Stats   Monthly and yearly, cum %
SCB   Monthly and yearly, cum, %
<MORE INFORMATION>
   Michael Hayes, The Dow Jones - Irwin Guide to Stock Market
Cycles, Dow Jones - Irwin, Homewood, Ill., 1977, pp. 56-57.

Standard & Poor's 500 Price-Earnings Ratio
<DESCRIPTION>
A measure of the value of the stocks listed in the Standard &
Poor's 500; more accurately, a measure of the speculative
nature of the purchases of those stocks.
<DERIVATION>
Five hundred companies are selected by Standard & Poor. The
earnings of those companies each quarter are summed and
divided by the summed market value of their common stocks at
the end of that quarter. The result is referred to as the
Standard & Poor Price-Earnings Ratio. Annual values are
derived by averaging the four quarterly values for each year.
<USE>
As a gage of speculative activity in the market and to
assess turning points of the market in the near term. The
higher the ratio, the more speculative the market is
considered to be because increased investment is not being
reflected in increased returns (earnings) from the
corporations' performances. Conversely, a lower ratio
indicates better value of purchases in the market.
<PUBLISHER>
Standard & Poor's Corporation
<ANNOUNCED IN>
Standard & Poor's Outlook
<ANNOUNCEMENT FREQUENCY>
Quarterly
<CUMULATIONS>
TABLES
MG Fin Wkly   Latest and year ago, nos.
EI   Monthly, weekly, yearly, cum, nos.
S&P Stats   Quarterly and yearly, cum, nos.
GRAPHS
MG Fin Wkly   Monthly, cum, nos.
EI   Yearly, cum, nos.
S&P Outlook   Yearly, cum, nos.

Standard & Poor's Composite Index [Frequently referred to
as the S&P 500]
<DESCRIPTION>
A measure of the change in aggregate market value of 500
common stocks, primarily (but not entirely) stocks traded on
the New York Stock Exchange, and for four subgroups:
industrial, financial, utility, and transportation stocks.

<DERIVATION>
The Standard & Poor's Corporation selects 500 stocks
(weighted in proportion to the total market value of stock
outstanding) and calculates their aggregate market value
hourly. The aggregate market value is calculated by
multiplying the price per share of each selected stock by the
number of shares listed for that stock; these values are then
totalled for all of the selected stocks, and the sum divided
by the market value on a base date (1941-1943). Appropriate
adjustments are made for stock dividends, splits,
consolidations, and similar events to ensure that the index
will reflect only price movements.
<USE>
Used as one of the components of the Leading Indicators
Composite Index and as a leading indicator because it
anticipates business cycle rises and declines.
<PUBLISHER>
Standard & Poor's Corporation
<ANNOUNCED IN>
Standard & Poor's Outlook
<ANNOUNCEMENT FREQUENCY>
Daily
<CUMULATIONS>
TABLES

Barron's	Daily, cum, index nos.
NYT	Daily, index nos.
WSJ	Daily, index nos.
S&P Stats	Daily, monthly, and yearly, cum, index nos.
S&P Outlook	Daily and weekly, cum, index nos.
S&P Outlook	Daily and weekly, cum, % change
WSJ	Latest and year ago, % change
S&P Corp Rec	Latest hourly and weekly, index nos.
Value Line	Latest week, index nos.
Value Line	Latest week, % change
Man Han	Latest week, index nos.
Man Han	Latest week, % change
EI	Monthly and yearly, cum, index nos.
SCB	Monthly and yearly, cum, index nos.
NYT	Weekly, high-lows, index nos.
S&P Stock	Yearly, cum, index nos.
Stat Abstr	Yearly, cum, index nos.

GRAPHS

NYT	Monthly, high-lows, index nos.
S&P Outlook	Monthly, cum, index nos.

<MORE INFORMATION>
   Keith V. Smith, "Stock Price and Economic Indexes for
Generating Efficient Portfolios," Journal of Business,
326-336 (July 1969).
   "Market Guides," Barron's, 9+ (Sept. 26, 1966).
   S. N. Levine (Ed.), Financial Analyst's Handbook, Vol. I,
Portfolio Management, Dow Jones - Irwin, Homewood, Ill.,
1975.
   Martin J. Pring, Technical Analysis Explained, An
Illustrated Guide for the Investor, McGraw-Hill, New York,
1980, p. 112.
   G. H. Moore and J. Shiskin, "Why the Leading Indicators
Really Do Lead," Across the Board, 71-75 (May 1978).

"Official Indicators: What Are They? Can They Predict the Future?" U.S. News and World Report, 66-67 (Aug. 16, 1976).

Standard & Poor's Municipal Bond Yields
<DESCRIPTION>
An arithmetic average of yields to maturity of 15 high-grade domestic municipal bonds.
<DERIVATION>
The Wednesday closing prices of 15 selected municipal bonds are noted and their yields to maturity averaged. Monthly figures are arithmetic averages of the weekly values for the months.
<USE>
Used as an indicator of the general trend of interest-rate changes and to compute price data for municipal bonds.
<PUBLISHER>
Standard & Poor's Corporation
<ANNOUNCED IN>
Standard & Poor's Outlook
<ANNOUNCEMENT FREQUENCY>
Weekly
<CUMULATIONS>
TABLES

BW	Latest week and year ago, %
S&P Cred Wk	Latest week, %
EI	Monthly, weekly, yearly, cum, %
SCB	Monthly and yearly, cum, %
S&P Corp Rec	Weekly, cum, %
S&P Outlook	Weekly, cum, %
S&P Stats	Weekly, cum, %

GRAPHS

S&P Cred Wk	Yearly, cum, %

Standard & Poor's Price-Earnings Ratio [See Standard & Poor's 500 Price-Earnings Ratio]

Standard & Poor's Stock Yields [See Standard & Poor's 500 Dividend-Price Ratio]

Status of ·the Labor Force [See Nonagricultural Employment; Total Unemployment; Unemployment Rate, Total; and Unemployment Insurance Programs, Initial Claims]

Steel Production
<DESCRIPTION>
Total number of tons of raw steel produced in the U.S. each week.
<DERIVATION>
The American Iron and Steel Institute receives production data from virtually all makers of ingots and steel for castings in the nation. Raw steel is defined as steel in the

first solid state after melting, suitable for further
processing or sale. In addition to ingots and castings, it
includes strand or pressure-cast blooms, billets, slabs, and
other product forms. The reported tonnages are totalled.
<USE>
Used as a gage of future activity of the heavy industry and
construction sectors of the economy.
<PUBLISHER>
American Iron and Steel Institute
<ANNOUNCED IN>
American Iron and Steel Institute news release
<ANNOUNCEMENT FREQUENCY>
Weekly
<CUMULATIONS>
TABLES

Barron's	Latest week and year ago, tons
Ind W	Latest week and year ago, tons
NYT	Latest week and year ago, tons
MG Fin Wkly	Latest week and year ago, tons
BW	Latest week and month and year ago, tons
Bus Stats	Monthly and yearly, cum, tons
S&P Stats	Monthly and yearly, cum, tons
SCB	Monthly and yearly, cum, tons
ASR (AISI)	Monthly and yearly, cum, tons
Hist Stats	Yearly, cum, tons
Min Ybk	Yearly, cum, tons
Pred Base	Yearly, cum, tons
Pred Fore	Yearly, cum, tons
Stat Abstr	Yearly, cum, tons

GRAPHS

Ind W	Latest week and year ago, tons

PROJECTIONS

Pred Fore	Yearly, tons

<MORE INFORMATION>
  Richard M. Snyder, Measuring Business Changes, Wiley, New
York, 1955, pp. 193-194.
  "The Rage for Faster Forecasts," Business Week, Oct. 18,
1982, pp. 135-138.

Stock Indexes [See Media General Stock Indexes]

Superbowl Predictor [See Appendix A. Nonquantitative
Indicators]

Surly Waiter Index [See Appendix A. Nonquantitative
Indicators]

Sutro Indicator
<DESCRIPTION>
An early warning signal of changes in the trend of the
economy based on the relative productions of consumer and
capital goods.

<DERIVATION>
Because the production of consumer goods leads that of capital goods, a ratio of the two respective industrial-production indexes (indexed to 100 for 1967) is taken to reflect the momentum of the economy, and the direction of the ratio is taken to indicate the stage of the business cycle. A one-month or three-month moving average of the ratio is used.
<USE>
Used as a long-lead warning of changes in economic and stock-market trends and to measure the shifts in production between the consumer- and capital-goods sectors within any one cycle. It typically leads the general economy by nearly two years at peaks and close to one year at troughs.
<PUBLISHER>
E. W. Axe & Co.
<ANNOUNCED IN>
Personal memos
<ANNOUNCEMENT FREQUENCY>
Monthly
<CUMULATIONS>
None
<MORE INFORMATION>
   "Extra, Extra!" MONY's Pension Investment Facilities, June 1983, pp. 2-3.

T

Technology Stock Index [See Hambrecht and Quist Technology Stock Index]

Ten-Day Auto Sales [See Automobile Sales]

Three-Month Treasury Bills
<DESCRIPTION>
An average interest rate expressed on a bank discount basis computed for issuances of U.S. securities auctioned weekly.
<DERIVATION>
Bids are accepted by the Treasury, and securities are auctioned weekly, usually on Tuesdays. Payment for the securities must accompany the bids; the securities are discounted (i.e., the interest for the full term is paid immediately; the principle is repaid at maturity). The computed average is based on varying prices at which portions of the issue are awarded to the highest bidders. Monthly cumulations are simple averages of the auction average rates for the issues sold during the month.
<USE>
Used to set the current interest rate for many money-market and other financial instruments.
<PUBLISHER>
Board of Governors of the Federal Reserve System
<ANNOUNCED IN>
Federal Reserve press release: Selected Interest Rates, Statistical Release G.13 (415)
<ANNOUNCEMENT FREQUENCY>
Weekly
<CUMULATIONS>
TABLES

MG Fin Wkly	Latest week, %
WSJ	Latest week and week ago, %
Wkly Econ	Latest week and month, %
Barron's	Latest two weeks and year ago, %
Ind W	Latest two weeks and year ago, %
FR Bull	Monthly and quarterly, cum, %
Bus Stats	Monthly and yearly, cum, %

EI	Monthly and yearly, cum, %
Econ Rept	Monthly and yearly, cum, %
FHLBBJ	Monthly and yearly, cum, %
S&P Stats	Monthly and yearly, cum, %
SCB	Monthly and yearly, cum, %
Moody's B&F	Quarterly and yearly, cum, %

GRAPHS

MG Fin Wkly	Monthly, cum, %
EI	Yearly, cum, %
Moody's Bond	Yearly, cum, %

PROJECTIONS

Wkly Econ	Monthly, %

<MORE INFORMATION>

Joint Economic Committee, 1980 Supplement to Economic Indicators, Historical and Descriptive Background, USGPO, Washington, D.C., 1980.

G. Munn, Encyclopedia of Banking and Finance, 8th ed., Bankers Publishing, 1983.

Total Unemployment

<DESCRIPTION>

An estimate of the number of unemployed persons in the U.S. during a given month.

<DERIVATION>

The total civilian labor force is estimated from decennial census figures and more-frequent benchmarks. Unemployment among this population is estimated from monthly surveys of a sample that includes 47,000 households nationwide. Employment of the members of the households is determined for the week including the twelfth day of the month. To be counted as unemployed, a person has to be 16 years of age or older and actively seeking work or awaiting recall to a position from which he or she had been laid off. The surveyed population includes the military and inmates of penal, welfare, and health institutions. All data are seasonally adjusted. The estimated total unemployment is then calculated from the perceived unemployment rate and the size of the labor force.

<USE>

Used as a major and highly current indicator of the general state of the U.S. economy, of the present activity in the manufacturing and commercial sectors of the economy, and as a predictor of the near-to-midterm sales of consumer goods and availability of money for saving. Total unemployment is inversely related to general business fluctuations and is considered a leading indicator at peaks and a lagging indicator at troughs.

<PUBLISHER>

U.S. Department of Labor

<ANNOUNCED IN>

Employment and Earnings

<ANNOUNCEMENT FREQUENCY>

Monthly

<CUMULATIONS>

TABLES

Barron's	Latest month and year ago, nos.
Ind W	Latest month and year ago, nos.

NYT	Latest quarter and year ago, nos.
BCD	Monthly, cum, nos.
BNA	Monthly, cum, nos.
Unemp Stats	Monthly, cum, nos.
Bus Stats	Monthly and yearly, cum, nos.
EI	Monthly and yearly, cum, nos.
Econ Rept Pr	Monthly and yearly, cum, nos.
Emp & Earn	Monthly and yearly, cum, nos.
FR Bull	Monthly and yearly, cum, nos.
MLR	Monthly and yearly, cum, nos.
SCB	Monthly and yearly, cum, nos.
SS Bull	Monthly and yearly, cum, nos.
Int Econ Ind	Quarterly and yearly, cum, nos.
Emp & Train	Yearly, cum, nos.
Hbk Lbr Stat	Yearly, cum, nos.
Hist Stats	Yearly, cum, nos.
Stat Abstr	Yearly, cum, nos.
GRAPHS	
BCD	Yearly, cum, nos.

<MORE INFORMATION>
   Counting the Labor Force, National Commission on Employment and Unemployment Statistics, Washington, D.C., 1978.
   Julius Shiskin, "Employment and Unemployment: The Doughnut or the Hole," Monthly Labor Review, 3-10 (Feb. 1976).
   Bureau of Labor Statistics, How the Government Measures Unemployment, Rept. 505, U.S. Department of Labor, Washington, D.C., 1977.
   National Bureau of Economic Research, The Measurement and Bevavior of Unemployment, Princeton Univ. Press, Princeton, N.J., 1957.
   Julius Shiskin, Labor Force and Unemployment, BLS Rept. 486, U.S. Department of Labor, Washington, D.C., 1976.
   Seymour L. Wolfbein, Employment and Unemployment in the United States, Science Research Assoc., Chicago, 1964.
   John E. Bregger, "Unemployment Statistics and What They Mean," Monthly Labor Review (June 1971).
   Gloria P. Green, "Measuring Total and State Insured Unemployment," Monthly Labor Review (June 1971).
   Bureau of Labor Statistics, Workers, Jobs, and Statistics, Rept. 698, U.S. Department of Labor, Washington, D.C., 1983.

TRIN [See Short-Term Trading Index]

Truck and Bus Factory Sales
<DESCRIPTION>
Monthly sales and inventories of manufacturers of trucks and buses.
<DERIVATION>
The Motor Vehicles Manufacturers Association surveys the industry monthly. Some small producers are not included in the survey. The numbers of units sold that month and the inventory are reported. Sales include imports of U.S. manufacturers but not motor coaches. A unit may be either a complete vehicle or a chassis sold separately. Sales data are

grouped by gross vehicle weight. Data are seasonally adjusted by the U.S. Department of Commerce, Bureau of Economic Analysis.
<USE>
Used as an indicator of capital-goods investment and of the strength of the transportation sector of the economy.
<PUBLISHER>
Motor Vehicle Manufacturers Association of the U.S.
<ANNOUNCED IN>
Survey of Current Business
<ANNOUNCEMENT FREQUENCY>
Monthly
<CUMULATIONS>
TABLES
Bus Stats   Monthly and yearly, cum, units
SCB   Monthly and yearly, cum, units
MVMA   Yearly, cum, units
Stat Abstr   Yearly, cum, units
WMVD   Yearly, cum, units

U

Unemployment [See Total Unemployment; Unemployment Insurance Programs, Initial Claims; and Unemployment Rate, Total]

Unemployment Insurance Programs, Initial Claims

<DESCRIPTION>
A measure of unemployment among workers covered by the employment-security programs of the Employment and Training Administration (ETA) of the Department of Labor. The figures give the number of certified workers filing claims for having been totally or partially unemployed during the previous week and those requesting a determination of eligibility. These data cover beneficiaries of state programs, the program of federal-state extended-unemployment compensation, the program for federal employees, the exserviceman's unemployment-compensation program, veteran's benefit programs, and temporary unemployment programs. Reported as the insured unemployment under state programs, initial claims under state programs, insured unemployment under all regular programs, and special unemployment benefit claims.

<DERIVATION>
Completed weeks of unemployment for which benefits are claimed are reported by the state employment security agencies and the Railroad Retirement Board to the ETA weekly. These figures are summed and seasonally adjusted. Initial claims (requests for a determination of eligibility) are also reported to and listed by the ETA, but they are not added into the tally of unemployed because they do not represent certified unemployed to whom benefits are paid. Monthly data are averages of the weekly data.

<USE>
Used as a major and highly current indicator of the general state of the U.S. economy, of the present activity in the manufacturing and commercial sectors of the economy, and as a predictor of the near-to-midterm sales of consumer goods and the availability of money for saving.

<PUBLISHER>
U.S. Department of Labor, Employment and Training Administration

<ANNOUNCED IN>
Unemployment Insurance Claims
<ANNOUNCEMENT FREQUENCY>
Weekly
<CUMULATIONS>
TABLES
BCD   Monthly, cum, nos.
Unemp Stats   Monthly, cum, nos.
Bus Stats   Monthly and yearly, cum, nos.
EI   Monthly and yearly, cum, nos.
Econ Rept Pr   Monthly and yearly, cum, nos.
SCB   Monthly and yearly, cum, nos.
SS Bull   Monthly and yearly, cum, nos.
Hist Stats   Yearly, cum, nos.
Stat Abstr   Yearly, cum, nos.
GRAPHS
BCD   Yearly, cum, nos.
<MORE INFORMATION>

Joint Economic Committee, 1980 Supplement to Economic Indicators, Historical and Descriptive Background, USGPO, Washington, D.C., 1980.

Bureau of Labor Statistics, How the Government Measures Unemployment, Rept. 505, U.S. Department of Labor, Washington, D.C., 1977.

National Bureau of Economic Research, The Measurement and Bevavior of Unemployment, Princeton Univ. Press, Princeton, N.J., 1957.

Julius Shiskin, Labor Force and Unemployment, BLS Rept. 486, U.S. Department of Labor, Washington, D.C., 1976.

Seymour L. Wolfbein, Employment and Unemployment in the United States, Science Research Assoc., Chicago, 1964.

John E. Bregger, "Unemployment Statistics and What They Mean," Monthly Labor Review (June 1971).

Gloria P. Green, "Measuring Total and State Insured Unemployment," Monthly Labor Review (June 1971).

Bureau of Labor Statistics, Workers, Jobs, and Statistics, Rept. 698, U.S. Department of Labor, Washington, D.C., 1983.

Unemployment Rate [See Unemployment Rate, Total]

Unemployment Rate, Total
<DESCRIPTION>
An estimate of the percentage of the U.S. workforce that is unemployed during a given month.
<DERIVATION>
The total civilian labor force is estimated from decennial census figures and more-frequent benchmarks. Unemployment among this population is estimated from monthly surveys of a sample that includes 47,000 households nationwide. Employment of the members of the households is determined for the week including the twelfth day of the month. To be counted as unemployed, a person has to be 16 years of age or older and actively seeking work or awaiting recall to a position from which he or she has been laid off. The surveyed population

includes the military and inmates of penal, welfare, and health institutions. All data are seasonally adjusted. The percentage of unemployment is then calculated from the survey results for the total population and for groups of the population according to sex, age, and race.

<USE>
Used as a major and highly current indicator of the general state of the U.S. economy, as an indicator of the present activity in the manufacturing and commercial sectors of the economy, and as a predictor of the near-to-midterm sales of consumer goods and availability of money for saving. The unemployment rate is inversely related to general business fluctuations.

<PUBLISHER>
U.S. Department of Labor
<ANNOUNCED IN>
Employment and Earnings
<ANNOUNCEMENT FREQUENCY>
Monthly
<CUMULATIONS>
TABLES

Man Han	Latest month, %
Stat Bull	Latest month, %
Barron's	Latest month and year ago, %
BW	Latest month and year ago, %
NYT	Latest month and year ago, %
Bus Stats	Monthly and yearly, cum, %
EI	Monthly and yearly, cum, %
FR Bull	Monthly and yearly, cum, %
S&P Stats	Monthly and yearly, cum, %
SCB	Monthly and yearly, cum, %
Pred Base	Yearly, cum, %
Pred Fore	Yearly, cum, %

GRAPHS

EI	Yearly, cum, %
Mo Econ Ind	Yearly, cum, %

PROJECTIONS

Stat Bull	Quarterly, %
S&P Outlook	Quarterly and yearly, % (irr)
Value Line	Quarterly and yearly, %
Bus Rev WF	Yearly, %
Pred Fore	Yearly, %

<MORE INFORMATION>
Counting the Labor Force, National Commission on Employment and Unemployment Statistics, Washington, D.C., 1978.

Julius Shiskin, "Employment and Unemployment: The Doughnut or the Hole," Monthly Labor Review, 3-10 (Feb. 1976).

Glen G. Cain, "The Unemployment Rate as an Economic Indicator," Monthly Labor Review, 24-35 (Mar. 1979).

Bureau of Labor Statistics, Workers, Jobs, and Statistics, Rept. 698, U.S. Department of Labor, Washington, D.C., 1983.

John E. Bregger, "Unemployment Statistics and What They Mean," Monthly Labor Review (June 1971).

Gloria P. Green, "Measuring Total and State Insured Unemployment," Monthly Labor Review (June 1971).

Bureau of Labor Statistics, How the Government Measures Unemployment, Rept. 505, U.S. Department of Labor, Washington, D.C., 1977.

National Bureau of Economic Research, The Measurement and Bevavior of Unemployment, Princeton Univ. Press, Princeton, N.J., 1957.

Julius Shiskin, Labor Force and Unemployment, BLS Rept. 486, U.S. Department of Labor, Washington, D.C., 1976.

Seymour L. Wolfbein, Employment and Unemployment in the United States, Science Research Assoc., Chicago, 1964.

Unfilled Orders [Also called Manufacturers' Unfilled Orders]
<DESCRIPTION>
An estimate of the orders placed with manufacturers of durable goods that remain unfilled at the end of a given month.
<DERIVATION>
Manufacturers of durable goods (items with a normal life expectancy of three years or more) are surveyed monthly and asked to report the sales value of orders for goods that have not been filled at the end of the month. Unfilled orders are defined as those that have not yet passed through the sales account. The value of any cancellations is to be deducted from the totals. Because some companies report only backlogs of unfilled orders and in order to maintain the distinction between orders and shipments, orders remaining unfilled at the end of the monthly reporting period are estimated directly and separately. Monthly estimates are derived by multiplying the previous month's estimate by the percentage change from the previous month to the current month for companies reporting in the current month. Values are benchmarked to a modified ratio of unfilled orders to shipments (the latter being annually benchmarked to the most recent level of the Annual Survey of Manufactures). The unfilled-orders data are seasonally adjusted. The totals are presented in current dollars.
<USE>
Used as a gage of the present and near-future state of the producer and consumer durable goods sectors of the economy.
<PUBLISHER>
U.S. Department of Commerce, Bureau of the Census
<ANNOUNCED IN>
Survey of Current Business
<ANNOUNCEMENT FREQUENCY>
Monthly
<CUMULATIONS>
TABLES

Barron's	Latest month and year ago, $
Bus Stats	Monthly and yearly, cum, $
EI	Monthly and yearly, cum, $
S&P Stats	Monthly and yearly, cum, $
SCB	Monthly and yearly, cum, $
BCD	Monthly, $

<MORE INFORMATION>
Joint Economic Committee, 1980 Supplement to Economic Indicators, Historical and Descriptive Background, USGPO, Washington, D.C., 1980.

United States International Transactions
<DESCRIPTION>
A summary of economic transactions between the residents of the U.S. and the residents of the rest of the world. These transactions are divided into current accounts and capital accounts. The current accounts include tabulations of merchandise imports and exports, investment receipts and payments, net military transactions, net travel and transportation receipts, the net of other services, and unilateral transfers (such as transfers, government grants, remittances, and pensions). The capital accounts are divided into the broad categories of U.S. assets abroad and foreign assets in the U.S. The U.S. assets abroad are subdivided into official reserves (gold, special drawing rights, convertible currencies, and the U.S. reserve position in the International Monetary Fund), other U.S. Government assets, and private assets. Foreign assets in the U.S. are subdivided into the assets of foreign official agencies and other foreign assets. Data on allocations of special drawing rights, the statistical discrepancy, and the value of the stock of U.S. official reserve assets at the end of the period are also included.
<DERIVATION>
Data for this indicator come from a broad range of sources. Data on merchandise imports and exports are received from the Bureau of the Census and are adjusted for coverage, valuation, and timing. U.S. companies with branches abroad provide quarterly reports of international transactions. Investments abroad and foreign investments in the U.S. are determined from benchmark surveys. The foreign transactions of U.S. Government agencies including grants, loans, purchases, and sales are directly reported. Reports are received from U.S. and foreign shipping lines and financial data from the Maritime Administration. U.S. travellers are surveyed about their expenditures abroad, and these data are compared with and supplemented by travel statistics from the Immigration and Naturalization Service. Reports on international claims and liabilities are received from the Treasury Department. All of these data are supplemented with data from questionnaires and government administrative data. The components of the data are seasonally adjusted if they display significant seasonal variation.
<USE>
Used to assess the international financial position of the United States and to compare that position with the economic strengths and weaknesses of other countries.
<PUBLISHER>
U.S. Department of Commerce, Bureau of Economic Analysis
<ANNOUNCED IN>
Survey of Current Business

<ANNOUNCEMENT FREQUENCY>
Quarterly
<CUMULATIONS>
TABLES
BCD   Quarterly, cum, $
EI   Quarterly and yearly, cum, $
Hist Stats   Yearly, cum, $
Stat Abstr   Yearly, cum, $
SCB   Quarterly and yearly, $
Bus Stat   Quarterly and yearly, $
GRAPHS
BCD   Yearly, cum, $
<MORE INFORMATION>
   Joint Economic Committee, 1980 Supplement to Economic
Indicators, Historical and Descriptive Background, USGPO,
Washington, D.C., 1980.

United States Merchandise Exports
<DESCRIPTION>
The dollar value of the goods exported from the U.S.,
reported on a free-alongside-ship basis. Three classes of
domestic exports of manufactured goods; crude materials and
fuels; and food, beverages, and tobacco are reported
separately and as a total. Total domestic and foreign (goods
imported into the U.S. and then exported) exports are also
reported.   A merchandise trade balance is calculated and
presented.
<DERIVATION>
Export statistics are obtained from the Shipper's Export
Declaration filed with U.S. Customs and forwarded by them to
the Bureau of the Census. Aggregate values of very-low-valued
shipments (e.g., $250 or less; limits vary with country of
destination)   are   estimated   with   factors   derived   from
statistical analyses of each country's importing history.
Low-valued shipments are sampled, and an estimate derived
from the results. All other shipments are considered
individually. Information on the export of military equipment
and supplies under the Military Assistance Program is
compiled from the records of the Department of Defense and is
adjusted to show the value at the U.S. port of exportation.
The data are adjusted for seasonal and working-day variation,
where appropriate.
<USE>
Used as an indicator of the movement of merchandise, a large
portion of the international payments comprising the balance
of payments.
<PUBLISHER>
U.S. Department of Commerce, Bureau of the Census
<ANNOUNCED IN>
United States Foreign Trade
<ANNOUNCEMENT FREQUENCY>
Monthly
<CUMULATIONS>
TABLES
BW   Latest month and year ago, $
NYT   Latest month and year ago, $

```
Highlights    Monthly, cum, $
SCB           Monthly, quarterly, and yearly, cum, $
EI            Monthly and yearly, cum, $
Exp Wkly      Monthly and yearly, cum, $
S&P Stats     Monthly and yearly, cum, $
Bus Stats     Quarterly and yearly, cum, $
Econ Rept Pr  Quarterly and yearly, cum, $
FR Bull       Quarterly and yearly, cum, $
Hist Stats    Yearly, cum, $
Pred Base     Yearly, cum, $
Pred Fore     Yearly, cum, $
Stat Abstr    Yearly, cum, $
PROJECTIONS
Value Line    Quarterly and yearly, % change
Pred Fore     Yearly, $
```
<MORE INFORMATION>
   Joint Economic Committee, 1980 Supplement to Economic
Indicators, Historical and Descriptive Background, USGPO,
Washington, D.C., 1980.
   Survey of Current Business, USGPO, Washington, D.C. (June
1978).
   John Kirk, "Economic Indicators: The How and the Why,"
Banking, 25-26 (July 1964).

United States Merchandise Imports
<DESCRIPTION>
The dollar value of the goods imported into the U.S.,
reported on a free-alongside-ship basis. Three classes of
domestic imports of manufactured goods; crude materials and
fuels; and food, beverages, and tobacco are reported
separately and as a total. A merchandise trade balance is
calculated and presented.
<DERIVATION>
Import statistics are obtained from the Import Entry Form
filed with U.S. Customs and forwarded by them to the Bureau
of the Census. Statistics covering low-valued imports are
estimated on the basis of a sample. Sampling procedures have
varied with time, value of import, and type of entry. The
data are adjusted for seasonal and working-day variation,
where appropriate.
<USE>
Used as an indicator of the movement of merchandise, a large
portion of the international payments comprising the balance
of payments.
<PUBLISHER>
U.S. Department of Commerce, Bureau of the Census
<ANNOUNCED IN>
United States Foreign Trade
<ANNOUNCEMENT FREQUENCY>
Monthly
<CUMULATIONS>
TABLES
```
BW            Latest month and year ago, $
NYT           Latest month and year ago, $
Highlights    Monthly, cum, $
```

```
EI           Quarterly and yearly, cum, $
Exp Wkly     Quarterly and yearly, cum, $
FR Bull      Quarterly and yearly, cum, $
S&P Stats    Quarterly and yearly, cum, $
SCB          Quarterly, monthly, and yearly, cum, $
Bus Stats    Quarterly and yearly, cum, $
Econ Rept Pr Quarterly and yearly, cum, $
Hist Stats   Yearly, cum, $
Stat Abstr   Yearly, cum, $
PROJECTIONS
Value Line   Quarterly and yearly, % change
```
<MORE INFORMATION>
Joint Economic Committee, 1980 Supplement to Economic Indicators, Historical and Descriptive Background, USGPO, Washington, D.C., 1980.
Survey of Current Business, USGPO, Washington, D.C. (June 1978).

U.S. News & World Report Weekly Index of Business Activity
<DESCRIPTION>
A weighted average of nine weekly measures of industrial production.
<DERIVATION>
Production figures for bituminous coal, crude petroleum, paperboard, steel ingots, carloadings, automobiles, trucks, electric power, and lumber are determined for the week and weights are selected based on national income figures. Each production value is seasonally adjusted. The carloadings value is periodically adjusted to reflect variation in boxcar capacity. The weighted values are then averaged.
<USE>
Designed to reflect weekly changes in business activity, particularly in the durable-goods sector of the economy as represented by the steel and automobile industries.
<PUBLISHER>
U.S. News & World Report
<ANNOUNCED IN>
U.S. News & World Report
<ANNOUNCEMENT FREQUENCY>
Weekly
<CUMULATIONS>
TABLES
US News   Latest week; week, month, and year ago; index nos.
GRAPHS
US News   Monthly, cum, index nos.

Utility Appropriations
<DESCRIPTION>
Estimated total appropriations and capital expenditures of investor-owned gas and electric utilities.
<DERIVATION>
Electric utility companies representing almost all of the plant investment and kilowatt-hour sales in the industry are

surveyed along with gas utilties representing more than half
of the revenues of such investor-owned utilities. Respondants
provide their opening backlog, appropriations, cancellations,
actual capital expenditures, and closing backlog. The data
are adjusted to reflect estimates for all investor-owned
electric and gas utilities. The data are presented before and
after seasonal adjustment. From these data, gross
appropriations, capital expenditures, and closing backlogs
are calculated for the two utilities separately and together.
<USE>
A leading indicator of future capital investment that is
extrapolated from the industry for which the data are derived
to other industries.
<PUBLISHER>
The Conference Board
<ANNOUNCED IN>
Utility Appropriations
<ANNOUNCEMENT FREQUENCY>
Quarterly
<CUMULATIONS>
TABLES
Util Approp   Quarterly, cum, $
GRAPHS
Util Approp   Quarterly and yearly, cum, $

V

Vacancy Rate, Prime Industrial Real Estate
<DESCRIPTION>
An estimate of the percentage of prime industrial buildings that are vacant.
<DERIVATION>
The Society of Industrial Realtors semiannually surveys its members in 76 industrial-market cities. The respondents rate the local vacancy situation (1) in six size categories based on square footage and (2) for prime high-technology property locations. Data are reported as the percentage of the total that is vacant. Prime industrial real estate is defined as that in the top 25% in desirability of the total, existing, industrial, general-use stock.
<USE>
Used as a leading indicator of future industrial activity.
<PUBLISHER>
Society of Industrial Realtors
<ANNOUNCED IN>
Industrial Real Estate Market Survey
<ANNOUNCEMENT FREQUENCY>
Semiannual
<CUMULATIONS>
TABLES
Ind W   Latest two periods and year ago, %
IREMS   Latest, %

Value Line Composite Average
<DESCRIPTION>
A geometric average of the prices of the stocks regularly reviewed in The Value Line Investment Survey indexed to a base value.
<DERIVATION>
Each market day, the closing price of each stock included in the survey is divided by the preceding day's close, with the preceding day set at an index with a base value of 100 for June 30, 1961. The resulting indices of change for that day are then geometrically averaged; that is to say, the N indices of change are multiplied together and the Nth root of

the product is taken. The preceding day's prices are adjusted
to reflect any stock splits or dividends, and the present
day's geometric average is then multiplied by the value of
the average for the preceding day to get the latest value. As
stocks are added to or dropped from the Survey, the average
is enlarged or decreased accordingly. The composite average
is broken down into major categories (industrials, utilities,
and rails) and into 146 subgroups.
<USE>
Used to estimate the price strength of a particular stock
relative to the overall performance of the market and the
relative price strength of an industry.
<PUBLISHER>
Value Line, Inc.
<ANNOUNCED IN>
Value Line Investment Survey
<ANNOUNCEMENT FREQUENCY>
Daily
<CUMULATIONS>
TABLES
Barron's   Daily, cum, index nos.
Value Line   Daily, cum, index nos.
Value Line   Daily, cum, % change
WSJ   Latest and year ago, index nos.
WSJ   Latest and year ago, % change
GRAPHS
Value Line   Yearly, cum, index nos.
<MORE INFORMATION>
   Arnold Bernhard, Value Line Methods of Evaluating Common
Stocks, Building and Maintaining a Portfolio, Arnold Bernhard
& Co., New York, 1979.
   "Market Guides," Barron's, 9+ (Sept. 26, 1966).

**Vendor Performance, Companies Reporting Slower
Deliveries**
<DESCRIPTION>
The percentage of Greater Chicago purchasing agents who are
experiencing slower deliveries in the current month than they
did in the previous month.
<DERIVATION>
Of the 1000 members of the Purchasing Management Association
of Chicago, 200 are surveyed monthly. These 200 are selected
from 15 types of industry in proportion to the size of the
local industry. They are asked to report whether deliveries
are faster than the previous month, the same, or slower. The
percentage of respondents reporting in each category is
calculated and tabulated.
<USE>
Used as one of the components of the Leading Indicators
Composite Index and as an indicator of the volume of business
being handled by the suppliers of the reporting agents.
<PUBLISHER>
Purchasing Management Association of Chicago
<ANNOUNCED IN>
Chicago Report

<ANNOUNCEMENT FREQUENCY>
Monthly
<CUMULATIONS>
TABLES
Stat Bull   Quarterly and year ago, % change
BCD   Monthly, cum, % change
S&P Stats   Monthly and yearly, cum, % change
GRAPHS
BCD   Yearly, cum, % change
<MORE INFORMATION>
  "Official Indicators: What Are They? Can They Predict the
Future?" U.S. News and World Report, 66-67 (Aug. 16, 1976).

Volume Momentum [See American Stock Exchange Volume
Momentum and New York Stock Exchange Volume Momentum]

W

Wharton Measures of Capacity Utilization

<DESCRIPTION>
Estimates of the percentage of use of plant and equipment in the manufacturing, mining, and utility industries.

<DERIVATION>
The production indexes published by the Federal Reserve System (see the entry Industrial Production, Major Market Groups and Selected Manufactures) of about ninety industries are inspected to determine the periods of peak output. A capacity utilization rate of 100% is assigned these peak outputs. Potential output is defined with a straight line from peak to peak. Beyond the peaks, the line is extrapolated with a constant slope. The utilization rate is defined as the ratio of actual to potential output. Actual output is taken to be the quarterly averages of the monthly Federal Reserve System indexes of industrial production. The individual utilization rates are then aggregated into 27 categories with the Federal Reserve production-index weights. Further weighting is performed to produce aggregate rates for manufacturing durables and nondurables, total manufacturing, mining, utilities, and all of these industries together.

<USE>
Used as sensitive indicators of business-cycle activity and as signals of inflationary pressure in the economy; can be used as explanatory variables for investment and price determination in econometric forecasting models.

<PUBLISHER>
Wharton Econometric Forecasting Associates

<ANNOUNCED IN>
Quarterly Model Outlook

<ANNOUNCEMENT FREQUENCY>
Wharton Econometric Forecasting Associates

<CUMULATIONS>
TABLES
Q Mod Outlk   Quarterly, cum, %

<MORE INFORMATION>
  The Wharton Index of Capacity Utilization, Economics Research Unit,   University of Pennsylvania, Philadelphia, Penn., 1966.

"The Wharton Indexes of Capacity Utilization: A Ten Year Perspective," Proceedings of the American Statistical Association, 1973.

Wholesale Trade
<DESCRIPTION>
Estimates of wholesale sales (after deducting returns, allowances, discounts, and services to customers) by and inventories (at cost) owned by and available for sale from merchant wholesalers.
<DERIVATION>
A sample of merchant wholesalers representing all kinds of wholesale-trade businesses is surveyed each month. The respondents provide dollar estimates of their sales and inventories. The sales and inventory data are adjusted for seasonal variation, and the sales data are also adjusted for trading-day variation.
<USE>
Used by business, industry, and government to assess the aggregate performance of American business because the data reflect the level of economic activity at an intermediate stage of the distributive process. The data are also used in determining the gross national product.
<PUBLISHER>
U.S. Department of Commerce, Bureau of the Census
<ANNOUNCED IN>
Current Business Reports
<ANNOUNCEMENT FREQUENCY>
Monthly
<CUMULATIONS>
TABLES
Bus Stats   Monthly and yearly, cum, $
EI   Monthly and yearly, cum, $
Mo Whol   Monthly and yearly, cum, $
SCB   Monthly and yearly, cum, $
Stat Abstr   Yearly, cum, $
<MORE INFORMATION>
   Joint Economic Committee, 1980 Supplement to Economic Indicators, Historical and Descriptive Background, USGPO, Washington, D.C., 1980.
   Bureau of the Census, Revised Monthly Retail Sales and Inventories: January 1967-December 1979, Department of Commerce, Washington, D.C., 1980.

Wilshire 5000 Equity Index
<DESCRIPTION>
The total dollar value in billions of dollars of all actively traded common stocks in the U.S.
<DERIVATION>
The price per share of each stock is multiplied by the number of shares listed to give the market value of that stock. The market values of all stocks are then summed, and the total is divided by the market value on the base date of Dec. 31, 1980. This quotient is then multiplied by the base value of

the index. Nonprice effects are eliminated by adjustments to the base-date market value. Monthly values are averages of daily values. The index is more volatile than other averages, such as the Dow Jones, because it includes smaller companies that are more susceptible to changes in valuation. Four other indexes are also derived from the Wilshire data base: their Capital Weighted Price Index, Equal Weighted Price Index, Capital Weighted Total Return Index, and Equal Weighted Total Return Index.

<USE>
Used as a measure of the value of the U.S. equity marketplace, to measure portfolio performance, and to calculate the net increase or decrease in the value of the marketplace.

<PUBLISHER>
Wilshire Associates

<ANNOUNCED IN>
Wilshire 5000 Equity Index

<ANNOUNCEMENT FREQUENCY>
Daily

<CUMULATIONS>
TABLES

Barron's	Latest month and week, year ago, $
Barron's	Latest month and week, year ago, % change
WSJ	Daily and year ago, $
WSJ	Daily and year ago, % change
Forbes	Latest month and year ago, % change

GRAPHS

Forbes	Monthly and yearly, cum, $

<MORE INFORMATION>
"The Least-Heralded Bull Market in History," Forbes, 37-38 (Oct. 13, 1980).

Workweek [See Workweek, Average Manufacturing]

Workweek, Average Manufacturing [Also called Average Manufacturing Workweek]
<DESCRIPTION>
An estimation of the average number of hours each production worker in manufacturing industries worked during the given week.

<DERIVATION>
The Bureau of Labor Statistics collects employment figures each month from a sample of employers for a specific pay period. The total hours of work paid for by each industry is divided by the number of manufacturing and related workers for that industry. The resulting values are then seasonally adjusted.

<USE>
Used as one of the components of the Leading Indicators Composite Index. The number of hours worked is also used to indicate future employment levels. After a recession, a rise in the number of hours worked indicates increased business activity and often precedes a rise in the number of employed

persons. During a peak in the business cycle, a drop in the number of hours worked indicates a possible slowdown in the economy.

\<PUBLISHER\>
U.S. Department of Labor, Bureau of Labor Statistics
\<ANNOUNCED IN\>
Employment and Earnings
\<ANNOUNCEMENT FREQUENCY\>
Monthly
\<CUMULATIONS\>
TABLES

Ind W	Latest two months and year ago, hr
Stat Bull	Latest and year ago, change in hr
BCD	Monthly, cum, hr
Bus Stats	Monthly and yearly, cum, hr
S&P Stats	Monthly and yearly, cum, hr
SCB	Monthly and yearly, cum, hr
Emp & Earn	Monthly and yearly, cum, hr
Pred Base	Yearly, cum, hr
Pred Fore	Yearly, cum, hr
Hbk Lbr Stat	Yearly, cum, hr
Stat Abstr	Yearly, cum, hr

GRAPHS

BCD	Yearly, cum, hr

PROJECTIONS

Pred Fore	Yearly, hr

\<MORE INFORMATION\>
Abraham Bluestone, "Overtime Hours as an Economic Indicator," Monthly Labor Review, 1024-1028 (Sept. 1956).

G. H. Moore and J. Shiskin, "Why the Leading Indicators Really Do Lead," Across the Board, 71-75 (May 1978).

Hazel M. Willacy, "Changes in Factory Workweek as an Economic Indicator," Monthly Labor Review, 25-32 (Oct. 1970).

R. C. Mendelssohn, "Three BLS Series as Business Cycle Turn Signals," Monthly Labor Review (Sept. 1959).

Gerhard Bry, The Average Workweek as an Economic Indicator, National Bureau of Economic Research Occasional Paper 69, New York, 1959.

Bureau of Labor Statistics, A Guide to Seasonal Adjustment of Labor Force Data, Bull. 2114, U.S. Department of Labor, Washington, D.C., 1982.

Bureau of Labor Statistics and Bureau of the Census, Concepts and Methods Used in Labor Force Statistics Derived from the Current Population Survey, BLS Rept. 463 and Current Pop. Rept. (Ser. P-23) 62, U.S. Department of Labor and U.S. Department of Commerce, Washington, D.C., 1976.

Bureau of Labor Statistics, Workers, Jobs, and Statistics, Rept. 698, U.S. Department of Labor, Washington, D.C., 1983.

APPENDIX A
NONQUANTITATIVE
INDICATORS

Bad Guess Theorem
<DESCRIPTION>
A nonquantitative predictor of stock market trends based on the inverse of the sentiments expressed by the advisory services.
<DERIVATION>
The sentiments of the leading investment-advisory services are surveyed by the user. A cynical attitude towards those advisory services is adopted, and an investment strategy opposite to that recommended by the clear majority of the services is selected.
<USE>
Used as a contrary indicator of future market performance. When the ratio of bull-to-bear sentiments of that coterie of experts is more than two, the market is expected to go down. When the ratio of sentiments is less than two-to-one, the market is expected to rise.
<PUBLISHER>
None
<ANNOUNCED IN>
Nowhere
<ANNOUNCEMENT FREQUENCY>
None
<CUMULATIONS>
None
<MORE INFORMATION>
James Russell, "Surly Waiters and Other Stock Predictors," Miami Herald, 1F ff. (Dec. 20, 1982).

Brokerage House Rule
<DESCRIPTION>
A nonquantitative and irreproducible predictor of near-term stock-market trends.
<DERIVATION>
A cynical attitude about the forecasting and planning abilities of brokerage firms is adopted by the user. Advertising by those firms for sales trainees, contracts awarded by those firms for remodelling or expansion of their

physical plants, and expansions of the labor forces of those firms are surveyed. If any of these conditions are noted, preparations are made for a sharp decline in the market.
<USE>
Used as a contrary indicator of the stock market's future performance.
<PUBLISHER>
None
<ANNOUNCED IN>
Nowhere
<ANNOUNCEMENT FREQUENCY>
None
<CUMULATIONS>
None
<MORE INFORMATION>
James Russell, "Surly Waiters and Other Stock Predictors," Miami Herald, 1F ff. (Dec. 20, 1982).

Drinking Couple Count
<DESCRIPTION>
A nonquantitative and irreproducible descriptor of current stock-market conditions and a predictor of near-term market trends.
<DERIVATION>
The user surveys the evening crowds at cocktail lounges frequented by participants in the stock market and counts the number of drinking couples. The ratio of drinking couples to individuals drinking alone or with someone of the same sex is calculated.
<USE>
Used as a direct indicator of present market performance. When the ratio of drinking couples is low, the market is depressed, and traders wish to drink alone. A rise in the market is to be expected shortly. When the ratio is high, market performance is considered to be good enough to brag about.
<PUBLISHER>
None
<ANNOUNCED IN>
Nowhere
<ANNOUNCEMENT FREQUENCY>
None
<CUMULATIONS>
None
<MORE INFORMATION>
James Russell, "Surly Waiters and Other Stock Predictors," Miami Herald, 1F ff. (Dec. 20, 1982).

Misery Index [Also called the Discomfort Index]
<DESCRIPTION>
A nonempirical estimation of the condition of the general economy as it affects the general public.
<DERIVATION>
The nationwide unemployment rate (expressed as a percentage) is added to the year-to-year change in the Consumer Price

Index (expressed as a percentage). The resulting Misery Index
is also expressed as a percentage. The origin of the index is
popularly ascribed to the late Arthur Okun, a member of the
President's Council of Economic Advisers.
<USE>
Often cited as a gage of the broad political reaction to be
expected as a result of current economic conditions. These
conditions are assumed to be closely associated with the
economic policies (and policy makers) under which they have
occurred. A high Misery Index is viewed as an indicator of
failure of economic policies (specifically governmental
policies) and as a harbinger of the replacement of elected
officials.
<PUBLISHER>
None
<ANNOUNCED IN>
Nowhere.
<ANNOUNCEMENT FREQUENCY>
None.
<CUMULATIONS>
None.
<MORE INFORMATION>
"Misery as an Indicator," NY Times (June 23, 1982).

Short-Skirt Index [Also called the Hemline Index]
<DESCRIPTION>
A nonquantitative predictor of stock-market performance.
<DERIVATION>
The average height of hemlines of women's skirts shown by
international fashion designers is observed and calculated by
the user.
<USE>
Considered to be a near- to midterm predictor of future stock
market performance. When hemlines are high, the market is
expected to rise. When they are low, the market is expected
to decline.
<PUBLISHER>
None
<ANNOUNCED IN>
Nowhere, although Women's Wear Daily is considered to be a
fruitful source of data.
<ANNOUNCEMENT FREQUENCY>
None
<CUMULATIONS>
None
<MORE INFORMATION>
"You Can Also Use Tea Leaves," Business Week, 120 ff. (Nov.
17, 1962).
James Russell, "Surly Waiters and Other Stock Predictors,"
Miami Herald, 1F ff. (Dec. 20, 1982).

Superbowl Predictor
<DESCRIPTION>
A psuedopredictor of the gross change in the stock market for
the following year based on the winner of the Superbowl.

<DERIVATION>
The winning of the Superbowl by one of the original National
Football League teams signifies an up year for the stock
market as measured by the Standard & Poor's 500 Index. The
winning of the Superbowl by one of the newer teams (those
franchised since 1963) indicates a decline of the market as a
whole during the following year.
<USE>
To predict the overall performance of the stock market for
the months from February to January.
<PUBLISHER>
The National Football League
<ANNOUNCED IN>
All newspapers, radio stations, and television stations.
<ANNOUNCEMENT FREQUENCY>
Annual
<CUMULATIONS>
Sports Ill   irr
<MORE INFORMATION>
J. Russell, "Surly Waiters and Other Stock Predictors," Miami
Herald, 1F ff. (Dec. 20, 1982).

Surly Waiter Index

<DESCRIPTION>
A nonquantitative indicator of the current performance of the
stock market.
<DERIVATION>
The user dines in three- and four-star restaurants and
observes the behavior of the waiters. The graciousness (or
lack thereof) of the waiters is graded on an arbitrary scale
for comparison across a time series.
<USE>
Considered to be a counter-cyclical coincident indicator.
When the market is depressed, waiters will be as
accommodating as possible to maximize tips and supplement
their major incomes, which are presumed to be derived from
playing the market. When the market is rising rapidly (and
due for a sharp reverse), no such accomodating nature is
needed or profferred.
<PUBLISHER>
None
<ANNOUNCED IN>
Nowhere
<ANNOUNCEMENT FREQUENCY>
None
<CUMULATIONS>
None
<MORE INFORMATION>
J. Russell, "Surly Waiters and Other Stock Predictors," Miami
Herald, 1F ff. (Dec. 20, 1982).

APPENDIX B
ABBREVIATIONS LIST AND
GUIDE TO SOURCES

Aero F&F
Aerospace Facts and Figures
Aerospace Industries Assoc. of America
1725 De Sales St., NW
Washington, D.C. 20036

Ag Charts
Handbook of Agricultural Charts
Superintendent of Documents
USGPO
Washington, D.C. 20402

Ag Charts S
Enlargements Handbook of Agricultural Charts
Superintendent of Documents
USGPO
Washington, D.C. 20402

Ag Prices
Agricultural Prices
Superintendent of Documents
USGPO
Washington, D.C. 20402

Ag Prices An
Agricultural Prices Annual Summary
Superintendent of Documents
USGPO
Washington, D.C. 20402

Ag Stats
Agricultural Statistics
Superintendent of Documents
USGPO
Washington, D.C. 20402

Ag Stats S
Agricultural Statistics Supplement
Superintendent of Documents
USGPO
Washington, D.C. 20402

Air Trans
Air Transport Facts and Figures
Air Transport Assoc. of America
1030 15th St., NW
Washington, D.C. 20036

AMEX
American Stock Exchange Statistical Review
American Stock Exchange
86 Trinity Pl.
New York, N.Y. 10006

Ann Retail
Retail Trade, Annual Sales, Year-End Inventories, and
Accounts Receivable by Kind of Retail Store
U.S. Department of Commerce
Bureau of the Census
Washington, D.C. 20230

ASR (AISI)
Annual Statistical Report
American Iron and Steel Institute
1000 16th St., NW
Washington, D.C. 20036

Auto News
Automotive News
Crain Automotive Group
965 E. Jefferson
Detroit, Mich. 48207

Barron's
Barron's National and Financial Weekly
22 Cortland St.
New York, N.Y. 10007

BCD
Business Conditions Digest
Superintendent of Documents
USGPO
Washington, D.C. 20402

BNA
Bureau of National Affairs Policy and Practice Series,
Compensation
Bureau of National Affairs,
Washington, D.C. 20037

Bond Buyer
The Bond Buyer
1 State St. Plaza
New York, N.Y. 10004

Budget Brief
The United States Budget in Brief
Superintendent of Documents
USGPO
Washington, D.C. 20402

Builder
Builder
National Assoc. of Home Builders
15th and M St., NW
Washington, D.C. 20005

Bus Exec Exp
Business Executives' Expectations
The Conference Board
845 3rd Ave.
New York, N.Y. 10022

Bus Rev WF
Business Review
Economics Dept.
Wells Fargo Bank, N.A.
475 Sansome St.
San Francisco, Calif. 94163

Bus Stats
Business Statistics
Superintendent of Documents
USGPO
Washington, D.C. 20402

BW
Business Week
McGraw-Hill Publishing Co.
1221 Avenue of the Americas
New York, N.Y. 10020

CABP
Consumer Attitudes and Buying Plans
The Conference Board
845 3rd Ave.
New York, N.Y. 10022

Cap Approp
Capital Appropriations
The Conference Board
845 3rd Ave.
New York, N.Y. 10022

Cap Util
Capacity Utilization in Manufacturing
Board of Governors of the Federal Reserve System
Washington, D.C. 20551

CCH Labor
Commerce Clearing House Labor Reports
Commerce Clearing House
4025 West Peterson Ave.
Chicago, Ill. 60646

Chem W
Chemical Week
McGraw-Hill Publishing Co.
1221 Avenue of the Americas
New York, N.Y. 10020

Coal Age
Coal Age
McGraw-Hill Publishing Co.
1221 Avenue of the Americas
New York, N.Y. 10020

Com Indx Rep
CRB Commodity Index Report
Commodity Research Bureau
1 Liberty Plaza
New York, N.Y. 10016

Comm Chart
Commodity Chart Service
Commodity Research Bureau
1 Liberty Plaza
New York, N.Y. 10006

Comm Yr Bk
Commodity Year Book
Commodity Research Bureau
1 Liberty Plaza
New York, N.Y. 10016

Const Repts
Construction Reports
Superintendent of Documents
USGPO
Washington, D.C. 20402

Const Rev
Construction Review
Superintendent of Documents
USGPO
Washington, D.C. 20402

D Money
Donoghue's Moneyletter
The Donoghue Organization
P.O. Box 411
Holliston, Mass. 01746

D&B Failure
The Business Failure Record
Dun & Bradstreet
99 Church St.
New York, N.Y. 10007

D&B Mon
Monthly Business Failure
Dun & Bradstreet
99 Church St.
New York, N.Y. 10007

Dun's Bus Mo
Dun's Business Month
Dun & Bradstreet
99 Church St.
New York, N.Y. 10007

Econ Rept Pr
Economic Report of the President
Superintendent of Documents
USGPO
Washington, D.C. 20402

EI
Economic Indicators
Superintendent of Documents
USGPO
Washington, D.C. 20402

Elect Mkt Db
Electronic Market Data Book
Electronic Industries Assoc.
2001 I St., NW
Washington, D.C. 20006

Emp & Earn
Employment and Earnings
Superintendent of Documents
USGPO
Washington, D.C. 20402

Emp & Earn S
Employment and Earnings Supplement
Superintendent of Documents
USGPO
Washington, D.C. 20402

Emp & Train
Employment and Training
Superintendent of Documents
USGPO
Washington, D.C. 20402

Energy Info
Energy Information Administration Annual Report to Congress
Superintendent of Documents
USGPO
Washington, D.C. 20402

Eng News-Rec
Engineering News-Record
McGraw-Hill Publishing Co.
1221 Avenue of the Americas
New York, N.Y. 10020

EP Mo
Electric Power Monthly
Superintendent of Documents
USGPO
Washington, D.C. 20402

Exp Wkly
U.S. Export Weekly
International Trade Reporter
Bureau of National Affairs
1231 25th St., NW
Washington, D.C. 20037

FAA Stats
FAA Statistical Handbook
Superintendent of Documents
USGPO
Washington, D.C. 20402

Facts File
Facts on File
Facts on File
460 Park Ave. So.
New York, N.Y. 10016

Farm Ind
Economic Indicators of the Farm Sector
Superintendent of Documents
USGPO
Washington, D.C. 20402

Farm L
Farm Labor
Crop Reporting Board
14th and Independence Ave., SW
Washington, D.C. 20250

Farm Pop
Farm Population of the United States
Superintendent of Documents
USGPO
Washington, D.C. 20402

FHLBBJ
Journal of the Federal Home Loan Bank Board
Superintendent of Documents
USGPO
Washington, D.C. 20402

Fin Ind
Financial Indicators and Corporate Financing Plans: A
Semiannual Survey
The Conference Board
845 3rd Ave.
New York, N.Y. 10022

Forbes
Forbes
Forbes, Inc.
60 5th Ave.
New York, N.Y. 10011

FR Bull
Federal Reserve Bulletin
Board of Governors of the Federal Reserve System
Washington, D.C. 20551

Govt Fin
Facts and Figures on Government Finance
Tax Foundation
1875 Connecticut Ave., NW
Washington, D.C. 20009

Hbk Lbr Stat
Handbook of Labor Statistics
Superintendent of Documents
USGPO
Washington, D.C. 20402

Highlights
Highlights of U.S. Export and Import Trade
Superintendent of Documents
USGPO
Washington, D.C. 20402

Hist Stats
Historical Statistics of the United States
Superintendent of Documents
USGPO
Washington, D.C. 20402

HUD Stats
Statistical Yearbook of the United States Department of
Housing and Urban Development
Superintendent of Documents
USGPO
Washington, D.C. 20402

Inc
Inc.
Inc. Publishing Corp.
38 Commercial Wharf
Boston, Mass. 02110

Ind Est
Industry Estimates of Orders, Shipments, and Backlogs
Superintendent of Documents
USGPO
Washington, D.C. 20402

Ind W
Industry Week
Penton
Penton Plaza
1111 Chester Ave.
Cleveland, Ohio 44114

Int Econ Ind
International Economic Indicators
Superintendent of Documents
USGPO
Washington, D.C. 20402

Int Energy
International Energy Annual
Superintendent of Documents
USGPO
Washington, D.C. 20402

Int Fin Stat
International Financial Statistics Yearbook
International Monetary Fund
Washington, D.C. 20431

Inv Guide
Investment Guide
American Investment Services
Great Barrington, Mass. 01230

Inv Intell
Investors Intelligence
2 East Ave.
Larchmont, New York 10538

IREMS
Industrial Real Estate Market Survey
Society of Industrial Realtors
777 14th St., NW
Washington, D.C. 20005

Key Coal
Keystone Coal Industry Manual
McGraw-Hill Pubishing Co.
1221 Avenue of the Americas
New York, N.Y. 10020

Man Han
The Manufacturers Hanover Financial Digest
Manufacturers Hanover Trust Co.
270 Park Ave.
New York, N.Y. 10017

Merch
Merchandising
Gralla Publications
1515 Broadway
New York, N.Y. 10036

MG Fin Wkly
Media General Financial Weekly
Media General Financial Services
333 E. Grace St.
Richmond, Va. 23219

Min Ybk
Minerals Yearbook
Superintendent of Documents
USGPO
Washington, D.C. 20402

MLR
Monthly Labor Review
Superintendent of Documents
USGPO
Washington, D.C. 20402

Mo Econ Ind
Monthly Economic Indicators
Chemical Bank
Economic Research Dept.
380 Madison Ave.
New York, N.Y. 10017

Mo En Rev
Monthly Energy Review
Superintendent of Documents
USGPO
Washington, D.C. 20402

Mo New Inc
Monthly New Incorporations
Dun & Bradstreet
99 Church St
New York, N.Y. 10007

Mo Retail
Monthly Retail Trade, Sales, Accounts Receivable, and
Inventories
U.S. Department of Commerce, Bureau of the Census
Washington, D.C. 20230

Mo Whol
Monthly Wholesale Trade, Sales, and Inventories
Superintendent of Documents
USGPO
Washington, D.C. 20402

Moody's B&F
Moody's Bank and Finance Manual
Moody's Investors Service
99 Church St.
New York, N.Y. 10007

Moody's Bond
Moody's Bond Record
Moody's Investors Service
99 Church St.
New York, N.Y. 10007

Moody's Ind
Moody's Industrial Manual
Moody's Investors Service
99 Church St.
New York, N.Y. 10007

Moody's Mun
Moody's Municipal & Government Manual
Moody's Investors Service
99 Church St.
New York, N.Y. 10007

Moody's Pub
Moody's Public Utility Manual
Moody's Investors Service
99 Church St.
New York, N.Y. 10007

Moody's Trans
Moody's Transportation Manual
Moody's Investors Service
99 Church St.
New York, N.Y. 10007

MVMA
MVMA Motor Vehicle Facts & Figures
Motor Vehicle Manufacturers Assoc. of the U.S.
300 New Center Bldg.
Detroit, Mich. 48202

Nation's Bus
Nation's Business
Chamber of Commerce of the U.S.
1615 H St.
Washington, D.C. 20062

Natl Income
National Income and Product Accounts of the United States,
1929-76, Statistical Tables
Superintendent of Documents
USGPO
Washington, D.C. 20402

NYSE Facts
Fact Book
New York Stock Exchange
11 Wall St.
New York, N.Y. 10005

NYT
The New York Times
The New York Times Co.
229 W 43rd St.
New York, N.Y. 10036

PPI
Producer Prices and Price Indexes
Superintendent of Documents
USGPO
Washington, D.C. 20402

Pred Base
Predicasts Basebook
Predicasts
11001 Cedar Ave.
Cleveland, Ohio 44106

Pred Fore
Predicasts Forecasts
Predicasts
11001 Cedar Ave.
Cleveland, Ohio 44106

Q Fin Rept
Quarterly Financial Report for Manufacturing, Mining, and
Trade Corporations
Superintendent of Documents
USGPO
Washington, D.C. 20402

Q Mod Outlk
Quarterly Model Outlook
Wharton Econometric Forecasting
University of Pennsylvania
Philadelphia, Penn. 19104

Rail Age
Railway Age
Simmons Boardman Publishing Co.
345 Hudson St.
New York, N.Y. 10014

S&L Source
Savings and Loan Sourcebook
United States League of Savings Associations
111 E. Wacker Dr.
Chicago, Ill. 60601

S&P Corp Rec
Standard & Poor's Corporation Records
Standard & Poor's Corp.
25 Broadway
New York, N.Y. 10004

S&P Cred Wk
Standard & Poor's Credit Week
Standard & Poor's Corp.
25 Broadway
New York, N.Y. 10004

S&P Outlook
Standard & Poor's Outlook
Standard & Poor's Corp.
25 Broadway
New York, N.Y. 10004

S&P Stats
Standard & Poor's Statistical Service
Standard & Poor's Corp.
25 Broadway
New York, N.Y. 10004

S&P Stock
Standard & Poor's Stock Guide
Standard & Poor's Corp.
25 Broadway
New York, N.Y. 10004

SCB
Survey of Current Business
Superintendent of Documents
USGPO
Washington, D.C. 20402

SS Bull
Social Security Bulletin
Superintendent of Documents
USGPO
Washington, D.C. 20402

Stat Abstr
Statistical Abstract of the United States, National Data Book
and Guide to Sources
Superintendent of Documents
USGPO
Washington, D.C. 20402

Stat Bull
Statistical Bulletin
The Conference Board
845 3rd Ave.
New York, N.Y. 10022

Stat Paper
Statistics of Paper, Paperboard, and Wood Pulp
American Paper Institute
260 Madison Ave.
New York, N.Y. 10016

Travel Ybk
Travel Market Yearbook
Ziff-Davis Publishing Co.
1 Park Ave.
New York, N.Y. 10016

Treas Bull
Treasury Bulletin
Superintendent of Documents
USGPO
Washington, D.C. 20402

UN Stat Year
United Nations Statistical Yearbook
United Nations Publications
801 U.N. Plaza
New York, N.Y. 10017

Unemp Stats
Unemployment Insurance Statistics
U.S. Unemployment Insurance Service
601 D St., NW
Washington, D.C. 20213

US Budget
Budget of the United States Government
Superintendent of Documents
USGPO
Washington, D.C. 20402

US News
U.S. News & World Report
2300 N St., NW
Washington, D.C. 20037

Util Approp
Utility Appropriations
The Conference Board
845 3rd Ave.
New York, N.Y. 10022

Value Line
The Value Line Investment Survey
Arnold Bernhard & Co.
711 3rd Ave.
New York, N.Y. 10017

Ward's Repts
Ward's Automotive Reports
Ward's Communications
28 W. Adams St.
Detroit, Mich. 48226

Wk Bond Buyr
The Weekly Bond Buyer
The Bond Buyer
1 State St. Plaza
New York, N.Y. 10004

Wkly Car
Weekly Carloading Reports
Assoc. of American Railroads
American Railroads Bldg.
1920 L St., NW
Washington, D.C. 20036

Wkly Econ
Weekly Economic Package
Economic Research Dept.
Chemical Bank
20 Pine St.
New York, N.Y. 10015

WMVD
World Motor Vehicle Data
Motor Vehicle Manufacturers Assoc. of the U.S.
300 New Center Bldg.
Detroit, Mich. 48202

World Fin M
World Financial Markets
Morgan Guaranty Trust Co. of New York
23 Wall St.
New York, N.Y. 10015

WSJ
The Wall Street Journal
Dow Jones & Co.
22 Cortland St.
New York, N.Y. 10007

Ybk Labor
Yearbook of Labour Statistics
International Labour Office
1750 New York Ave., NW
Washington, D.C. 20006

Ybk Rail
Yearbook of Railroad Facts
Assoc. of American Railroads
American Railroad Bldg.
1920 L St., NW
Washington, D.C. 20036

APPENDIX C
LIST OF COMPILERS OF
INDICATORS

Aerospace Industries Assoc. of America
1725 De Sales St., NW
Washington, D.C. 20036

Air Transport Assoc. of America
1030 15th St., NW
Washington, D.C. 20036

American Iron and Steel Institute
1000 16th St., NW
Washington, D.C. 20036

American Paper Institute
Paperboard Group
260 Madison Ave.
New York, N.Y. 10016

American Railway Car Institute
303 E. Wacker Dr.
Chicago, Ill. 60601

American Stock Exchange
86 Trinity Pl.
New York, N.Y. 10006

Association of American Railroads
1920 L St., NW
Washington, D.C. 20036

Association of Home Appliance Manufacturers
20 N. Wacker Dr.
Chicago, Ill. 60606

E. W. Axe & Co.
400 Benedict Ave.
Tarrytown, N.Y. 10591

Barron's National and Financial Weekly
22 Cortland St.
New York, N.Y. 10007

Board of Governors of the Federal Reserve System
Washington, D.C. 20551

Bond Buyer
1 State St. Plaza
New York, N.Y. 10004

Business Week
McGraw-Hill Publishing Co.
1221 Avenue of the Americas
New York, N.Y. 10020

Chartcraft, Inc.
2 East Ave.
Larchmont, N.Y. 10538

Commodity Research Bureau
1 Liberty Plaza
New York, N.Y. 10016

The Conference Board
845 3rd Ave.
New York, N.Y. 10022

F. W. Dodge Div.
McGraw-Hill Information Systems Co.
1221 Avenue of the Americas
New York, N.Y. 10020

The Donoghue Organization, Inc.
P.O. Box 411
Holliston, Mass. 01746

Dow Jones & Co.
22 Cortland St.
New York, N.Y. 10007

Dun & Bradstreet, Inc.
99 Church St
New York, N.Y. 10007

Federal Home Loan Bank Board
1700 G St, NW
Washington, D.C. 20552

Forbes, Inc.
60 5th Ave.
New York, N.Y. 10011

Hambrecht & Quist, Inc.
235 Montgomery St.
San Francisco, Calif. 94104

McCann-Erikson, Inc.
485 Lexington Ave.
New York, N.Y. 10017

McGraw-Hill Economics
1221 Avenue of the Americas
New York, N.Y. 10020

McGraw-Hill Information Systems Co.
1221 Avenue of the Americas
New York, N.Y. 10020

Media General Financial Services, Inc.
333 E. Grace St.
Richmond, Va. 23219

Moody's Investors Service
99 Church St.
New York, N.Y. 10007

Motor Vehicle Manufacturers Assoc. of the U.S.
300 New Center Bldg.
Detroit, Mich. 48202

National Association of Securities Dealers
1735 K St., NW
Washington, D.C. 20006

National Conference of States on Building Codes and Standards
481 Carlisle Dr.
Herndon, Va. 22070

National Forest Products Association
1619 Massachusetts Ave., NW
Washington, D.C. 20036

National Machine Tool Builders Association
7901 Westpark Dr.
McLean, Va. 22102

New York Stock Exchange
11 Wall St.
New York, N.Y. 10005

Office of Management and Budget
Executive Office Bldg.
Washington, D.C. 20503

Purchasing Management Association of Chicago
201 N. Wells St.
Chicago, Ill. 60604

Society of Industrial Realtors
777 14th St., NW
Washington, D.C. 20005

Sotheby's
1335 York Ave.
New York, N.Y. 10021

Standard & Poor's Corp.
25 Broadway
New York, N.Y. 10004

U.S. Department of Agriculture
Economic Research Service
14 St and Independence Ave., SW
Washington, D.C. 20250

U.S. Department of Agriculture
Economics, Statistics, and Cooperatives Service
14 St and Independence Ave., SW
Washington, D.C. 20250

U.S. Department of Commerce
Bureau of Economic Analysis
10 St. Between Constitution Ave. and E St., NW
Washington, D.C. 20230

U.S. Department of Commerce
Bureau of the Census
14 St. Between Consitution Ave. and E St., NW
Washington, D.C. 20230

U.S. Department of Commerce
International Trade Administration
Office of Planning Research
14 St. Between Constitution Ave. and E St, NW
Washington, D.C. 20230

U.S. Department of Energy
Energy Information Administration
Forrestal Bldg.
Washington, D.C., 20585

U.S. Department of Labor
Bureau of Labor Statistics
200 Constitution Ave., NW
Washington, D.C. 20210

U.S. Department of the Treasury
15th St and Pennsylvania Ave., NW
Washington, D.C. 20220

U.S. Department of Transportation
Federal Aviation Agency
800 Independence Ave., SW
Washington, D.C. 20591

U.S. News & World Report
2300 N St., NW
Washington, D.C. 20037

Value Line
711 3rd Ave.
New York, N.Y. 10017

Ward's Communications, Inc.
28 W. Adams St.
Detroit, Mich. 48226

Wharton Econometric Forecasting
University of Pennsylvania
Philadelphia, Penn. 19104

Wilshire Associates
100 Wilshire Blvd.
Santa Monica, Calif. 90401

INDEX

Advertising

Help-Wanted Index
McCann-Erikson National Advertising Index

Agriculture

Agricultural Employment
Farm Employment
Farm Income
Index of Prices Paid by Farmers for Commodities and
    Services,
    Interest, Taxes, and Farm Wage Rates
Index of Prices Received by Farmers
Parity Index
Parity Ratio

Banking and Finance

Average Prime Rate Charged by Banks
Bank Debits
Change in Business Loans
Change in Total Liquid Assets
Commercial and Industrial Loans Outstanding, Weekly
    Reporting Large Commercial Banks
Constant Maturities Treasury Securities
Consumer Installment Credit
Current Assets and Liabilities of Nonfinancial
    Corporations
Deposit Turnover
Federal Funds Rate
Federal Reserve Discount Rate
Loans and Investments
Margin Debt
Money Stock Measures and Liquid Assets
Money Supply M2 Deflated
New York Stock Exchange Firms' Free Credit Balance
Personal Saving
Prime Commercial Paper

Reserves and Borrowing
Six-Month Treasury Bills
Standard & Poor's 40 Financial Index
Three-Month Treasury Bills

Bonds

Barron's Confidence Index
Bond Buyer Twenty-Bond Index
Constant Maturities Treasury Securities
Dow Jones 20-Bond Average
High-Grade Municipal Bond Yields
Moody's Corporate Aaa Bond Yield Averages
Standard & Poor's Municipal Bond Yields

Building, see Construction

Business

Average Prime Rate Charged by Banks
Business Failures
Change in Business Loans
Consumer Confidence Index
Corporate Profits
Current Assets and Liabilities of Nonfinancial
    Corporations
Dun & Bradstreet's Profits Optimism Index
Dun & Bradstreet's Sales Optimism Index
Expenditures for New Plant and Equipment
Forbes Index
Gross Domestic Product
Gross National Product
Gross National Product Implicit Price Deflator
Heller/Roper Small Business Barometer
Inventory Change
Inventory-Sales Ratio
Net Business Formation
Net National Product
New Business Incorporations
Productivity and Related Data, Private Business Sector
Retail Trade
Sources and Uses of Funds, Nonfarm Nonfinancial
    Corporate Businesses
U.S. News & World Report Weekly Index of Business
    Activities
Wholesale Trade

Capacity Utilization

Manufacturers' Capacity Utilization: Bureau of
    Economic Analysis
Manufacturers' Capacity Utilization: Federal Reserve
    Board
Wharton Measures of Capacity Utilization

Capital Investment, see Investment, Capital

Commodities

Carloadings
Change in Sensitive Prices
Chemical Week Weekly Index of Chemical Prices
Coal Production (Bituminous)
Gold Prices
Industrial Raw Materials Price Index
Lumber Production
Petroleum Production

Composite Indexes

Building Cost Index
Business Week Index
Business Week Leading Index
Chemical Week Weekly Index of Chemical Prices
Coincident Indicators Composite Index
Consumer Price Index
Consumer Prices, Major Industrial Countries
Diffusion Index
Forbes Index
Gross National Product
Gross National Product Implicit Price Deflator
Lagging Indicators Composite Index
Leading Indicators Composite Index
Net National Product
U.S. News & World Report Weekly Index of Business
   Activities

Construction

Building Cost Index
Construction Contract Awards
Construction Cost Index
Contracts and Orders for Plant and Equipment
Housing Permits
Housing Starts
New Construction
New Construction Planning

Consumption

Aircraft Shipments
Disposable Personal Income
Disposition of Personal Income
Personal Consumption Expenditures

Earnings, see Wages and Earnings

Employment (See also Unemployment)

Accession Rate, Manufacturing
Agricultural Employment
Average Weekly Hours
Farm Employment

Help-Wanted Index
Labor Turnover
Nonagricultural Employment
Workweek, Average Manufacturing

Expenditures

Capital Expenditures
Corporate Financing Plans
Expenditures for New Plant and Equipment
Personal Consumption Expenditures
Utility Appropriations

Exports, see Foreign Trade

Federal Government Income and Outlays

Federal Budget Receipts by Source and Outlays by
   Function
Federal Budget Receipts, Outlays, and Debt
Federal Sector, National Income Accounts Basis
Fiscal Thrust

Foreign Trade

Balance of Trade
United States International Transactions
United States Merchandise Exports
United States Merchandise Imports

Housing

Building Cost Index
Housing Permits
Housing Starts
Mobile Home Sales
New Home Mortgage Yield
New Private Housing: Units Authorized by Permit Places

Imports, see Foreign Trade

Income

Average Hourly and Weekly Earnings
Disposable Personal Income
Disposition of Personal Income
Farm Income
National Income
Parity Ratio
Sources of Personal Income

Interest Rates

Average Prime Rate Charged by Banks
Constant Maturities Treasury Securities
Federal Funds Rate

Federal Reserve Discount Rate
High Grade Municipal Bond Yields
New Home Mortgage Yield
Prime Commercial Paper
Six-Month Treasury Bills
Three-Month Treasury Bills

Inventory

Inventory Change
Inventory-Sales Ratio
Inventory-Shipments Ratio
Manufacturers' Inventories
Wholesale Trade

Investment, Capital

Capital Appropriations
Capital Expenditures
Change in Business Loans
Commercial and Industrial Loans Outstanding, Weekly
    Reporting Large Commercial Banks
Expenditures for New Plant and Equipment
Gross Private Domestic Investment
Utility Appropriations

Labor

Accession Rate, Manufacturing
Agricultural Employment
Average Hourly and Weekly Earnings
Average Weekly Hours
Building Cost Index
Labor Turnover
Layoff Rate, Manufacturing
Nonagricultural Employment
Quit Rate, Manufacturing
Total Unemployment
Unemployment Insurance Programs, Initial Claims
Unemployment Rate, Total
Workweek, Average Manufacturing

Manufacturing

Accession Rate, Manufacturing
Aircraft, New Orders
Automobile Output
Automotive Factory Sales
Average Hourly and Weekly Earnings
Coal Production (Bituminous)
Contracts and Orders for Plant and Equipment
Inventory-Shipments Ratio
Layoff Rate, Manufacturing
Machine Tool Orders
Manufacturers' Capacity Utilization: Bureau of
    Economic Analysis

Manufacturers' Capacity Utilization: Federal
   Reserve Board
Manufacturers' Inventories
Manufacturers' Orders
Manufacturers' Shipments
New Orders, Nondefense Capital Goods
Paperboard Production
Quit Rate, Manufacturing
Truck and Bus Factory Sales
Unfilled Orders
Workweek, Average Manufacturing

Monetary Aggregates

Money Stock Measures and Liquid Assets
Money Supply M2 Deflated

Nonquantitative Indicators

Bad Guess Theorem
Brokerage House Rule
Drinking Couple Count
Misery Index
Short-Skirt Index
Superbowl Predictor
Surly Waiter Index

Opinion Polls

Advisory Service Index
Buying Plans Index
Capital Appropriations
Consumer Confidence Index
Corporate Financing Plans
Dun & Bradstreet's Profits Optimism Index
Dun & Bradstreet's Sales Optimism Index
Heller/Roper Small Business Barometer
New Construction Planning

Orders

Aircraft, New Orders
Contracts and Orders for Plant and Equipment
Freight Car Orders
Machine Tool Orders
Manufacturers' Orders
New Orders, Nondefense Capital Goods
Unfilled Orders

Prices

Building Cost Index
Change in Sensitive Prices
Chemical Week Weekly Index of Chemical Prices
Construction Cost Index
Consumer Price Index

221

Consumer Prices, Major Industrial Countries
Gold Prices
Gross Domestic Product
Index of Prices Paid by Farmers for Commodities and
    Services, Interest, Taxes, and Farm Wage Rates
Index of Prices Received by Farmers
Industrial Raw Materials Price Index
Parity Index
Parity Ratio
Producer Price Indexes

Production

Aircraft, New Orders
Appliance Factory Sales
Automobile Output
Automotive Factory Sales
Business Week Index
Coal Production (Bituminous)
Electric Power Production
Gross Domestic Product
Gross National Product
Gross National Product Implicit Price Deflator
Industrial Production, Major Industrial Countries
Industrial Production, Major Market Groups and
    Selected Manufactures
Lumber Production
Paperboard Production
Petroleum Production
Productivity and Related Data, Private Business Sector
Steel Production
Sutro Indicator
U.S. News & World Report Weekly Index of Business
    Activities

Profits

Corporate Profits
Dun & Bradstreet's Profits Optimism Index

Purchasing

Buying Plans Index
Vendor Performance, Companies Reporting Slower Deliveries

Real Estate

New Home Mortgage Yield
Vacancy Rate, Prime Industrial Real Estate

Revenue

Federal Budget Receipts by Source and Outlays by Function
Federal Budget Receipts, Outlays, and Debt
McCann-Erikson National Advertising Index
Revenue Passenger Miles

Sales

Aircraft Shipments
Appliance Factory Sales
Automobile Sales
Automotive Factory Sales
Dun & Bradstreet's Sales Optimism Index
Inventory-Sales Ratio
Inventory-Shipments Ratio
Manufacturers' Shipments
Mobile Home Sales
Retail Trade
Truck and Bus Factory Sales
Wholesale Trade

Stocks

Advisory Service Index
American Stock Exchange Advance-Decline Line
American Stock Exchange Big Block Activity
American Stock Exchange Market Value Index
American Stock Exchange Odd-Lot Index
American Stock Exchange Price-Earnings Ratio
American Stock Exchange Seat Sales
American Stock Exchange Short Interest Ratio
American Stock Exchange Volume
American Stock Exchange Volume Momentum
Barron's Fifty-Stock Average
Barron's Group Stock Averages
Barron's Twenty Low-Priced Stocks Index
Dow Jones Composite Average
Dow Jones Industrial Average
Dow Jones Transportation Average
Dow Jones Utilities Average
Hambrecht & Quist Technology Stock Index
High-Low Differential
Margin Debt
Media General American Stock Exchange Equal-Investment
    Index
Media General American Stock Exchange Market Value Index
Media General Composite Equal-Investment Index
Media General Composite Market Value Index
Media General New York Stock Exchange Equal-Investment
    Index
Media General New York Stock Exchange Market Value Index
Media General Over-the-Counter Market Value Index
New York Stock Exchange Advance-Decline Line
New York Stock Exchange Big Block Activity
New York Stock Exchange Composite Index
New York Stock Exchange Firms' Free Credit Balance
New York Stock Exchange Firms' Margin Accounts
New York Stock Exchange Members' Short Sells Ratio
New York Stock Exchange Nonmembers' Short Sells Ratio
New York Stock Exchange Odd-Lot Index
New York Stock Exchange Odd-Lot Sales
New York Stock Exchange Odd-Lot Short Sales and
    Purchase Index

New York Stock Exchange Price-Earnings Ratio
New York Stock Exchange Seat Sales
New York Stock Exchange Short Interest Ratio
New York Stock Exchange Volume
New York Stock Exchange Volume Momentum
Over the Counter Index
Price-Earnings Ratio for Over the Counter Stocks
Price Momentum
Short-Term Trading Index
Speculation Index
Standard & Poor's 20 Transportation Index
Standard & Poor's 40 Financial Index
Standard & Poor's 40 Utilities Index
Standard & Poor's 400 Industrial Index
Standard & Poor's 500 Dividend-Price Ratio
Standard & Poor's 500 Price-Earnings Ratio
Standard & Poor's Composite Index
Value Line Composite Averages
Wilshire 5000 Equity Index

Technical Indicators (Nonstock)

Donoghue's Money Fund Averages
Money Stock Measures and Liquid Assets
Money Supply M2 Deflated
Six-Month Treasury Bills
Sotheby's Art Index
Sutro Indicator
Three-Month Treasury Bills

Transportation

Aircraft, New Orders
Aircraft Shipments
Automobile Output
Automobile Sales
Automotive Factory Sales
Carloadings
Dow Jones Transportation Average
Freight Car Orders
Revenue Passenger Miles
Standard & Poor's 20 Transportation Index

Unemployment (See also Employment)

Labor Turnover
Layoff Rate, Manufacturing
Quit Rate, Manufacturing
Total Unemployment
Unemployment Insurance Programs, Initial Claims
Unemployment Rate, Total

Utilities

Dow Jones Utilities Average
Electric Power Production

224

Standard & Poor's 40 Utilities Index
Utility Appropriations

Wages and Earnings

Average Hourly and Weekly Earnings
Farm Employment
Hourly Earnings Index
National Income

About the Authors

FREDERICK M. O'HARA, JR., currently is a consultant in technical communication. Earlier he served on the staff of the Oak Ridge National Laboratory and the University of Illinois' Institute of Communications Research.

ROBERT SICIGNANO is a Business and Industry Librarian at the Lawson McGhee Library in Knoxville, Tennessee. He is the author of the *Special Issues Index* (Greenwood Press, 1982).